Jora

The practical guide to waste management law

with a list of abbreviations and acronyms,
useful websites and relevant legislation

Waste seeks its sanctuary
in the dawn wasteland,
the afforested morning rides,
the afternoon sunlit bubbling culvert
and the evil oubliette of the midnight manhole cover.

'In a Dark Mood' by Richard Hawkins

The practical guide to waste management law

with a list of abbreviations and acronyms, useful websites and relevant legislation

R. G. P. Hawkins and H. S. Shaw

 Thomas Telford

Published by Thomas Telford Publishing, Thomas Telford Ltd, 1 Heron Quay, London E14 4JD
URL: http://www.thomastelford.com

Distributors for Thomas Telford books are
USA: ASCE Press, 1801 Alexander Bell Drive, Reston, VA 20191-4400
Japan: Maruzen Co. Ltd, Book Department, 3–10 Nihonbashi 2-chome, Chuo-ku, Tokyo 103
Australia: DA Books and Journals, 648 Whitehorse Road, Mitcham 3132, Victoria

First published 2004

A catalogue record for this book is available from the British Library

ISBN: 0 7277 3275 7

Typeset by Helius, Brighton and Rochester
Printed and bound in Great Britain by MPG Books, Bodmin, Cornwall

Preface

In 2004 the Government is facing challenges on many fronts in the context of environmental management, and will be under pressure to meet its agreed specific waste management goals for at least the next 15 years. Targets selected in Brussels either by the European Commission or the European Parliament will, on the best evidence available, not be met.[1] Some current difficulties are illustrated in the Summary of the February 2004 House of Commons Environment, Food and Rural Affairs All Party Select Committee Report:

> In particular we conclude that Government handling of the End of Life Vehicles (ELV) Directive and, to a slightly lesser extent, the Waste Electrical and Electronic Equipment (WEEE) Directive has been characterised by a lack of guidance and clarity. The result has been the stakeholders, particularly the recycling industry have not been clear about what is expected of them – and so have not, for example, been able to make decisions about investments.

> We again question whether Defra possesses enough of the specialist skills it needs to deal with this sort of Directive, particularly in terms of legal capacity. Some of our witnesses commented that Government lacks a proper understanding of the waste and recycling sector. A number of our recommendations are aimed at improving its level of expertise.

The Sustainable Development Commission's April 2004 End of Term Report judged the Government's progress on transport and waste to be 'dreadful'. It is therefore all the more important for existing waste management law to be clear and, as important, to be understood in straightforward, practical terms by not only engineers and managers but by all elected representatives at any tier of local, regional or national government.[2] Perhaps even the better informed of their constituents?

---

[1] This was unequivocally the view expressed in paragraph 37 of the House of Commons All Party Environmental Audit Committee 5th Report, *Waste — An Audit*, April 2003.

The aim of this practical guide is to provide public and private sector practitioners, together with their performance auditors, and all, for example, who are striving for a waste awareness certificate who do not have a formal legal training, with an understanding of operational waste management law and the practical implications of non-compliance. The authors' legal and engineering backgrounds have allowed them to be selective in compiling a concise source book. For a full understanding of this complex subject, practical examples are given and key topical issues are summarised in the 20 tables and 80 text boxes taken from contemporary media reports. Website references for all the leading subjects have been carefully researched and provided for further reference.

This is a guide for the farmer concerned about the new agricultural waste regulations, for the construction site manager unsure about what to do with discarded oil, waste batteries or an accidental spillage, and the golf course designer apprehensive about whether the material stored for his landscaping has unexpectedly increased in the summer darkness. It is also for the wary bank manager considering whether to advance money for brownfield site redevelopment, the yoghurt carton supplier concerned about changes to packaging regulations, or a victim of commercial arson wanting his insurance company to allow him to clear his site of debris and begin reconstruction as soon as possible.

Of course, this book is also for the Environment Agency regulator seeking promotion through passing an examination, the engineer undertaking continued professional development, a graduate studying for a professional interview, or a trainee lawyer wishing to specialise in environmental and waste management. The related sourced and indexed text can provide valuable material for postgraduate training modules in the field of waste management and environmental law and other accredited vocational programmes.

But the field of waste management covers a very broad range of disciplines, including chemical engineering, microbiology, hydrology, innovative engineering, transportation economics, noise abatement, epidemiology and human resources. There is a thin line dividing some subject areas from intrinsic waste management law, and certain topics that are related to waste management are subjects in their own right, and are covered by the appropriate specialists texts. Therefore, some matters can only be briefly summarised, albeit with a website reference.

Whilst every public and private sector, environmental and waste manager is dogged by the ever-increasing plethora of EU and national employment laws and codes of practice—indeed there are over 130,000 employment tribunal cases in the UK each year—this specialism has to be an area without this small book in the same way that private finance practices affecting a waste

---

[2] Please see Box 1.1 for a summary of some groups affected by waste management law, and Figure 7.1 for an example of the fundamental changes already being imposed.

management project must remain the province of the merchant banker. Of course, the current provisions and restrictions on landfill tax are covered.

The legal definitions of an employee can, however, be as important as that of waste itself. Managing recruitment and selection professionally (possibly the most important priority for waste managers in 2005 if, as they must be, recruitment standards are to be improved), as well as maintaining a fair level of disciplined management through to dismissal, are all difficult and sometimes painful skills to acquire. Experience overseas shows that companies must give their employees clear advice on the steps to be followed when they suspect that bribes are being offered or demanded. No matter how well drafted and equitably enforced environmental law is, if carefully designed internal audit procedures cannot flush out bribes, disguised as perhaps agents' commission, then the corporate infection will spread into growing disrespect from external environmental lawyers and agencies. In southern Europe, Africa, Central and South America, and the Far East, corruption is a cancer paralysing healthy waste management development, although few, *nota bene* the European Commission, try to assess its impact.

The subject of health and safety is very complementary to waste management law as is seen by the recent fusion between the positions of environmental and health and safety mangers. The Robens Report,[3] which in the most simple of terms described the duty to take reasonable care both within and outside the workplace, is *primus inter pares* of all important review documents preceding any legislation in this country in the last 50 years. Whilst there have been grave concerns powerfully expressed, in some cases having to be qualified later by leaders in certain medical journals, this practical guide does not deal specifically with the possible epidemiological effects of waste management.

In any apparent observations on the performance of EU or UK Government departments, courts, institutes or associations, etc., one of the objectives of this practical guide is to inform the reader of what sometimes would appear to be the continuance of antediluvian practices and attitudes which are certainly changing, but not with the dispatch which some may have hoped. Likewise, ambitious and not always wholly necessary environmental standards are being set in stone, whilst law extant for often a decade has not been adequately enforced or the extent of that enforcement audited and reported. The UK Government faces a rocky undulating path of progress, not by any means all of its own making, over the next decade, and needs practical field support through constructive criticism and innovative solutions.

There can be few who will not be affected by the new planning regime and its regional implications, the new Integrated Pollution Prevention and Control

---

[3] *Report of the Committee on Safety and Health at Work* (Chairman Lord Robens). The Stationery Office (HMSO), 1972.

regime, the Waste and Emissions Trading Act 2003, the Household Waste Recycling Act 2003, the reclassification of Special into 91/689 Hazardous waste, non-natural agricultural becoming Controlled waste,[4] the Waste Electronic and Electrical Equipment and End of Life Vehicle Regulations, the EU ADR Regulations becoming 2004 UK law, the proposed EU Biowaste Directive, the Duty of Care amendments, the Water Act 2003, or the proposed environmental liability Directive. It is for these people that this book has been written.

The law and practice as set out in this practical guide is a summary principally of England, Wales and the EU, and contains much that is applicable to Scotland and Northern Ireland.[5]

Richard Hawkins MA Barrister FCIWM FRGS FRSA

Richard Hawkins has been an international field operational lawyer advising environmental authorities on the content and enforcement of waste management law and codes of practice in Hong Kong, the RSA, and Botswana, at the same time controlling companies' financial liabilities in the UK, Israel, the UAE and the Gulf States through proper contractual and standard operating procedures for avoiding pollution damage. A former advisor to the European Parliament, he was one of the founder members of the UK Waste Management Industry Training and Advisory Board (WAMITAB), and the UK Environmental Law Association (UKELA), and has authored or co-authored five books, including the *Concise Lexicon of Environmental Terms*, 1st and 2nd Editions.

Heidi Sarah Shaw BEng(Hons) PhD

Dr Shaw is a consultant engineer for Gifford and Partners, where she is responsible for business development in the field of waste management. Before joining Gifford in December 2003 she was responsible for the University of Southampton MSc Sustainable Waste Management Course. During this time she worked closely with the waste management industry to establish the successful part-time modular course, which was awarded CIWM accreditation in 2003. The course is well recognised by industry as one of the leading vocational postgraduate waste management training courses in the UK, and is attended by practitioners from local authorities, government agencies, private consultants, technical operators and environmental charities. Dr Shaw is now a Visiting Research Fellow with the School of Civil Engineering and the Environment at the University of Southampton.

Richard G. P. Hawkins
Heidi S. Shaw

---

[4] Please see www.defra.gov.uk/environment/waste/topics/agwaste.htm.
[5] Please see Appendix E for the relevant countries' websites.

Acknowledgements

In compiling this practical guide, the authors wish sincerely to thank those who read some of our imperfect chapter texts, tables and boxes.

We are grateful in particular to Ian Avery, Douglas Benjafield, Andrew Bryce, Roger Davies, Martin Edwards, Ray Parmenter, Reuben Shaw, David Tarrant, Stephen Tromans, Gill Weeks and John Wilkinson for their comments. Also, thanks to Sylvia and Snap my dog.

Any errors or omissions, however, are solely the responsibility of the authors. All ideas and specific suggestions to improve the second edition will be acknowledged.

The authors would like to thank Gifford and Partners Consulting Engineers for their positive help and encouragement in the researching and writing of this practical guide. Gifford (www.gifford.uk.com) was founded some 50 years ago and today employs over 500 staff worldwide, covering a broad range of civil, structural and environmental engineering disciplines. The practice has a well earned reputation for environmental innovation, particularly in its more sustainable approaches to building design. Its new Southampton headquarters incorporate many novel structural, service and architectural features which integrate the building with the surrounding rural environment and make it one of the more energy efficient buildings in the country.

Authors' textual notes

- All EU Directives in the text have the year before the Directive number. For example the 75/442 EEC Waste Framework Directive was passed in 1975, and is Directive number 442. When a Directive is first mentioned in a chapter it is set out in full, and thereafter referred to in shortened form, e.g. the 75/442 Directive, for ease of the reading. EU Regulations have the number and then the year, e.g. Regulation 2037/2000 on Ozone Depleting Substances.

- Instead of repeating the names of well-known UK Acts in full, they are abbreviated if mentioned repeatedly in a chapter, e.g. the Environmental Protection Act 1990 is the EPA 1990. Likewise, for the Transport of Dangerous Goods (Safety Advisors) Regulations 1999 (Statutory Instrument 1999 No. 257) the Statutory Instrument number is abbreviated to SI 257. References to sections of Acts are also abbreviated for convenience, so section 34 of the Environmental Protection Act 1990 becomes s.34 EPA 1990.

- When specific Regulations are referred to, a capital R is used, but regulations in general are spelt with a small r.

- It has been a matter of considerable regret that for 40 years there has never been a consensus that the term 'Special waste' should have a capital 'S'. Likewise, for the consistent use of a capital 'C' in the terms 'Controlled waste' and 'unControlled waste', which refer to specific waste types controlled under specific legislation. Similarly, the term 'Controlled waters' has a statutory meaning. In this practical guide, capitals have been used for clarity of meaning.

- When the term 'hazardous' is used to refer to Hazardous waste as defined by the 91/689 Hazardous Waste Directive, it is spelt with a capital 'H'.

- Website references have been checked as assiduously as possible. For very lengthy website addresses the home page address is often given, in case the link to a particular web page or publication is changed. In such cases the reader will need to navigate the website or use the site search facility.

- There can be confusion for the reader in the superseding of the Part I EPA 1990 Integrated Pollution Control by the 96/61 IPPC Directive and the PPC Act 1999. Likewise, there can be confusion between the LAPC under Part I of the EPA 1990 and the LAPPC under the PPC Act. The explanatory text and footnote for these very adjacent abbreviations is given in Chapter 8, but the possible initial confusion has been high-lighted here for the convenience of the reader.

- For brevity, 'he' means 'he' or 'she'.

Abbreviations and acronyms

ABPO 1999	Animal By-Products Order 1999
ABPR 2003	Animal By-Products Regulations 2003
ACL	Approved Carriage List
ACP	Advisory Committee on Packaging
ADR	Accord Européen Relatif au Transport International des Marchandises Dangereuses par Route (international regulations relating to the transportation of dangerous goods) alternative dispute resolution
AMDEA	Association of Manufacturers of Domestic Electric Appliances
AMR	annual monitoring reports
ATF	authorised treatment facility
BAT	Best Available Technique(s)
BATNEEC	Best Available Technique(s) Not Entailing Excessive Cost
BMW	biodegradable municipal waste
BNFL	British Nuclear Fuels Ltd
BPEO	Best Practicable Environmental Option
BPM	Best Practicable Means
BS	British Standards
BS EN	British Standards European Norm
BSI	British Standards Institution
BVIO 2003	Local Government (Best Value) Performance Indicators and Standards 2003
CA	civic amenity
CAWR 2002	Control of Asbestos at Work Regulations 2002
CBI	Confederation of British Industries
CCL	climate change levy
CDG	carriage of dangerous goods
CEN	Comité Européan de Normalisation

CHIP	Control of Hazardous Chemical (Hazard Information and Packaging for Supply) Regulations
CHP	combined heat and power
CIA	Chemicals Industries Association
CIS	Common Implementation Strategy
CIWEM	Chartered Institution of Water and Environmental Management
CIWM	Chartered Institution of Wastes Management
CLER 1983	Classification and Labelling of Explosives Regulations 1983
COMAH	Control of Major Accident Hazards Regulations
COPA 1974	Control of Pollution Act 1974
COP(A)A 1989	Control of Pollution (Amendment) Act 1989
COSHH	Control of Substances Hazardous to Health Regulations 2002
COTC	Certificate of Technical Competence
CQE	Certificate of Qualifying Experience
CWR 1992	Controlled Waste Regulations 1992
DEFRA	Department for Environment, Food and Rural Affairs
DETR	Department of the Environment, Transport and the Regions
DFID	Department for International Development
DfT	Department for Transport
DGL	Dangerous Goods List
DGSA	dangerous goods safety advisor
DoE	Department of the Environment (then into DETR, after FMD now DEFRA and ODPM)
DPD	development plan documents
DPWA 1972	Deposit of Poisonous Waste Act 1972
DTI	Department for Trade and Industry
DTLR	Department for Transport, Local Government and the Regions
DVLA	Driver and Vehicle Licensing Agency
DVR	differential and variable rate
EA	Environment Agency
EA 1995	Environment Act 1995
EAC	Emergency Action Code (transport) Environmental Audit Committee
EC	European Community (now EU) European Commission
ECA	European Chemicals Agency European Court of Auditors

ECHR	European Convention on Human Rights
ECJ	European Court of Justice
ECSE	European Coal and Steel Community
EEC	European Economic Community
EFRA	Environment, Food and Rural Affairs (House of Commons Select Committee)
EfW	energy from waste
EHO	environmental health officer
EHS	Environment and Heritage Service (for Northern Ireland)
EIA	environmental impact assessment
EIC	Environmental Industries Commission
ELV	end of life vehicles
ELVR 2003	End of Life Vehicles Regulations 2003
EMS	environmental management system
EPA 1990	Environmental Protection Act 1990
ES	environmental statement
ESA	Environmental Services Association (formerly the National Association of Waste Disposal Contractors)
ETS	Emissions Trading Scheme
EU	European Union
EWC	European Waste Catalogue
FA 1996	Finance Act 1996
FMD	foot-and-mouth disease
FSA	Food Standards Agency
GES	good ecological status
HASAWA 1974	Health and Safety at Work etc. Act 1974
HHW	household Hazardous waste
HID	Hazardous Installations Directorate
HIN	hazard identification number
HLW	high-level waste (radioactive)
HMCCE	Her Majesty's Commissioners of Customs and Excise
HMIP	Her Majesty's Inspectorate of Pollution (now the Environment Agency)
HMWB	heavily modified water body
HPA	Health Protection Agency
HRA 1998	Human Rights Act 1998
HSC	Health and Safety Commission
HSE	Health and Safety Executive
HWC	Hazardous Waste Catalogue
HWD	Hazardous Waste Directive
HWI	hazardous waste incineration
HWL	Hazardous Waste List

HWRA 2003	Household Waste Recycling Act 2003
ICE	Institution of Civil Engineers
ICER	Industry Council for Electronic Equipment Recycling
IEEP	Institute for European Environmental Policy
ILW	intermediate-level waste (radioactive)
IPC	Integrated Pollution Control
IPP	Integrated Product Policy
IPPC	Integrated Pollution Prevention and Control
ISO	International Standards Organisation
ISWA	International Solid Waste Association
LA	local authority
LAPC	Local Air Pollution Control
LAPPC	Local Air Pollution Prevention Control
LARAC	Local Authority Recycling Advisory Committee
LATS	Landfill Allowance Trading Scheme
LAWDCS	local authority waste disposal companies
LCPD	Large Combustion Plants Directive
LDD	local development documents
LDF	local development framework
LDS	local development scheme
LFD	Landfill Directive
LFR 2002	Landfill (England and Wales) Regulations 2002
LFT	landfill tax
LTCS	Landfill Tax Credit Scheme
MAFF	Ministry of Agriculture, Fisheries and Food (now DEFRA)
MARPOL 73/78	International Convention for the Prevention of Pollution from Ships 1973
MBT	mechanical and biological treatment
MEA	multilateral environmental agreement
MEP	Member of the European Parliament
MP	Member of Parliament
MRF	materials recovery facility
MSFUR	Merchant Shipping and Fishing Vessels (Port Waste Reception Facilities) Regulations 2003
MSW	municipal solid waste
mtpa	million tonnes per annum
NAO	National Audit Office
NEC	New Engineering Contract
NFU	National Farmers' Union
NGO	non-governmental organisation
NI	Northern Ireland
NRA	National Rivers Authority (now the Environment Agency)

NSCA	National Society for Clean Air
NVQ	National Vocational Qualification
OCD	operations control document
ODP	ozone-depleting potential
ODPM	Office of the Deputy Prime Minister
ODS	ozone-depleting substance
OECD	Organisation for Economic Co-operation and Development
OFGEM	Office of Gas and Electricity Markets
OPRA	operator pollution risk appraisal [now called (EP)OPRA]
PBB	polybrominated biphenyl
PCA 1991	Planning and Compensation Act 1991
PCB	polychlorinated biphenyl
PCPA 2004	Planning and Compulsory Purchase Act 2004
PCT	polychlorinated terphenyl
	Primary Care Trust
PERN	Packaging Waste Export Recovery Note
PFI	private finance initiative
PPC	Pollution Prevention and Control (regime)
PPCR 2000	Pollution Prevention and Control Regulations 2000
PPE	personal protective equipment
PPG	Planning Policy Guidance
PPP	public–private partnership
PPS	Planning Policy Statement
PRN	Packaging Recovery Note
PWR 1997	Producer Responsibility Obligations (Packaging Waste) Regulations 1997
RCEP	Royal Commission on Environmental Pollution
RCU	regional coordination unit
RDA	regional development agency
RDR	Coal Mines (Respirable Dust) Regulations 1975
REACH	Registration, Evaluation and Authorisation of Chemicals
REPIC	Recycling Electrical Producers Industry Consortium
RIA	Regulatory Impact Assessment
RICS	Royal Institute of Chartered Surveyors
RID	Règlements Internationale Relatif au Transport des Marchandises Dangereuses par Chemin de Fer (international regulations relating to the transportation of dangerous goods)
RIDDOR	Reporting of Injuries, Diseases and Dangerous Occurrences Regulations 1995
RIU	Regulatory Impact Unit
RLF	recycled liquid fuel

ROC	Renewables Obligation Certificate
RoHS	Restriction of the Use of Certain Hazardous Substances in Electrical and Electronic Equipment (Directive)
RPB	regional planning body
RPG	regional planning guidance
RSA 1993	Radioactive Substances Act 1993
RSS	regional spatial strategies
RTAB	regional technical advisory bodies
s.	section
ss.	sections
SA	Sustainability Appraisal
SA 1998	Scotland Act 1998
SCI	Society of Chemical Industry
	statement of community involvement
SEA	Strategic Environmental Assessment
SEPA	Scottish Environment Protection Agency
SI	Statutory Instrument
SIC	Standard Industrial Classification
SME	small and medium-sized enterprise
SMMT	Society of Motor Manufacturers and Traders
SNWP	Scottish National Waste Plan
SPD	supplementary planning documents
SRM	specified risk material
SSI	Scottish Statutory Instrument
SVQ	Scottish Vocational Qualification
SWEN	Special Waste Explanatory Note
SWF	Strategic Waste Fund
SWR 1996	Special Waste Regulations 1996
t/y	tonnes per year
TAC	Technical Adaptation Committee
TCPA 1990	Town and Country Planning Act 1990
TEC	see TREMCARD
TEU	Treaty on the European Union
TFS	transfrontier shipment
TFSR 1994	Waste Transfrontier Shipment Regulations 1994
TLP	tradeable landfill permit
TREMCARD	transport emergency card
TSE	transmissible spongiform encephalopathy
UA	unitary authority
UKAS	United Kingdom Accreditation Service
UKELA	United Kingdom Environmental Law Association
USEPA	United States Environmental Protection Agency

VOSA	Vehicle Operator Services Agency
VTC	vocational training certificate
WAC	waste acceptance criteria
	waste awareness certificate
WAMITAB	Waste Management Industry Training and Advisory Board
WAP	waste acceptance procedures
WCA	waste collection authority
WDA	waste disposal authority
WEEE	waste electrical and electronic equipment
WEEE 2004	Waste Electrical and Electronic Equipment Regulations 2004
WETA 2003	Waste Emissions Trading Act 2003
WFD	Waste Framework Directive
WIA 1991	Water Industry Act 1991
WID	Waste Incineration Directive
WINTO	Waste Industry National Training Organisation
WIP	Waste Implementation Programme
WM	waste management
WML	waste management licence
WMLR 1994	The Waste Management Licensing Regulations 1994
WMP	Waste Management Paper
WPA	waste planning authority
WRA	waste regulation authority
WRA 1991	Water Resources Act 1991
WRAP	Waste and Resources Action Programme
WTN	Waste Transfer Note

Contents

List of boxes

List of tables

List of figures

Chapter 1

The historical background

The waste management sector in the UK manages and engineers more than 120 million tonnes of waste per year, excluding agricultural waste, with an annual turnover of over £4.2 billion, and involving the operation of approximately 2000 facilities. Over 800 MW are generated from some of these facilities, for example through engineered methane delivery. Waste management projects demand highly qualified multidisciplinary teams, comprising, *inter alia*, engineers, geochemists, scientists, planners, surveyors, chemists, lawyers and project finance analysts. However, as waste management is increasingly regulated (some would say over-regulated and under-enforced), many more groups are finding their activities affected by environmental and waste management law.

Waste management practice has a distinctive history, and the legacy from its early days has been a hindrance for waste professionals. It is, alas, still an albatross. The field of waste management has inherited labels such as dumping and tipping, which are far from accurate descriptions of most, but not all, of today's practices, in England and Wales, and unfairly distracts from the science behind most of contemporary waste management technology. Recent developments in European Union (EU) environmental law have had far-reaching effects on many people, from the compost site operator to the supermarket supplier and to the consumer, who presently has little or no knowledge of the packaging regulations. The actual implementation of new EU waste management law is providing civil servants with economic, social and engineering application challenges.

Section 1.1 examines the history of waste management practice and regulation, and provides the reader with an original insight into the origins of today's culture. It describes how the disciplines of British waste management contracting, engineering and transportation law have evolved, and explains why, deservedly from past historical practices, the industry is now so heavily regulated. Understanding this historical background will hopefully influence and provide a balance for Parliament's scrutiny and decisions on proposed EU law

Box 1.1: Summary of some groups affected by waste management law

Academics	Food retailers
Accountants and financiers	Haulage and supply chain managers
Airports	Health and safety personnel
Animal feed manufacturers and	Hydrologists
suppliers	Insurers
Auditors	Investors
Catering outlets	Managers and administrators
Charity workers (education,	Manufacturing industry
community networks)	Marketing personnel
Civil servants	Medical practitioners
Civil, environmental, mechanical,	Mining and quarrying practitioners
chemical and geotechnical	Professional institutions (e.g. ICE,
engineers	RICS, CIWM, CIWEM)
Climatologists	Regulators
Collection authorities	Retail
Compliance officers	Slaughterhouses
Consultants in many disciplines	Small and medium-sized enterprises
Councillors and politicians	Sociologists
Customs and Excise	Students (WAMITAB, Btech, NVQ,
Disposal authorities	undergraduates and postgraduates)
Ecologists	Surveyors
Economists	Tanneries
Enforcers	Technical research and development
Entrepreneurs	Town planners
Environmental consultants	Transportation economics
Environmental scientists	Waste contractors, managers and
Exporters and importers	transporters
Farmers	Waste producers, commercial,
Food manufacturers	domestic and industrial

for the future (please see Box 1.2).[1] Field operational environmental professionals need to inform themselves of whether the new challenges set by the European Commission (EC) are achievable, and satisfy crude cost–benefit analyses. Their involvement in the decision-making process is crucial if the UK is to make informed future decisions; they have not been as involved as they should have been in Brussels in the past, as most of them now admit.

---

[1] See also the House of Commons All Party EFRA Select Committee Report 2002 on Hazardous waste, paragraph 22: 'We recommend that the minister takes this discussion forward and instigates a thorough review of the process by which environmental legislation is arrived at in the European Commission'.

Box 1.2: The fridge fiasco

The 2037/2000 Ozone Depleting Substances Regulation was adopted by the European Council in June 2000. In 2001, ill-equipped to implement the EU 2037/2000 Regulation, the UK saw a build-up of waste fridges and increased fly-tipping, dubbed by the media the 'fridge fiasco'. In April 2002 the Environment Minister told the House of Commons All Party Environment, Food and Rural Affairs (EFRA) Select Committee that the cost of processing the backlog of fridges could be of the order of £40 million. An inquiry undertaken by the Select Committee (4th Report, Session 2001–2002) later stated that 'We recommend that Regulations such as 2037/2000 should in future not be agreed to until the practical implications have been clarified'. In addition the UK Government should also:

- not agree to ill-conceived legislation in the first place
- consult industry early when assessing the implications of proposed legislation
- ensure that all points are clarified before signing
- look again at the plethora of forthcoming Regulations and Directives as a matter of urgency.

One must hope that the Government has heeded this all-party warning.

Source: House of Commons All Party Environment, Food and Rural Affairs Committee (2002), 4th Report, Session 2001–2002, *Disposal of Refrigerators*.

1.1. A short history of waste management legislation in England and Wales, 1306–2004

1.1.1. The evolution of waste management law

Contemporary waste management practices are of course only an evolution of the attitudes and importance that society has taken through the ages towards the protection of public health and the necessity for environmental pollution control. So it is often frequently said and sometimes reiterated to cliché status that those who cannot remember the past are condemned to repeat it.

Today's legal system began for all practical purposes in the reign of King Henry II, from 1154 to 1189. The first formal legislation to protect the aerial environment in the UK was passed in the 14th century, the Royal Proclamation Against Using Sea Coal in London, in 1306. This was followed 80 years later by Britain's first waste legislation, an Act of Richard II: removal of refuse on pain of forfeits, in 1388. Since Geoffrey Chaucer was Clerk of Works (1389–1391) to this king's cultured court, the forfeits could be both innovative and hurtful.

Before the 19th century, polluting deposits of waste or refuse more frequently led to private litigation than to public prosecution, and sometimes more robust remedies cloaked by night. The common law tort of nuisance gave a landowner the right to bring an action for damages, although his chance of success had to be measured by a standard of nuisance or annoyance that was inevitably crude and subjective as well as being exercised against a declining feudal background.

In 1848 for the first time the general public, as distinct from the private land-owner, received a form of code of protection under the Public Health Act 1848. This was the first source of control for the general public over the activities of people depositing waste in modern times. But why the long gap from 1388 to 1848? In the early phases of industrialisation the rights of large sections of society were disregarded, who as a result simply had to tolerate their environment. It is important to understand the extent of the historical squalor in our cities.

The Industrial Revolution, which began in the 1720s, brought about a change in society. The nation became occupied with the results of the invention of steam power, namely smelting, milling, engineering and increased manufac-turing. In the last 100 years we have become appalled at children down the mines, but from the forge floor to the whiteish collar offices, Britains living during the Industrial Revolution were proud of their achievements, which were reflected in the expansion of the British Empire and the national wealth. This wealth encouraged school and hospital building, and living standards inevitably began unequally to increase through most, but certainly not all, ranks of society.

When in 1862 Lord Derby was asked to chair the Select Committee on the Amelioration of Invisible Gaseous Pollution, it was an unusual move for the state to become involved with industrial processes, since many felt (including most political parties in the House of Commons) that Government initiatives to control pollution would have a damaging effect on national prosperity. When air pollution in London, and in particular the smell wafting onto the terraces of parliamentary Westminster, became intolerable, the Alkali Act 1863 was reluc-tantly passed.

The Alkali Act 1863 was more than just another statute as a result of Government intervention. It introduced the concept of Best Practicable Means (BPM), which required operators to reduce to the minimum the discharge of noxious or offensive gases. BPM is the basis of section 3 of the Pollution Prevention and Control Regulations 2000 SI 1973, which require operators to apply the Best Available Technique (BAT) to reduce emissions and the impact on the environment as a whole. This is referred to in today's Department for Environment, Food and Rural Affairs (DEFRA) policy guidance as the Best Practicable Environmental Option (BPEO).

The 1863 Act also introduced the origins of the Environment Agency and its present relationship with the waste management industry. In 1863 a new inspec-torate, the Alkali Inspectorate, was set up to cooperate with industry. Until 1862, Parliament and local authorities had attempted to deal with such nuisances by banning them, without making constructive suggestions as to how to abate them. When new problems became apparent, the remit was widened, and the Alkali Act 1863 consolidated into the Alkali Act 1906. Likewise, the Public Health Act 1875 gave enlarged powers to public authorities to enforce the Public Health Act 1848, the 19th century equivalent of the Environment Act 1995, which empowers today's Environment Agency.

Despite these improvements, legislation still focused on directly perceptible public health issues (e.g. the Smoke Abatement (London) Acts of 1853 and 1856). Even as late as the 19th century the connection between health and air and water pollution remained unproven, and little was done to control environmental damage as a result of industrialisation. There were, however, other influences. Poets began to emphasise the importance of nature and the individual. Artists began to make people look at their environment in a different way, portraying the dark satanic mills and blackened churches as images of oppression and despair. Hard-working people coming up in the world did not want their honest efforts associated with the decline of river or air quality. Still, even in the late 19th and early 20th centuries there remained throughout society an almost uncritical belief in continued unregulated progress.

So when did the environment become a consideration for the planners, at least, if not the public? As late as 1946 *Green Belt Cities* (F. Osborn, published byAdams, 1969)[3] gave a checklist on pp. 60–62 of 18 considerations for the very first stages of surveying and planning for a new town, yet there is not a single reference to environmental checks. Throughout the 200-page book there is no reference to pollution or the importance of sound municipal or commercial waste disposal practices. Extraordinary.

The Town and Country Planning Act 1909 gave limited power for authorities' schemes so as to control land as yet undeveloped. Sadly, this had no effect on the Thames Alps, huge mounds of municipal rubbish from Southwark to Dartford, the putrid smell of which unforgettably wafts out of the text of Dickens.[2] It was not until the 1930s that local authorities were extremely concerned about preventing a proliferation of refuse dumps within their boundaries from waste arising from outside their catchment areas. The South Hornchurch Dumps in Essex were three-quarters of a mile in length, one-third of a mile in breadth, and over 90 feet high. However, to protect uncontrolled dumping, counties neighbouring London passed a number of local Acts (e.g. the Surrey County Council Act 1932 (section 94), the Essex County Council Act 1933 (section 146) and the Hertfordshire County Council Act 1935 (Section 26)). In order to deposit waste arising from outside of a county, permission had

---

[2] See both *David Copperfield*, Chapter XLVII, 'At the riverside', and *Oliver Twist*, Chapter L, 'The pursuit and escape'.

[3] Osborn, F., *Green Belt Cities*, Evelyn, Adams & Mackay, London, 1969.

to be sought, subject to conditions. Waste contractors could of course dispose of waste arising from within their county area.

The Public Health Act 1936 placed local authorities under a duty (not an option nor a power nor a right, but a *duty*) to inspect their areas from time to time for statutory nuisances, which included premises in an obnoxious state or which emitted smells or dust that were prejudicial to health or amounted to a nuisance. Health authorities were given the power to prosecute and to serve abatement notices. When a notice was not complied with, the local authority could apply to a magistrates' court to make a nuisance order requiring abatement with no recurrence and/or a fine.

New legislation would normally be gradually and consistently implemented from the magistrates' courts with the guidance of a body of coherent case law, as, for example, has been the case with careless driving, under successive Road Traffic Acts. However, well before the outbreak of the Second World War, in 1938, air raid shelters had to be dug, air raid wardens and midnight fire watchers recruited, and superficially trained, gas masks and identity cards issued and town halls sandbagged, with all windows rendered as bomb-shatterproof as possible. So there was little time for councils to exercise their new 1936 powers, especially since most public sector officers were awaiting their call-up papers.

However, the 1936 Public Health Act only introduced a system of regulation and not of prevention. Local authorities were given no power to stop deposits being formed; they could only act after a nuisance had been created. Moreover, the powers given under the 1936 Act related only to individual sites which were in some way unsanitary or substandard. There was still no scope to take a comprehensive view of an area as a whole and regulate the pattern and formation of land uses therein. As far as the problem of waste management was concerned, population densities were not high, so filling gravel pits with rubbish (often contiguous with the groundwater) was little charge on the rates. Thus the culture began of out of sight, out of mind, against a background succinctly described as 'no votes in rubbish for councillors'. The pejorative labels of dumping and tipping unsurprisingly became common currency, which could only give a lasting impression to the media and the general public of lack of order and operational indiscipline.

The Town and Country Planning Act 1947 had regard to the social consequences associated with the redevelopment of a war-ravaged country. It did not advance or regress the cause of better national or local waste management planning, partly because the volume of waste materials was severely reduced owing to food rationing, restrictions on coal supply and packaging and little residues from the limited coal allowances for the household grate. In the following 25 years of the Cold War, little, if any, attention was paid to the dumping and tipping of wastes. 'Take it down to the tip' was a common request. This resulted in the desecration of a not inconsiderable part of the UK's countryside, albeit concealed sometimes in remote sites at the end of country lanes or in the hinterland of now disused RAF or US Air Force airfields.

Why was there so little progress during the 1950s and 1960s? The early 1950s was a time of unique optimism. Postwar euphoria prevailed. Everest was climbed, the Comet jet went into service,[4] with a popular young queen crowned. Widespread environmental damage following the war did not fit the conventional narrative. Britain was moving forward and away from austerity; people did not want to be reminded of bad things — the dust and noise from rebuilding after severe cratering bomb damage and the Korean war from 1950 to 1953 were enough. The advancement of modern conveniences added to the sense of freedom, and the 1950s and 1960s saw a social liberation reflected in music, fashion (the 'new look') and family life. People had suffered during the war, and technological progress was a good way to feel confident and forget previous vulnerability. As in the Industrial Revolution, people did not want their growing standard of living associated with environmental degradation — but the recovery in population and the growth of the consumer society were beginning to produce environmental problems.

In January 1953 a freak combination of climatic conditions in the North Atlantic caused an intensive storm compounded by a low-pressure surge that barrelled across Scotland, down the East Coast and across to the Netherlands. More than 300 people in Britain were killed, thousands of homes were destroyed and whole towns were flooded with their own diluted sewage. The death toll in Holland was more than 1000. Yet there was no culture of victimhood as there is today. Perhaps there should have been, but there was not. This was also shown in the then public phlegmatic attitude towards environmental depredations. A mother lost her daughter to hypothermia on Canvey Island and was bluntly told by her own mother and mother-in-law inland 'you've buried her, now you've got to forget her' — an emotional legacy of the Second World War, unacceptable in the 21st century. The same harsh view was taken of environmental bruising in those initial postwar years.

The Mines and Quarries (Tips) Act 1969 was a direct result of the deaths of 40 children in their schoolroom in the shadow of the rain soaked, poorly drained and unstable coal tips of Aberfan in the Welsh Valleys. So the first priority was public health and safety. The Health and Safety at Work etc. Act 1974 was derived from the excellent Robens Report. It recommended sweeping away intricate complex regulations and imposing a general duty on employees as well

---

[4] The jet roar over Hatfield was a reassuring sound of apparent aircraft design success and thus not only easily tolerated but indeed welcomed by the town and its environs. Never forget that noise is a sound that somebody else makes!

as employers to take all reasonable care of each other as well as members of the public on which their work might impinge.

1.1.2. Waste management practice reformed

Until 1972, and in practice for some time thereafter, the disposal of materials which seemingly had no further use was a localised service throughout the UK. It was the responsibility of small, mainly public but also private, organisations with few resources. The deposit of industrial or other waste substances was either undertaken by the manufacturer itself (producer responsibility before its formal time), often by dumping the wastes within the factory's curtilage, or by a small local quasi-specialist haulier who would be contracted to collect the materials for which no further use had been found. Materials were typically no more precisely defined than in a tea-stained and pocket-crumpled docket, pencil-inscribed 'chemical wastes', and left to entrepreneurial skills to arrive at a suitable grave. The dumping and tipping label would have made it all the more acceptable compared with the discipline of the shop floor.

The contractor therefore provided what was essentially a transportation service, and the majority had little technical understanding of the nature of the wastes or the environmental danger that could result from their disposal in an uncontrolled fashion. Many thousands of disposal sites were in use, and the wastes received therein in the same disparate form as the consideration invested to obtain their entrance. Sites were selected for their proximity and their convenience more than their geophysical suitability. Their interrelationship with the considerable national problem of the restoration of derelict land was wholly ignored, and many were extremely small and quite incapable of being administered efficiently or in an environmentally acceptable manner in relation to their contamination potential. Unless people's rights were affected, their interest was that of a benign observer, an attitude reflected later in the administration of the recent foot-and-mouth disease slaughter.

However, early in 1972 an incident involving the concealment of cyanide waste in drums found by children (fortuitously with no harm to human health) in the industrial Midlands of England became a national issue and this raised demands for tighter legislative control.

The Deposit of Poisonous Waste Act 1972 (DPWA 1972) was drafted in 3 weeks in May and was followed by enforcing Regulations in August, less than 3 months later. The Act made it an offence, at last, to deposit or abandon poisonous, noxious or polluting waste on land where it might give rise to an environmental hazard. It became a hazard if it were present in sufficient quantity or concentration to *threaten* death or injury to animals (e.g. bees, flies or hedgehogs) or persons (e.g. a poacher), or if it were to contaminate a ground or surface water supply. Deposit of the waste in containers was not to be taken as excluding the risk of such a threat, and the degree of risk was to be assessed by having regard to any measures which the owner or occupier might have taken to mini-mise such a risk and from preventing children from tampering with the waste. The phrase 'poisonous, noxious or polluting' came straight from the Rivers (Preven-tion of Pollution) Act 1951 from which there had been but minimal case law.

1.1.3. The potential effects of the Deposit of Poisonous Waste Act 1972

Under the DPWA 1972 a person charged with an offence could have broadly pleaded that either he acted under instructions from an employer or relied on information from others, providing that he honestly believed that the waste was acceptable to deposit. The Act made offenders liable for any resultant damage. Section 3 established a system of document notification procedures to alert the authorities of vehicle and materials' movements in connection with the removal or deposit of waste, and for connected purposes. This is the basis of today's Waste Transfer Note system. The DPWA 1972 was the first such Act in the world to be implemented and it had a number of significant effects:

- if the regional water authorities and the local authorities assiduously collected the notified data and intelligently analysed it, the size of the hazardous UK waste problem could be estimated, and recruitment, train-ing and planning integration could follow
- the potential elevation from a parish pump level of the UK industrial waste minimisation and recycling problem could be anticipated with the direct involvement of the county and metropolitan authorities, who would have to look hard at the problem and on the basis, as stated before, that their electorate were not concerned with successful rubbish management
- increased professional standards in the waste management industry resulting from recruitment at a higher educational level and achievement
- closure of many fly-blown, rodent-infested, litter-scattered sites, many of which doubled up as children's urban or rural playgrounds
- development of applied techniques for the selection and evaluation of landfill sites
- regional plants for the treatment and destruction of all forms of more intractable materials.

The DPWA 1972 was repealed and replaced by the Control of Pollution (Special Waste) Regulations 1980, superseded now by the Special Waste Regu-lations 1996, which in July 2004 in their turn are now subject to the Regulations under the EU Hazardous Waste Directive 91/689.

1.1.4. Developments in the UK following accession to the European Community

During the second half of the 20th century, developments in Europe (Table 1.1) established the European Economic Community (EEC), which later became the

Box 1.3: What is waste? Do not expect a simple litmus test

There is no decisive test as to whether or not something is waste, there are merely a number of indicators: 'waste is what falls away when one processes a material or an object and is not the end-product which the manufacturing system directly seeks to produce' (paragraph 32 in the 2002 European Court of Justice case C-90/00, *Palin Granit Oy* v. *Vehmassalon kansanterveystyön kuntayhtymän hallitus* 2 CMLR 24). This was a confused decision following inconsistent logic and legal precedent.

European Community (EC) and then the European Union (EU). The UK first applied to join the EEC in 1961. After more than a decade of negotiation and the French veto, the UK finally joined by ratifying and signing the Treaty of Accession in Brussels in 1972. Each new Member State had to sign an Act of Accession, to provide for EU legislation to form part of that Member State's national law. In the UK this was the European Communities Act 1972. The passing of this Act became a defining moment in the history of UK waste management law, since, after 1972, UK laws became an amalgamation of UK initiatives and EU Directives, and, when passed, certainly subordinate to the latter.

The Control of Pollution Act 1974 (COPA 1974) was the first statute regulating the disposal of waste to land and the discharge of effluent to watercourses and sewers. The COPA 1974 gave a definition of waste (paragraph 30(1)), which appears almost word for word in today's legislation (please see Chapter 2). The Act states that 'anything which is discarded or otherwise dealt with as if it were waste shall be presumed to be waste unless the contrary was proved'. The COPA 1974 inspired the European 75/442 Waste Framework Directive. Article 1(a) of the 75/442 Directive states that waste means 'any substance or object which the holder disposes of or is required to dispose of pursuant to the provisions of national law in force'. The 75/442 Directive was later amended by Directive 91/156, which changed the word 'dispose' to 'discard'.

In the 75/442 Directive Annex IIA (as amended by the 91/156 Directive) disposal includes 'the collection, sorting, transport and treatment of waste as well as storage pending tipping above or under ground or incineration'. Note how the non-technical word 'tipping' appears here in international law. According to Directive 75/442, disposal also included transformation operations necessary for its reuse, recovery or recycling. Directive 75/442 set out four key obligations:

- each Member State must designate a competent authority to be responsible for waste management
- each waste-competent authority must have a waste management plan

- all facilities to treat, store or dispose of waste must have a permit
- the polluter pays (which in practice, he often does not, e.g. car exhausts or farmers' fertilizers leaching into neighbouring streams).

Whilst individual sections of the Environmental Protection Act 1990 (EPA 1990) are explained simply in individual chapters, such as in Chapter 10 on the s.34 EPA Duty of Care requirements, and the collection and disposal duties of local authorities arising from this Act, which are described in Chapter 4, an overview of the contents of the EPA 1990 is provided below.

To implement the requirements of the 75/442 Directive, new legislation had to be introduced in the UK, and this is recounted in more detail in the following chapters of this practical guide. The EPA 1990 was the culmination of long discussions of amendments to environmental law, covering a wide range of topics not all relevant to waste management. The EPA 1990 was the most comprehensive piece of environmental legislation introduced in the UK.[5] Prior to the EPA 1990, pollution to the air, water and land had been subject to separate legislative regimes.

Part I of the EPA 1990 introduced an integrated pollution control approach, by which releases into all parts of the environment by factories etc. engaged in industrial and certain other processes are subject to a single authorisation system. This was the system of Integrated Pollution Control, which is applicable to the release of pollutants to air, water and land from certain processes, and established under s.7 the criteria of Best Available Techniques Not Entailing Excessive Cost (BATNEEC), explained more fully in Chapter 8. Integrated Pollution Control is currently being replaced by the Integrated Pollution Prevention and Control regime, but fundamental requirements for BATNEEC, now abbreviated to just BAT, still apply.

Part II of the EPA 1990 (ss.29–78) replaced and strengthened the waste disposal law in the COPA 1974. Part III, ss.79–85, consolidated and reformed the law on statutory nuisances (please see Chapter 9 of this guide). Part IV, ss.86–98, replaced the Litter Act 1983, which dealt with the offence of leaving litter, and added new powers. Part V made a number of amendments to the Radio Active Substances Act 1960. Part VI, ss.106–127, introduced a new legal regime governing the use of genetically modified organisms. Part VII replaced the Nature Conservation Council and the Countryside Commission. Part VIII made provision for public registers of land which may be contaminated, hazardous substances, pollution at sea and stubble burning.

---

[5]*The Environmental Protection Act 1990 (Current Law Statutes Annotated Reprints)*, by S. R. Tromans, provides a fully annotated and explained copy of the Act.

Also under the EPA 1990, hazardous waste is called Special waste,[6] although England and Wales have recently adopted the EU term Hazardous waste to conform with the definition given in the European Waste Catalogue and the 91/689 Hazardous Waste Directive. COPA 1974 was superseded by Part II of the Environmental Protection Act 1990 (EPA 1990), the Environment Act 1995 (EA 1995), the Water Resources Act 1991 (WRA 1991) and the Water Industry Act 1991 (WIA 1991), although the latter two have recently been amended by the Water Act 2003.

Under the Control of Pollution (Amendment) Act 1989 supplemented by the Controlled Waste (Registration of Carriers and Seizure of Vehicles) Regulations 1991 (as amended) it is an offence to carry Controlled waste, now called Directive waste (because the definition of waste given in the EU 75/442 Directive, amended by 91/156, is now used), without being registered with the Environment Agency. In order to comply with the Duty of Care (s.34 EPA 1990), recipients of waste have to check carriers' registrations on a regular basis, even if using a firm which they continually employ, since registrations can be revoked, unknown to them. The Controlled Waste Regulations 1992 SI 588 describe waste to be treated as household waste, and provide criteria for the types of household waste for which a charge for collection may be made. The EA 1995 makes provisions for the implementation of producer responsibility. It established the Government regulatory and enforcement bodies, the Environment Agency and the Scottish Environment Protection Agency. It also introduced the contaminated land regime, the sections of which were transferred to be s.78A–78YC in Part IIA of the EPA 1990. An unusual procedure.

In Scotland almost all matters relating to the environment are within the legislative competence of its Parliament, save for those reserved matters such as pollution relating to oil and gas transportation, marine transport, and nuclear energy, given in Schedule 8 of the Scotland Act 1998. For Wales, the Westminster Parliament has the exclusive competence to make primary environmental legislation. The Welsh National Assembly has powers to make secondary legislation. For Northern Ireland, as long as Stormont's powers have been diverted to Westminster, there lies the competence. (Please see also Chapter 4.)

The 90/313 Freedom of Access to Information on the Environment Directive was implemented in the UK via the Environmental Information Regulations 1992 SI 3240. This gave the public a limited statutory right to access

---

[6] The term 'Special' in the old Department of the Environment language was spelt with a small 's', which became the source of some confusion, particularly amongst overseas environmental experts, from, for example, the US Environmental Protection Agency (USEPA). It would have been helpful if the statutory description of the waste could have been spelt with a capital 'S' to distinguish it from terms such as 'special care' or 'special notice'.

environmental information held by public authorities and other bodies. The 90/313 Directive was replaced in January 2003 by the 2003/4 (*sic*) Public Access to Environmental Information Directive. (Please see footnote 1 in Chapter 13.)

The European Convention on Human Rights (ECHR) 1950 (and its five Protocols in the following decade) is an agreement derived from the Council of Europe to protect the rights and freedoms of everyone. However, under the ECHR, plaintiffs have to take their case to the European Court of Human Rights in Strasbourg, which is time-consuming and expensive. The Human Rights Act 1998 (HRA 1998) allows the rights already covered under the ECHR UK to be pursued under the UK legal system, hopefully making those rights more accessible. UK cases must take into account previous decisions in Strasbourg under the ECHR. There are several sections in the HRA 1998, but the key areas affecting waste management activities are: Article 6, the right to a fair trial (this can affect planning inquiries); Article 7, retrospective crimes; and Article 8, the right to privacy (this can affect waste analysis projects).

The implementation into the UK of the HRA 1998 is best illustrated by the 'business as usual' attitude adopted by the courts in such cases as *Alconbury Developments* v. *The Secretary of State for the Environment, Transport and the Regions* (House of Lords 1998 — for more detail please see Box 4.2). In effect, so long as measures are in place to safeguard the fairness of the proceedings and the decision is subject to ultimate judicial control, the tribunal does not have to be truly independent in that it can be appointed by the Government. (Please see Chapter 4.)

1.2. The rise of the European environmental influence

The period from the 1300s to the 1800s saw the birth of waste legislation, starting with the regulation of the midden of the Middle Ages and ending with the Alkali Act of 1863, which introduced, as we have seen, the concept of BPM to minimise harmful discharges. Historical evidence shows that these changes were driven by prosperity, the growing population and the need to protect public health. The first initiative was taken by the Crown, as we have related, in the form of a Royal Proclamation in 1306, then a Royal Act in 1388. In the gap between 1388 and 1848 England was busy. The nation fought against foreign invasion, the king was excommunicated from the Catholic Church, our merchant fleets explored the world and Europe experienced the renaissance of art, literature and science. But why is all of this important? Because it is necessary to understand that the EU comprises individual Member States, many of which have differing legal systems. It may thus be a problem incorporating the 200 EU environmental legislative instruments passed to date into the legal systems of the 10 May 2004 accession countries. Table 1.1 summarises the evolution of the EU.

Table 1.1: The evolution of the EU

Signed/ approved	Into force	Summary	Key outcomes
1951	1952	The Treaty of Paris established the European Coal and Steel Community (ECSC)	1. ECSC
1957	1958	The Treaty of Rome established the European Economic Community (EEC), with the aim of forming a common agricultural policy and common industrial market	2. EEC 3. Single Market
1965	1967	A treaty was signed in Brussels to merge the EEC, European Atomic Community (Euratom) and the ECSC under a single organisation, the European Community (EC), and also to establish a single Council and a Commission for the Member States	4. EC 5. European Council and European Commission
1972	1973	The UK, Ireland and Denmark signed the Treaty of Accession to join the EC	6. The UK accedes to join the EC
1972	1973	The European Communities Act 1972 provided for legislation passed within the EC to form part of British national law	7. EC law is supreme over UK law
1972	–	Member States asked the European Commission to draw up an environmental policy. The policy was approved by the Council in 1973	8. EC first action programme
1986	1987	The Single European Act amended the Treaty of Rome to include the aim of Environmental Protection Article 130r(2)	9. Principles for environmental policy set out

Table 1.1: Contd

Signed/ approved	Into force	Summary	Key outcomes
1989	–	The first EC Waste Management Strategy was drawn up	10. First European Waste Management Strategy
1992	1993	The Maastricht Treaty changed the name of the EC to the European Union (EU)	11. EC became the EU
1996	–	A revised version of the European Commission's waste strategy was adopted	12. European Waste Management Strategy revised
1997	1999	The Amsterdam Treaty amended the Treaty on European Union (TEU) and other EU and EC treaties	13. EU and EC treaties merged
2001	2003	The Treaty of Nice merged the former treaties of the EU and the EC, and set out reforms and time-frames in preparation for EU enlargement in May 2004	
2003	2004	Ten new countries signed the 2003 Treaty of Accession (Athens) to join the EU, eight of which are from the ex-Communist Bloc. This is the lengthiest EU treaty yet, containing 4900 pages, and potentially increasing the number of Member States to 27 in 2007	14. EU membership to increase from 15 Member States (population of 375 million) to approximately 25 (population of ~ 450 million)

In May 2004 it is difficult to envisage that the 1958 Treaty of Rome contained no direct provision for an environmental policy; it was amended by the Single European Act 1986[7] to include the aim of environmental protection (numbered at the time as Article 130r). The Treaty of Rome as amended by the

[7] The Single European Act established a single European market to allow for the free movement of goods, people and services between Member States.

Single European Act was further amended by the Treaty of Amsterdam (Article 130r is now Article 174). European environmental policy has five key features:

- prevention is better than remedial measures
- environmental damage should be remedied at source
- the polluter pays
- environmental policies must be integrated into other EC policies
- regard should be paid to the proximity principle.

These principles must be taken account of in the preparation of all EU environmental legislation, although the third feature is not consistently applied. To propagate these principles, the EU has developed a number of environmental strategies.

1.3. EU strategies

There are two main EU strategies that affect waste management:

- the Waste Management Strategy
- the EU Sustainable Development Strategy.

The EC recently carried out a review of the development of EU environmental policy from 2001 to 2003. According to the report, the key challenge is to 'decouple economic growth from environmental pressures'.

1.3.1. The EU Waste Management Strategy

In 1972 the Member States asked the EC to draw up its first environmental action programme. The first EC Waste Management Policy was set out in the EC's 1989 Waste Management Strategy. This had three key features:

- the waste hierarchy (reduce, reuse, recycle, recover energy, dispose)
- the proximity principle
- waste disposal self-sufficiency.

The proximity principle requires waste to be recovered, treated or disposed of as near to the source as possible. Waste disposal self-sufficiency, in broad terms, means that each country and its regions should, where possible, manage its own waste materials. A legal framework for the implementation of this strategy was set out in the 75/422 Waste Framework Directive, later amended by the 91/156 Waste Directive.

A revised version of the Waste Management Strategy was adopted by the EU in 1996. This reaffirmed the waste hierarchy and emphasised that waste reduction is a first priority. The EU has undertaken a series of action programmes to implement the environmental policies, the most recent of which, the 6th Community Environmental Action Programme, was set out in 2002 in

EU Council Decision 1600/2002. The programme aims to develop seven priority areas as Thematic Strategies, one of which is Waste Prevention and Recycling.

1.3.2. The EU sustainable development strategy

Every public and private sector environmental manager should know that Dr Brundtland, invited in 1983 to chair the World Commission on Environment and Development, defined sustainable development as development that 'meets the needs of the present without compromising the ability of future generations to meet their own needs.' The EU Sustainable Development Strategy stipulates that sustainable development must be at the core of all Member States' policies, a little like every government's imprecation that the environment should be at the heart of all its policies. Certainly well intentioned, but what in practice does it mean?

The term 'sustainable' now appears in public inquiries (e.g. planning appeals) and the statute books. In England and Wales, under s.4(1) EPA 1995, one of the principal aims of the Environment Agency is to carry out its duties 'so as to make an appropriate contribution towards achieving sustainable development'. In practice, the term 'sustainable development' is poorly defined and inconsistently applied. Sustainable development is now sometimes abbreviated to sustainability, but, alas, with no greater definition in meaning.[8] However, it is commonly accepted that sustainable development balances the costs and benefits of three criteria:

- economic
- social
- environmental.

The difficulty lies in determining the balance between the need for environmental protection and social and economic progress.

1.4. Implementation of the EU strategies

Once the EC has developed its strategies, its Member States must then implement them. The key methods are:

- legislation
- coercive measures (bans, restrictions, phase-outs)

---

[8] For a discussion on the application and general usefulness of the phrase see Hawkins R. G. P and Shaw H. (2004), 'Is sustainable development environmentally sustainable?', *CIWM Wastes Management Journal*, Feb. See also Hawkins R. G. P and Shaw H. (2004), 'Sustainable development: 'a monument for eternity'?', *Proc. ICE Engng Sustain.*, **2**.

- financial incentives (e.g. the landfill tax)
- voluntary measures
- education and information
- assessment techniques (e.g. environmental impact assessment).

Principles from EU strategies such as the proximity principle have now entered UK laws and courts, principally through legislation. The three key sources of EU law that affect waste management activities are:

- regulations
- directives
- decisions.

1.4.1. Regulations
Regulations are used to legislate for the whole of the EU. Once approved by Members of the European Parliament at the proposal of the EC, regulations then have the force of law without having to be implemented by individual national legal systems, e.g. the 1774/2002 Animal By-Products Regulation. Just because regulations apply to all Member States, the interpretation in each Member State is not necessarily uniform.

1.4.2. Directives
Directives are the key mechanism for waste management legislation. They set out legally binding objectives, but individual Member States can chose the form they take in the national legal system and the methods for achieving the objectives. Probably the most important Directives affecting waste management are the 75/442 Waste Framework Directive (as amended by the 91/156 Directive) and the 99/31 Landfill Directive.

If a Directive's objectives are not met by a given deadline then Member States can be fined. For example, the UK is currently at risk of a £180 million per year fine for not fully implementing the requirements of the Landfill Directive by the given deadline, and so are several other EU countries.[9]

The average GDP per capita of the 10 new Member States (the 'accession countries') is currently at 40% of existing EU levels. If England and Wales have been dilatory in complying with the succession of EU waste management legislation, how will the accession countries fare even if some have been granted derogations for implementing certain Directives for a number of years?

---

[9] See the Government Strategy Unit publication *Waste Not Want Not* (www.number-10.gov.uk/su/waste/report/01.html).

1.4.3. Decisions

Decisions are legally binding, and are used when the EC concludes that a particular activity is contrary to a particular EU policy. The decision is addressed to a particular Member State, organisation or even an individual; for example, proceedings were taken against Greece for the pollution of Cretan waters (please see Box 4.3).

1.5. The Waste Framework Directive

The 75/442 Waste Framework Directive, as amended by the 91/156 Directive, has six key features:

- It defines the meaning of waste.
- It requires Member States to encourage the waste hierarchy (reduce, reuse, recycle, recover energy, dispose).
- Waste must be managed without harm to human health or the environment.
- Member States must establish an integrated network of facilities using the BAT (please see Chapter 8), and must strive for self-sufficiency in waste disposal.
- A competent authority must be designated to implement the Directive (e.g. the Environment Agency or Scottish Environmental Protection Agency).
- All disposal and recovery operations must be permitted (licensed) by the competent authority.

The 75/442 Directive (as amended by the 91/156 Directive) provides lists of materials which are waste when discarded, and activities classed as disposal or recovery operations (please see Chapter 2).

Directives relating to specific issues that come under a Framework Directive are called Daughter Directives, for example the 94/62 Packaging and Packaging Waste Directive. Recent European case law has ruled that provisions for the

---

Box 1.4: Article 4 of the 75/442 Directive

Member States shall take the necessary measures to ensure that waste is disposed of without endangering human health and without harming the environment, and in particular without:

- risk to water, air, soil and plants and animals
- causing a nuisance through noise or odours
- adversely affecting the countryside or places of special interest.

See the important interpretation of 'without risk' in *R* v. *Daventry DC* ex parte *Thornby Farms* 2001 EHLR 94, p. 106, summarised in Box 6.1 of Chapter 6.

definition of waste in a Daughter Directive will prevail over the 75/442 Framework Directive definition in cases concerning the material which the Daughter Directive specifically sought to regulate.

1.6. The principle of subsidiarity

Article 5 of the 75/442 Waste Framework Directive states that the network of waste management facilities must 'enable the Community as a whole to become self-sufficient in waste disposal and the Member States to move towards that aim individually, taking into account geographical circumstances or the need for specialised installations for certain types of waste.'

The definition of subsidiarity is slightly obfuscated by the EU language in which it is written. The original Treaty on the European Union (TEU) signed in Maastricht on 7 February 1992, which came into force on 1 November 1993, was amended at an intergovernmental conference in 1997 in Amsterdam. From this amended TEU came the *acquis communautaire* for which there is no formal definition, but which goes beyond the formal acceptance of EU law to include rules which have no binding force. These would include opinions and resolutions of the Council and Commission. The term has more of a political than a legal meaning, implying acceptance of the fields of cooperation in foreign policy, justice and home affairs.

Subsidiarity[10] is described in the Treaty of Amsterdam, which states that there is a process of creating an ever closer union among the people of Europe in which decisions are taken as directly as possible to the citizens, in accordance with the principle of subsidiarity. The Treaty of Amsterdam also has a protocol on the application of the principle of subsidiarity and proportionality. However, Article 5 states that the Community shall take action in accordance with the principle of subsidiarity, only if and insofar as the objectives of the proposed action cannot be sufficiently achieved by the Member States individually, and can therefore by reason of the scale or effect of the proposed action be better achieved by the Community. Therefore, the onus is on the EC to justify at a Community level the actions arising from its proposals rather than leaving it to the Member States. There may well be challenges in the future in the European Court of Justice on the grounds that a particular proposed EC measure offends against the principle of subsidiarity.

---

[10] This was certainly an early argument of the UK Government; for example, the statement of the Environment Minister of State, Tim Yeo, in 1993, just over a decade ago, argued that industrial states should be free to make decisions on how to dispose of their own waste in their own country.

Many may consider that the landfill option would have been managed better by the Member States individually, since many geological and geophysical characteristics are unique to specific countries. Instead, the principle of harmonised law was followed, and all the Member States were subject to the same targets and requirements. The problem is that the individual performance target dates were chosen without a clear rationale, let alone an open and transparent cost–benefit analysis.

Closer to home, the principle of subsidiarity is nowhere better illustrated than in the UK. Like the English/Welsh national waste strategy, the Scottish national waste strategy concludes that the current dependence on landfill (in 2004, there are about 240 licensed sites in Scotland) is unsustainable. However, the Scottish strategy needs to take account of the widely varying topography and population densities throughout the Highlands and islands, the lowlands down to the Clyde and across to the Borders, as well as its different energy profile. Over 50% of energy is derived from nuclear generation, and there are abundant reserves of hydroelectricity. Yet all Member States are subject to the same landfill targets. It is difficult, therefore, to understand how the European Parliament thought that this would be practicable. All in all, the Landfill Directive provided too much detail, which will be unevenly implemented throughout the 25 Member States. A cautionary tale for future EC proposed legislation.

Chapter 2

Defining waste

All waste managers from the public or private sector, whether producers, engineers, transporters or regulators, even of minimal experience, know that the definition of waste is crucial, because its correct application in each and every circumstance dictates which activities are subject to the exigent and complex UK and EU regulatory regimes. The penalties for getting it wrong can mean not only the loss of a waste management licence, but the loss of the status to hold one. Compared with the loss of the rice bowl, financial sanctions can be secondary.

The definition of waste is the most perplexing question in waste management law. The fundamental questions, however, are simple:

- When does a material become waste?
- When does a material cease to be waste?

2.1. How the definition of waste has developed

Table 2.1 sets out the tortuous chronological list of events in attempting to establish a modular process for determining the meaning of waste, first in the UK courts, and then in the European Court of Justice (ECJ).

The statutory definition of waste, according to English law, is shown in Box 2.1. This definition, based on s.30 COPA 1974, appears relatively straightforward; the wording states that a waste is something that has been discarded. But even this definition can be subjective. If a beer is left undrunk by a parting guest and so discarded in its glass, and then someone else picks it up and starts drinking it, then the half-full glass no longer is waste, at least in the mind of the consumer. If the landlord, against all public health decency and many consumer protection and licensing laws, tips the hall-filled glass back into the keg, then when has it changed its status from waste?

Table 2.1: The evolution of the definition of waste

Date	Regulation	Type	Summary
1974	Section 30 of the Control of Pollution Act 1974 (COPA 1974)	Primary legislation	Waste was originally defined in s.30 COPA 1974
1975	Waste Framework Directive 75/442	European Directive	Directive 75/442 (based on COPA 1974) provided a definition of waste with an emphasis on ascertaining the intention of the original owner to discard the material
1990	Section 75 of the Environmental Protection Act 1990 (EPA 1990)	Primary legislation	The s.30 COPA 1974 definition was transposed almost verbatim into s.75 EPA 1990, and s.30 COPA 1974 was repealed
1974–1994	English case law	Case law	English case law (e.g. *Kent County Council v. Queenborough Rolling Mill* 1990) interpreted certain words and phrases from the COPA 1974, equally applicable to the wording of the EPA 1990, but before the ECJ decisions
1991	91/156 Waste Directive	European Directive	The 91/156 Directive amended the 75/442 Directive, replacing the term 'dispose' with 'discard'

Between 1975 and 1994 the statutory definition of waste in the UK did not accord with the requirements of the 75/442 Waste Framework Directive. Under the European Communities Act 1972 the UK had to transpose the 75/442 Directive fully into domestic legislation. Extant legislation is shown below

Year	Title	Type	Description
1994	The Waste Management Licensing Regulations 1994 SI 1056 (WMLR 1994)	Secondary legislation	The WMLR 1994 included provisions to implement the 75/422 Directive. Regulation 19 states that Schedule 4 shall have effect, which contains a list of all substances or objects that are waste when discarded. Schedule 4 relates directly to Annex I of the 75/422 Directive
1994	Department of the Environment (DoE) Circular 11/94	Circular	Circular 11/94 provides, *inter alia*, Government (DoE) guidance on the definition of waste, and an attempt to clarify the position in relation to the WMLR 1994. A (very) different Circular may perhaps be issued in 2005
1994	The 94/62 Packaging and Packaging Waste Directive	European Directive	The definition of recycling is given in the 94/62 Directive. This definition was used in the 3rd Mayer Parry Recycling 2003 case, see below
1996	Part III of the Finance Act 1996 (FA 1996)	Primary legislation	According to s.64 FA 1996 landfill tax must be paid on any material that is disposed of as a waste at a landfill. The definition is based on whether the owner has the intention of discarding the material
1997	Producer Responsibility Obligations (Packaging Waste) Regulations 1997 SI 648	Secondary legislation	The 94/62 Directive was implemented through the (Packaging Waste) Regulations 1997 SI 648 Producer Responsibility Obligations
1998–today	ECJ case law	European case law	Since the WMLR 1994, UK Courts have had fully to apply the 75/422 Directive definition of waste. In case of judicial difficulty, cases have been referred to the ECJ. It can take up to 2 years or more for a final decision

Box 2.1: The waste definition in s.75 EPA 1990

> **75.**—(1) The following provisions apply for the interpretation on this part.
>
> (2) 'Waste' includes
>
>   (a) any substance which constitutes a scrap material or an effluent or other unwanted surplus substance arising from the application of any process; and
>
>   (b) any substance or article which requires to be disposed of as being broken, worn out, contaminated or otherwise spoiled;
>
> but does not include a substance which is an explosive within the meaning of the Explosives Act 1875.
>
> (3) Anything which is discarded or otherwise dealt with as if it were waste shall be presumed to be waste unless the contrary is proved.

Following the COPA 1974, a body of UK case law developed, which interpreted the wording of the COPA 1974/EPA 1990 definition of waste. Although much of this case law is now largely superseded by ECJ judgements (see below), it provides a useful background for the waste manager's imagination, instinct and personal judgement.

- *Ashcroft* v. *Michael McErlain Ltd* (1985). Section 30 of the COPA 1974 stated that when a material is discarded and deposited by its producer it becomes waste. Excavated material, whilst usually considered to be waste awaiting further use, was held here not to be so since the material was taken directly from the site for use at a paddock. An outlet for the waste is usually found in advance to avoid double handling. This case relied on the dictionary definition of waste, in which a material must be thrown aside for it to become waste. Since the material was not placed by the roadside or into a skip, but taken straight to the recipient, it was not classed as waste. (This case shows both common sense and its age.)

- *Berridge Incinerators Ltd* v. *Nottinghamshire County Council* (1987). This case was essentially a dispute over the validity of Berridge Incinerators' planning permission, and whether a waste disposal licence could be issued under the COPA 1974. The person receiving a material discarded by a producer receives waste. The judge observed that:

  > If I have an old fireplace to dispose of to a passing rag and bone man, its character as a waste is not affected by whether or not I can persuade the latter to pay me 50 pence for it. In my judgement, the correct approach is to regard the material from the point of view of the person who produces it ....

  This statement is a fundamental principle for today's definition of waste.

- *Kent County Council* v. *Queenborough Rolling Mill* (QRM) (1990) (when the COPA 1974 definition was the law). QRM wanted sorted material to raise the level of their land adjacent to the River Medway. But the imported material, which had been previously discarded at an old pottery site, was deemed to be waste, even though QRM had found a use for the material, albeit sometime after it had originally been discarded. The material also remains a waste even if it is reclaimed and undergoes intermediate processing (such as sorting or grinding), since the nature of the material remains the same. Thus, QRM was required to have a waste disposal licence under COPA 1974.

- *R* v. *Rotherham Magistrates* (1990). Discarded detritus was deposited on a golf course. Mr Justice Shiemann[1] described the continuing difficulty to define precisely what waste is (and on which many hundreds of thousand of pounds can rest through the landfill tax or conforming to licensing requirements). He said it was comparable to looking at a Victorian Escher patterned vase, when first from one angle you can see birds, and then from another, those birds have turned to fishes.

2.2. The current statutory definition of waste

The task of providing a definition of waste would be easier if the aforementioned UK body of case law had been built on and refined. But, alas, the UK Government were rightly taken to task by the European Commission in that neither the COPA 1974 nor the EPA 1990 definition fully conformed to the 75/422 Waste Framework Directive. To avoid EU financial sanctions, the then Department of the Environment (DoE) drafted the Waste Management Licensing Regulations 1994 (WMLR 1994), which invoked the 75/442 Directive European definition (amended by the 91/156 Directive).

Box 2.2: The 75/422 EC Waste Framework Directive definition of waste

Article 1	(a) **waste** means any substance or object which the holder disposes of or is required to dispose of pursuant to the provisions of national law in force
	(b) **disposal** means the collection, sorting, transport and treatment of waste as well as its storage and tipping above or under ground, - the transformation operations necessary for its re-use, recovery or recycling.

---

[1] Lord Justice Schiemann has been promoted to the ECJ, where he will hopefully bring some intellectual rigour to the judgement process.

Matters have, however, become more complex, not only because of the incorporation of the EU definition into UK law but also because under the 91/156 Directive Article 1(a) is rephrased and reworded so that waste means:

> any substance or object in the categories set out in Annex I which the holder discards or intends or is required to discard.

The 91/156 Directive includes several Annexes giving lists of substances or objects which are waste when discarded, and activities deemed to be waste recovery operations. These Annexes are referred to verbatim in Schedule 4 of the WMLR 1994.

- Substances or Objects which are Waste When Discarded (WMLR 1994 Schedule 4 Part II, Annex I 75/442 Directive)
- Waste Disposal Operations (WMLR 1994 Schedule 4 Part III, Annex IIA 75/442 Directive)
- Waste Recovery Operations (WMLR 1994 Schedule 4 Part IV, Annex IIB 75/442 Directive).

All materials or objects that come under Schedule 4 Part II that a person discards, intends to discard, or is required to discard are called Directive Wastes.

The wording of Q16 in Box 2.3 shows how difficult it is to determine exactly the true definition of waste according to Directive 75/442.

DoE Circular 11/94 attempted to explain the meaning of waste according to the WMLR 1994 75/442 definition. In summary, a material was waste if it is:

- consigned to a waste disposal operation
- illegally disposed of, or abandoned
- consigned to a specialised recovery operation
- the product from a specialised recovery operation
- that a producer pays to have a material removed, which usually indicates that it is waste
- sold for commercial use or given away in circumstances where it can be expected to be reused and should not be regarded as 'discarded' and so cannot be waste (thus an Oxfam plastic sack contents are not waste).

Complementary to the EU attempt to define waste is the 94/62 Packaging and Packaging Waste Directive, which defines the term 'recycling'. This term determines the point at which a substance ceases to become waste. Article 3(7) of the 94/62 Directive defines recycling as 'the reprocessing in a production process of the waste materials for the original purpose or for other purposes including organic recycling but excluding energy recovery'. The definition of waste according to a Daughter Directive takes precedence over the 75/442 definition if the material to which the Daughter Directive refers is in question. As more recycling Daughter Directives take effect, the need for a clear definition will become all the more crucial.

Box 2.3: Substances or objects which are waste when discarded (WMLR 1994 Schedule 4 Part II, Directive Wastes)

1. Production or consumption residues not otherwise specified in this part of this schedule (Q1).
2. Off-specification products (Q2).
3. Products whose date for appropriate use has expired (Q3).
4. Materials spilled, lost or having undergone other mishap, including any materials, equipment, etc., contaminated as a result of the mishap (Q4).
5. Materials contaminated or soiled as a result of planned actions (e.g. residues from cleaning operations, packing materials, containers, etc.) (Q5).
6. Unusable parts (e.g. reject batteries, exhausted catalysts, etc.) (Q6).
7. Substances which no longer perform satisfactorily (e.g. contaminated acids, contaminated solvents, exhausted tempering salts, etc.) (Q7).
8. Residues of industrial processes (e.g. slags, still bottoms, etc.) (Q8).
9. Residues from pollution abatement processes (e.g. scrubber sludges, baghouse dusts, spent filters, etc.) (Q9).
10. Machining or finishing residues (e.g. lathe turnings, mill scales, etc.) (Q10).
11. Residues from raw materials extraction and processing (e.g. mining residues, oil field slops, etc.) (Q11).
12. Adulterated materials (e.g. oils contaminated with PCBs, etc.) (Q12).
13. Any materials, substances or products whose use has been banned by law (Q13).
14. Products for which the holder has no further use (e.g. agricultural, household, office, commercial and shop discards, etc.) (Q14).
15. Contaminated materials, substances or products resulting from remedial action with respect to land (Q15).
16. Any materials, substances or products which are not contained in the above categories (Q16).

(The reference in parentheses at the end of each paragraph of this part of this schedule is the number of the corresponding paragraph in Annex I to Directive75/442, as amended by Directive 91/156.)

Source: www.hmso.gov.uk.

In practice the DoE Circular 11/94 has not been sufficient for determining whether materials are waste or not. Whilst the Government and the Environment Agency may provide guidance, Circular 11/94 clearly states in paragraph 2.12 that the interpretation of the Directive definition is a matter for the courts to decide. Each case needs to be decided upon the particular facts. In recent years a number of high-profile cases have been referred to the ECJ[2] for determination,

---

[2] The ECJ should not be confused with the European Court of Human Rights or the European Court of Auditors.

and part of Circular 11/94 has been superseded by ECJ judgements. The supremacy of the ECJ over the English legal system has meant that the interpretation of the definition of waste has changed, often as a result of the lack of clear definition of key terms. The ECJ judges, generally, do not have judicial experience in advance, and, in any event, have naturally not been trained in or had the experience of the English and Welsh legal system.

2.3. EU case law

Many of the prior English cases involved the reuse or recycling of materials, which the supplier had never regarded over the years to be waste, and this trend continues today in the ECJ. More recent case law has interpreted the term 'discard' to mean unwanted by the original owner, or not needed for the original purpose from the point of view of the original owner (regardless of whether someone else has a use for the materials later). But the ECJ, through its judgements as we shall see below, does not propound one single template for the definition of waste. Sometimes the ECJ has arrived at a more visceral than a logical forensic judgement in classifying certain materials as waste, with the apparent intent, albeit superficially praiseworthy, of protecting the public health by making them subject to the EC waste legislation. The inconsistent definitions, let alone delays of two or more years before the ECJ comes to a decision, result in general uncertainty for business and, even more important, detriment to the environment, since capital expenditure for the development, manufacture and engineering of materials-handling equipment may be delayed.

Mayer Parry Recycling Ltd (MPR) is a large international recycling company, which ran a facility to sort and shred scrap metal (partly from packaging), and transform it into a grade 3B material, which could then be sold on to make steel ingots. MPR's 5-year legal ordeal involved a series of cases, which started with the question of whether the premises required a waste management licence. The first case was brought by the Environment Agency in November 1998 in the Chancery Division, which ruled that the material did fall within the WMLR 1994.

Scrap metal that has not been completely recycled clearly cannot be allowed to circulate freely around the EU uncontrolled according to the Schengen agreement on border controls.[3] The process must produce a new product, not just a raw material, so that a high level of environmental protection is achieved. The metal packaging processed by MPR contained paint and other contaminants, and these had to be removed before the steel mill could use them. Even though the processed material had economic value, it was still deemed to be waste. Some important outcomes of the MPR case are:

---

[3] For background information on the Schengen agreement see: news.bbc.co.uk/1/hi/special_report/1997/schengen/13508.stm.

Box 2.4: The EU legal system takes over 2 years to define recycling

1998 UK Chancery Division. In this case the word 'discard' in the 75/442
Directive meant 'to get rid of', and was generally concerned with materials no
longer required for their original use. The purpose of the 75/442 Directive was
to control the disposal and recovery of such materials. Therefore, materials to
be reused, as opposed to being finally disposed of, and requiring no disposal
operation before their reuse, were not waste. Likewise, materials prepared for
reuse by a recovery operation. So, those MPR materials that required a
recovery operation remained waste until the recovery operation was complete.
Recycling or reclamation of metals was a listed recovery operation, and so
long as materials were in the process of recovery, they remained waste.

2000 UK Queen's Bench Division. The Environment Agency and the Secretary
of State sought a declaration that MPR was not entitled to issue packaging
waste recovery notes (PRNs), because the material did not cease to be waste
after MPR had finished processing it, only ceasing to be waste after the steel
producers had processed it. The case was referred to the ECJ.

2003 ECJ. The ECJ determined that recycling in the 94/62 Packaging and
Packaging Waste Directive excluded the reprocessing of metal packaging
waste when it is transformed into a secondary raw material, but not when it is
used to produce ingots, sheets or coils as a primary raw material for a steel
mill, so the MPR processed material remained a waste, even when transformed
into the grade 3B material. Can this be the final judgement for MPR?

For further information see:

www.lawreports.co.uk/ecjjunc0.2.htm
The Times Online Legal Archive, 14 July 2003
R (MPR) v. *The Environment Agency*[a] and *others* judgement, 19 June 2003
(ECJ case C-444/00).

[a] The decision in *MPR* v. *The Environment Agency* does not bind other competent
authorities outside England and Wales, and their views on the definition of waste must
also be complied with.

- waste recycling may involve a series of stages, and further stages may be
needed before the recycling process is complete
- a material is fully recycled (and thus no longer waste) when it is at a stage
where it can take the place of a raw material in forming a product[4]
- for the purpose of recycling, the 94/62 Packaging Directive definition
overrides the 75/442 Directive definition

---

[4] This definition is not robust; for example, where a material is waiting to be burned, although it
is ready for use as a replacement raw material, regulatory control is still needed.

- clarity and uniformity are essential for effective implementation of the 75/442 Directive, and the definitions should be distinct to avoid the double-counting of targets.

The wilderness of mirrors in which the ECJ wanders, ignoring the very important commercial and legal maxim that the law must be as certain as possible, is no better demonstrated than the contrast between the judgements in the MPR and Palin Granit Oy cases (Box 2.5).

The 1990 *Kent County Council* v. *Queenborough Rolling Mill* case had ruled that a discarded material remained waste while its nature remained the same. The 2002 ECJ Palin Granit case demonstrates the opposite, in that two materials of the same nature can be classed as waste or non-waste. The issue with MPR had been the completeness of the recovery operation. According to the MPR judgement, a material is waste if it does not need anything done to it to make it a product. But in the Palin Granit case, the ECJ was concerned with the certainty and foreseeability of future use of the left-over material, and deemed that a material, even if useful, and left lying around, is waste — even if it presents no risk to human health or the environment.

So the definition of waste itself is not only opaque but the outcome of court cases can be inconsistent and illogical. The ECJ recent rulings imply the necessity for regulations and controls to be imposed at the expense of a logical evolution of the definition. It has become more and more difficult to anticipate the decisions of courts. The uncertainty surrounding EU environmental law brings a lack of confidence into the system (and, at times, respect for it). EU environmental law is also brought into disrepute. Public sector officers and commercial and industrial managers need consistent and rigorous criteria in order to determine whether the input and outputs are waste, recyclate or partially processed recyclate.

Eight years before the Palin Granit case, Annex 2 on the definition of waste in Circular 11/94 gave the DoE understanding of Article 1 of the 91/156 Directive. The DoE made it abundantly clear in paragraph 2.12 that the interpretation of the Directive definition of waste is a matter for the courts to decide. Nevertheless the then DoE decided that the purpose of the Directive is to treat as waste, and accordingly to supervise the collection, storage, recovery and disposal of substances or objects which fall outside of the commercial cycle or the chain of utility.

The House of Lords Select Committee on the EU 47th Report Session 2002/3 European Waste Management Policy (18 November 2003) stated that:

the overlaps and inconsistencies between Directives (especially the definitions of 'waste' and 'recycling'), as well as inconsistencies in practice between Member States in relation to the same Directive should be reviewed by the Commission.

Box 2.5: The definition of waste is open to wider interpretation

The Finnish company Palin Granit Oy applied for a licence to manage a granite quarry. Surplus stone was held by the local administrative court to be a waste, even though the company planned to use it as a gravel fill, for embankments or coastal defence works in the future. The storage area for the surplus stone was held to be a landfill, requiring a separate licence. There was no environmental or public health threat, and the stone certainly had economic value.

The ECJ ruled that 'waste is what falls away when one processes a material or an object and is not the end-product which the manufacturing system directly seeks to produce'. Palin Granit Oy argued that the left-over stone was stored ready for further use, so it was not discarded and thus not a 75/442 waste. Nevertheless the ECJ, whilst accepting that this interpretation was consistent with that of the 75/442 Directive, decided that the definition of waste should be open to a wider interpretation to fulfil the purported objective of avoiding pollution. The reuse must be a certainty, not just a possibility. The irony of this case is that the court held that the location of the storage, the material composition and the absence of a risk to human or environmental health were irrelevant. Not the original intent of the European Parliament or, indeed, the Commission.

Source: *Palin Granit Oy* v. *Vehmassalon kansanterveystyön kuntayhtymän* [2002] 2 CMLR 24, case C-90/00.

2.4. Contemporary tentative guidelines

It has not been possible to provide a definitive two- or three-line answer to the question of what exactly is waste. The current statutory definition is given in Article 1 of the 75/442 Waste Framework Directive (as amended by the 91/156 Directive) and the accompanying annexes, which is implemented under the Waste Management Licensing Regulations 1994. However, every circumstance will be subject to a background of changing court decisions. The sensible option is to follow the outcome of future cases in the UK and EU courts. Also, consult www.lawreports.co.uk, curia.eu.int (the ECJ website) www.environment-agency.gov.uk, www.ends.co.uk and www.telegraph.co.uk, and you should be up to date to determine the scope of your own particular waste definition problem before consulting your own well-versed lawyer.

This practical guide offers the following very tentative guidelines. It is difficult to draft even a few exemplars with certainty, if only because of the Palin Granit decision, and the intention of the original owner can be very relevant:

- A mattress that has been discarded and then abandoned in a ditch is waste.

33

- Today's newspaper placed in a waste receptacle for collection by the local authority is waste.
- An object being sent to a specialised recovery operation is waste, e.g. scrap metal sent to a sorting facility.
- An empty wine bottle unbroken placed in a bottle bank is waste, because it is to be sent to a specialist recovery unit to be crushed and melted into new glass bottles.
- On the other hand, an unbroken milk bottle left for the milkman's morning collection is not waste, although it has been discarded, because it will not be subject to a specialist recovery operation (washing out and refilling with milk is not considered a specialist recovery operation). A milk bottle has also not fallen out of the commercial cycle or chain of utility.
- Compact discs consigned to a treatment or disposal operation (e.g. to a composting site, landfill or incinerator) are waste.
- A beer bottle which the owner discards on a park bench is waste, but an empty pint glass left on a beer garden seat for washing is not. It is still part of the chain of utility.
- Stable straw and manure from a mucked out stable is waste.
- But if that stable straw and manure is spread onto agricultural land for recognised beneficial use as a soil conditioner, then it is no longer waste.
- Discarded material on a bonfire awaiting 5 November is waste.
- A used car which is taken to a scrap-yard where a fee is, or is not, paid for it to be destroyed is waste, because it is discarded, since it is of no further use to the owner.
- But a used car which is taken to a second-hand dealer for resale is not waste. It is still in the chain of utility.
- A cardigan with a hole in its sleeve consigned for resale at a charity shop is not waste, even though it is of no further use to the original owner, and might be thought to have been discarded. It is still in the chain of utility.
- A material ceases to be waste when it has been reworked into a useable material which can take the place of a raw material in the production process, e.g. plastic granules ready for remoulding in a factory.

When you confront a difficulty write as soon as possible to your MEP or MP with a brief summary of the facts and two or three supporting documents, and request a surgery appointment. In this way, clarity through bureaucratic and parliamentary pressure may be eventually brought to the law. Please remember it is your regional assembly and national parliament as it is your environment and that of your grandchildren. The parliamentary members are there to help solve your problems.

Other useful ECJ judgements to consult are:

- *ARCO Chemie Netherland Ltd (ACN)* v. *Minister van Volkshulsvesting, Ruimtellike Ordening en Milieubaheer (MVROM)* [2002], case C-418/ 97. (Please see Section 6.1 on incineration later in this guide.)
- Avesta Polarit Chrome Oy, case C-114/01 — available online at curia.eu.int/ jurisp/cgi-bin/form.pl?lang=en. (Please see Section 3.3.1 on mining waste later in this guide.)

2.5. What happens if it is waste?

According to Article 4 of the 75/442 Waste Framework Directive 'Member States shall take the necessary measures to ensure that waste is recovered or disposed of without endangering human health and without using processes or methods which could harm the environment'. This fundamental principle was implemented under the EPA 1990. If a material is classed as waste and arises from the household, or industrial or commercial activity, then it is likely to be classified as a Controlled waste, and regulated under the EPA 1990. Other environmental controls affecting waste are set out in the Town and Country Planning Act 1990, the Environment Act 1995 and the Pollution Prevention and Control Act 1999. For regulated waste materials, the following general points apply:

- anyone who produces, carries, stores, treats or disposes of the waste has a Duty of Care to prevent escape of the waste (please see Chapter 10)
- the material must be transported by a registered waste carrier with the correct documentation (please see Chapter 11)
- the material may be subject to some material specific recovery and recy- cling targets (please see Chapter 5)
- facilities for treatment or disposal of the waste will need planning permissions and most likely a permit or a licence to operate (please see Chapters 7 and 8)
- if it is disposed of at a landfill site, then the material is liable for landfill tax (please see Chapter 6).

Chapter 3

Waste classification

3.1. Introduction

3.1.1. Sources of waste

A waste will enter the environment from its source either by deposition on or in land, through flow or seepage into a water body (rivers, sea, aquifers, etc.), or by emission to air (Table 3.1). The sources of waste listed in the Waste Strategy 2000 (England and Wales) are household, industry and commerce, agriculture, and mines and quarries (www.defra.gov.uk/environment/waste/strategy/). Waste from a particular source can be homogeneous (e.g. mining waste), or it can be extremely varied (e.g. household waste). Waste can come under different legislation because of its source (e.g. ship waste), or because of its properties (e.g. Hazardous waste).

3.1.2. Controlled and unControlled wastes

Some wastes are Controlled under the Environmental Protection Act 1990 (EPA 1990)[1] while others are unControlled or subject to other legislation. Household, industrial and commercial wastes are Controlled under the EPA 1990. Special waste is any waste with specified hazardous properties. Special waste is covered under EPA 1990, but is now subject to the 91/689 Hazardous Waste Directive and European Waste Catalogue definition of hazardous.

Agricultural waste from natural and non-natural sources and waste from mines and quarries, including discarded machinery or pit props, are presently known as unControlled wastes. However non-natural agricultural waste will shortly be subject to new controls, and there is a proposed EU Directive to control mining waste. Some wastes not covered by the EPA 1990 are subject to their own specific legislation, such as explosives under the Explosives Act 1896 or radioactive waste under the Radioactive Substances Act 1993.

---

[1] To view the EPA 1990 online see www.hmso.gov.uk/acts/acts1990/Ukpga_19900043_en_1.htm.

Table 3.1: The four forms of waste

State	Example	Typical route to the environment	Example regulations
Solid	Demolition rubble	Deposited on or in land	The Landfill Regulations 2002 SI 1559
Liquid	Oil, landfill leachate. Liquids may be volatile (rapidly vaporising)	Seepage into groundwater, inland water bodies or the sea	Oil Storage Pollution Control Regulations 2001 SI 2954
Gas	Carbon dioxide emissions, dioxins, furans	Emission into the atmosphere via an incinerator stack	Pollution Prevention and Control Regulations 2000 SI 1973
Putrescible	Plant or animal material that can decompose, undergoing chemical breakdown, e.g. catering waste, green waste or animal by-products	Spreading of decomposed material onto land, or the emission of landfill gas due to anaerobic biodegradation	The Landfill Regulations 2002 SI 1559 The Animal By-Products Regulations 2003 SI 1482

3.2. Waste controlled by the Environmental Protection Act 1990

In s.75(4) EPA1990, Controlled wastes are:

- household
- industrial
- commercial waste.

Household waste is from a domestic property or living accommodation, caravan (on a caravan site), residential home, university or educational establishment, hospital (non-Hazardous only) or nursing home. Household waste excludes minerals, synthetic oil or grease, asbestos and clinical waste, and Special or Hazardous waste (please see Section 3.5) from a laboratory or hospital. Industrial waste arises from a factory, public transport or utility premises, or public postal or telecommunications service premises. Commercial waste is from premises used wholly or mainly for business, trade, recreation or entertainment, excluding household and industrial waste, and mines, quarries and agricultural waste.

Controlled wastes are defined in s.75 EPA 1990, and further details are set out in the Controlled Waste Regulations 1992 SI 588 (CWR 1992). Under the CWR 1992, as amended by the Waste Management Licensing Regulations 1994 SI 1056, Controlled waste is also called Directive waste. The CWR 1992 are available online at www.hmso.gov.uk/si/si1992/Uksi_19920588_en_1.htm.

3.2.1. Construction and demolition waste

Construction and demolition waste is a subgroup of commercial and industrial waste. The latest Office of the Deputy Prime Minister (ODPM) survey estimated annual England and Wales construction and demolition waste arisings of 93.9 million tonnes, 48% of which is recycled and 48% beneficially reused (mainly for layering or topping at landfill sites and backfilling quarries), with the remainder landfilled (see www.defra.gov.uk/environment/statistics/waste/wrconstruc.htm).

3.2.2. Municipal waste

The term municipal waste is used to describe all wastes that come under the control of local authorities (e.g. street litter, collected recyclate, waste from parks and gardens, household, council offices and some small-scale commercial waste, and dog waste). According to the Landfill Regulations 2002 SI 1559 municipal waste includes household waste and wastes from other sources which, due to their nature, have similar properties to household waste.

Municipal waste can be extremely varied and include a wide range of materials, making it difficult for local authorities to manage. Waste within local authority control can be subject to its own laws or byelaws, for example fast-food retailers being required to keep the area in the vicinity of their outlets litter-free. Under Part IV of the EPA 1990, littering is a criminal offence, and local authorities have a duty to keep roads for which they are responsible free from litter.

Household and municipal waste can contain Hazardous waste, which can have unstable and often threatening characteristics. For example, in 2003 two dustmen conducting a normal collection round were taken to hospital suffering from chemical burns from sulphuric acid, which leaked from residential bins. The problem is difficult to regulate and enforce.

3.3. UnControlled waste

The UK originally interpreted the 75/442 Waste Framework Directive (as amended by the 91/156 Directive) not to include agricultural and mining and quarrying waste. These wastes were therefore known as unControlled under the EPA 1990. However, according to the European Commission (EC), agricultural waste should be managed in line with the 75/442 Directive. To avoid EU financial sanctions, the UK must now draft new legislation and codes of practice so that most agricultural, mining and quarrying wastes are regulated according to the objectives contained in the preamble to the 75/442 Directive. How this will be done is now subject to consultation papers. In 2002 the vice-president of the National Farmers' Union (NFU) said that 'All concerned with these regulations must strive to ensure that where controls are necessary, they are proportionate to the risks .... We see our role as helping to find realistic and least-cost solutions to the problem of agricultural waste and we seek to play an active part in the National Agricultural Waste Stakeholder Forum'. The new Regulations directly affect the 155 000 working farms in England and Wales, many of which have been financially affected by both the foot-and-mouth and BSE crises.

3.3.1. Mining

In June 2003 the EC adopted a proposal for a Directive on the management of waste from the extractive industries, as a supplement to the 75/442 Waste Framework Directive. The Directive aims to prevent or reduce, as far as possible, the risk of any adverse effects on the environment or human health following the management of waste from the extractive industries. The Government issued consultation papers in November 2003. For further information see the ODPM planning website (www.odpm.gov.uk).

Health and safety in the mining industry comes under the regulatory responsibility of the Hazardous Installations Directorate. For further information see www.hse.gov.uk/hid/index.htm. Dust generated from mining is currently covered by the Coal Mines (Respirable Dust) Regulations 1975 SI 2001, although these are at present subject to consultation and will shortly be revised (see www.hse.gov.uk/mining/legislat.htm).

Box 3.1: The threat to human health or the environment is irrelevant in determining whether a material is waste or not

> Avesta Polarit Chrome Oy, a Finnish mining company, extracted chrome by boring and crushing rock and ore, annually averaged at 8 million tonnes for 100,000 tonnes of ore. The company appealed that the left-over rock and sand was not waste within the 75/442 Directive (as amended by the 91/156 Directive). The European Court of Justice (ECJ) followed the decision in Palin Granit (please see Chapter 2) in that the test was whether the holder of the residual rock discarded or intended to discard the left-over rock.
>
> The composition of the left-over rock and whether it was any risk to human health or the environment were not relevant criteria. If, however, the company used the rock and sand for refilling their mine galleries, and could identify the materials for that purpose, then it would probably not be defined as waste.
>
> Avesta Polarit Chrome Oy (formerly Outokumpu Chrome Oy), ECJ case C-114/01.

3.3.2. Agricultural waste

This is waste generated from agricultural premises, which are defined in the Agriculture Act 1947 and include nurseries, horticultural activities, fruit growing, livestock breeding and keeping, dairy farming, grazing and meadow land, market gardens, and the use of land for woodlands as a supplement to farmland. Wastes ranging from plastics to tractor engine oil are presently exempt from waste management law if arising on a farm. Seventy per cent of farmers are currently storing some form of waste with no plans for disposal. Agricultural waste is expected to become Controlled waste in 2005, in order to comply with the 75/442 Waste Framework Directive. The new Regulations will affect all non-natural waste produced on farms, including:

- animal health products
- building waste
- plastic and films (silage wrap waste).

The new Regulations will:

- prohibit on-farm deposit of agricultural non-natural waste
- prohibit open burning of non-natural waste on farms

The Regulations will be phased in, with the ban on deposit taking immediate effect. Farmers will have to chose to:

- transfer waste using a registered carrier
- return waste to the supplier or
- dispose of waste under a waste management licence or permit.

The last option will be particularly costly for most farms.

In 2003 the Environment Agency (EA) carried out an agricultural waste survey, with the following findings:

- it was estimated that the 180,000 farms in England and Wales produce 300,000 tonnes of non-natural waste per year
- 600,000 tonnes of scrap metal, tyres and asbestos are stored on farms
- 38% of holdings have tips and 29% have active tips
- approximately 90% of disposal methods currently used by farmers will become illegal under the new Regulations
- waste becomes the responsibility of the land owner where no offender is identified.

Movements of animal by-products must be recorded in writing for the EA, except manure transported between two points on the same farm, or locally between farms and users in the same country.

The Agricultural Waste Stakeholders' Forum, comprises the Department for Environment, Food and Rural Affairs (DEFRA), the EA, the NFU and other organisations, and meets every 2–3 months to discuss the agricultural waste consultation and inform the Government of progress. The forum website is at www.defra.gov.uk/environment/waste/agforum.

Under the Sludge (Use in Agriculture) Regulations 1989 SI 1263, sludge can only be applied to land if:

- the sludge has been tested according to specified procedures
- the soil on which it is to be applied has been tested according to specified procedures
- the land is a dedicated site
- the soil is relatively acidic
- no fruit or vegetable crops (except fruit trees) are growing or being harvested in the soil at the time of the use
- the average annual rate of sludge application does not exceed the level specified in the Regulations.

Under the Farm Waste Grant (Nitrate Vulnerable Zones) (England) Scheme 2003 SI 562, Government grants are available for up to 40% of the expenditure on improved farm waste facilities (up to £85,000 in aggregate). Funding is available for the provision, replacement or improvement of:

- facilities for handling and storing manure, slurry and silage effluent
- disposal activities for slurry and silage effluent
- facilities for the separation of clean and dirty water, where those facilities reduce the need to store slurry.

The current scheme is for the period 16 April 2003 to 31 October 2005. For further information see www.defra.gov.uk/corporate/regulat/forms/agri_env/nvz/nvz8.pdf. There are no similar schemes for solid waste management on farms.

The Waste (Foot and Mouth Disease) Regulations 2001 SI 1478 were passed in reaction to the outbreak in 2001. Although the foot-and-mouth crisis is over, due to the difficulties of the Ministry of Agriculture, Fisheries and Food (now

Box 3.2: The cost of the new Regulations for farmers

According to the NFU, in 2003 approximately 2000 farmers per year were going out of business because of low prices. One of the largest milk producers in the UK, the Co-op Group, recently abandoned dairy farming because the cost of production is greater than the price earned on its 20 million litres produced each year. The new rules for agricultural waste will have financial implications for farmers, and the NFU is pressing for realistic, cost-effective farm waste solutions.

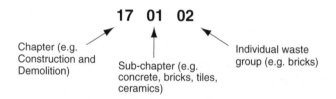

Figure 3.1: Explanation of the EWC six-digit code

DEFRA) in controlling farm animal victim disposal, it may be necessary in the future to examine the historical interment of dead animal dumps.

3.4. Waste classification systems

The European Waste Catalogue was originally introduced in the 94/3 Commission Decision,[2] which established a list of wastes under Article 1a of the 75/442 Waste Framework Directive. The 94/904 Council Decision[3] established a Hazardous Waste Catalogue (HWC), which defined the scope of the 91/689 Hazardous Waste Directive (HWD). The two lists were combined and a harmonised European Waste Catalogue (EWC), in which Hazardous wastes are identified with an asterisk, was published (the 2000/532 Decision, as amended).

The EWC comprises 20 chapters, which are based on a particular industry, material or process. Each chapter has a two-digit code between 01 and 20, and two further digits denote the subchapter, and two more the individual waste group (Figure 3.1). The EWC is given in Appendix A of the EA's Technical Guidance WM2, *Hazardous Waste: Interpretation of the Definition and Classification of Hazardous Waste* (available from www.environment-agency.gov.uk).

Until recently the UK waste classification system did not conform to the 75/442 Waste Framework Directive, the 91/689 Hazardous Waste Directive or the EWC. Article 4 of the 2000/532 Decision states that all Member States must comply with the harmonised EWC. There has for some time been a conflict between the EU definition of Hazardous waste and the UK system of identifying waste with hazardous properties under the Special Waste Regulations 1996. This is currently being resolved and the EU definition of Hazardous and the EWC are being phased in. The Landfill (England and Wales) Regulations 2002 SI 1559 use the EWC for the purpose of landfill regulation. Regulation 19 of the

---

[2] The 94/3 Directive is no longer in force, and the original EWC was later replaced by an updated version under Commission Decision 2001/118, as amended by 2001/119.
[3] Note here that one is a Commission Decision (the executive of the EU), and the other is a Council Decision (designated parliamentary ministers from the Member States).

Landfill Regulations 2002 SI 1559 amends the Environmental Protection (Duty of Care) Regulations 1991 so that waste must be identified on the Waste Transfer Note by reference to the appropriate six-digit codes in the EWC. New Hazardous Waste Regulations are expected to be published in late 2004 and to become law in 2005.

Some EA documentation and clients may request a description of waste according to the Standard Industrial Classification (SIC) code. SIC codes are used to identify the business sector from which the waste is generated. The codes are given in the indexes to the *United Kingdom Standard Industrial Classification of Economic Activities 1992*, which were published by the Office for National Statistics in 1997. SIC codes are also referred to in legislation such as the Producer Responsibility Obligations (Packaging Waste) Regulations 1997 (as amended).

3.5. Special (Hazardous) waste

Until recently, the UK used its own waste classification system, and the term Special was used to describe waste with hazardous properties. This posed:

- legal difficulties, since it was in breach of the 91/689 Hazardous Waste Directive
- practical difficulties, since requirements in EU law relate to Hazardous waste as defined according to the EU system, not the UK system.

For example, the 99/31 Landfill Directive required all Member States to reclassify landfill sites as Hazardous, non-Hazardous or Inert according to the waste they accept. This was impractical in the UK, since the term 'Special' did not encompass the same waste types as the EU term 'Hazardous'. The Landfill Regulations 2002 use the 91/689 Directive definition of Hazardous and the EWC, and other changes are being phased in to bring UK terminology and regulations in line with EU law. The new Hazardous Waste Regulations are anticipated to become law in 2005. The Regulations may also in the future include Hazardous waste from agriculture, mines and quarries.

In order to understand the changes to the classification of Hazardous waste it is necessary to recite the former disciplines under the Special Waste Regulations 1996. The new Regulations, when introduced, may still use references from the old Regulations. In Scotland the term 'Special' has been retained under the Special Waste Amendment (Scotland) Regulations 2004 SI 112 (please see Section 3.5.4).

3.5.1. Special waste

Waste that is considered to pose a danger to human health or the environment had been termed in the UK Special waste. In 1999 the three largest Special waste streams were oils and oil and water mixtures (1 million tonnes per annum), construction and demolition (1 million tonnes per annum) and wastes arising from organic chemical processes (540,000 million tonnes per annum). More than 6 million tonnes of Special waste were disposed of in England and Wales in 2000, from 200,000 producers, 90,000 of which regularly produced Special waste. In 2003, 2.1 million tonnes of Special waste were landfilled.

Section 62 of the EPA 1990 sets out special provisions for any waste deemed by the Secretary of State to be 'so dangerous or difficult to treat, keep or dispose of that special provision is required for dealing with it'. Section 75(9) of the EPA 1990 states that '"Special waste" means Controlled waste as respects which Regulations are in force under section 62 above'. Details for Special waste were set out in the secondary legislation:

- Special Waste Regulations 1996 SI 972 (SWR 1996)
- Special Waste (Amendment) Regulations 1996 SI 2019
- Special Waste (Amendment) Regulations 1997 SI 251.

Under the Special Waste Regulations 1996 a waste is Special if it:

- is listed in Part 1 of Schedule 2 of the Regulations
- has one or more of the 14 hazardous characteristics shown in Box 3.3 and Table 3.2.

Box 3.3: Hazardous characteristics for Special waste (Special Waste Regulations 1996)

H1	Explosive
H2	Oxidising
H3A	Highly flammable
H3B	Flammable
H4	Irritant
H5	Harmful
H6	Toxic
H7	Carcinogenic
H8	Corrosive
H9	Infectious
H10	Teratogenic[a]
H11	Mutagenic
H12	Substances that will release toxic gases in contact with water, air or acid
H13	Substances which, after disposal, are capable of yielding another substance (e.g. a leachate) which possesses any of the characteristics in this box
H14	Ecotoxic

[a] A substance causing abnormal embryos.

45

Table 3.2: Thresholds for Special waste

Hazardous property	Additional information	Threshold
Highly flammable	–	Liquid with a flashpoint of 21°C or less
Irritant	Risk phrases R36–R38	20%
Irritant	Risk phrase R41	10%
Harmful	–	25%
Very toxic	–	0.1%
Toxic	–	3%
Carcinogenic	Category 1 or 2	0.1%
Corrosive	Risk phrase R34	5%
Corrosive	R35	1%

Wastes with hazardous properties are given in the Hazardous Waste List (HWL) in Schedule 2 of the Special Waste Regulations 1996 (www.hmso.gov.uk/si/si1996/Uksi_19960972_en_5.htm). Thresholds for hazardous properties are given in Schedule 3, and this may prove more than useful if there is any question in future years of their exhumation in the remediation of contaminated land.

The Special Waste Regulations 1996 do not apply to:

- householders[4]
- explosives (covered by the Explosives Act 1875)
- agricultural waste
- mines and quarry waste
- radioactive waste due to its radioactivity (however, if in addition it possesses one of the properties in Box 3.3, then it is also Special waste).

Typical examples of Special waste are asbestos, solvents, infected dressings, lead–acid batteries, oil filters and oily sludges, chemicals and pesticides. There are many other types of waste that are hazardous that are not described as Special. One of the facts of life, however regrettable, not faced up to by the waste industry or the Department of the Environment (DoE) or the public sector is that all waste can be hazardous in certain circumstances or concentration. You can, alas, drown in the sloping shallow end of a well-cleaned swimming pool if you cannot swim.

---

[4] Except asbestos, clinical waste and household waste produced by laboratories and hospitals, in which case the Special Waste Regulations do apply.

The preferred method for identifying Special wastes is to use the EA assessment flow diagram (see www.environment-agency.gov.uk/netregs). The EA has published Special Waste Explanatory Notes (SWENs) which provide guidance on particular assessment matters relating to the criteria in the Special Waste Regulations 1996. SWEN provide the EWC code in parentheses, and are available from the EA website www.environment-agency.gov.uk/business. Special waste movements are monitored by the EA through the Special Waste Regulations 1996 consignment note system. The transportation of Special waste is explained in Chapter 11.

3.5.2. The 91/689 Hazardous Waste Directive

The 91/689 Hazardous Waste Directive (HWD) aims to:

- establish a precise and uniform definition of Hazardous waste across Member States
- ensure the correct management and regulation of Hazardous waste.

Hazardous wastes are marked in the European Waste Catalogue (EWC) with an asterisk. These entries have a mirror entry, which is the same substance, but without the hazardous properties. An excellent summary of the EWC and a tool for the identification of Hazardous wastes is given in the BIFFA Waste Services publication *European Waste Catalogue and Hazardous Waste List* (www.biffa.co.uk/pdfs/EWC_Paper-v1.09.pdf or contact BIFFA on 01494 521 221).

Other waste law affected by the 91/689 definition of Hazardous waste are the:

- Pollution Prevention and Control (England and Wales) Regulations 2000
- End of Life Vehicles Regulations 2003 SI 2635
- Waste Electrical and Electronic Equipment Regulations 2004.

3.5.3. Treatment and disposal of Hazardous waste

Under the Basel Convention on Transboundary Movements of Hazardous Waste the UK must deal with Hazardous waste arising within the country. Some Hazardous wastes such as solvents, oils and metals can be recycled or reused. Others are landfilled or incinerated. In 2002, of the 5 million tonnes of Hazardous waste generated in England and Wales:

- 39% of was landfilled (5% less than in 2001)
- 40% was recycled or treated
- 5% was incinerated
- 16% was temporarily stored before treatment or disposal.

Under the Landfill Regulations 2002 certain transitional arrangements were made for existing landfills. As of 16 July 2004 all of the Landfill Regulations 2002 are relevant to all new and existing landfills. In particular:

- more stringent technical standards apply to landfill sites accepting Hazardous waste
- co-disposal (or commingling) of Hazardous and non-Hazardous waste is banned
- all Hazardous waste will require pre-treatment prior to landfilling in order to reduce its quantity or hazardous nature.

In 2002 there were 1430 landfills in England and Wales, of which 241 accepted Hazardous waste. In July 2004 this was reduced to fewer than 30 sites (around a 90% reduction). DEFRA anticipates that there will be no Hazardous waste landfills available in Wales or the Thames region after August 2004. It is inevitable that some waste on the borderline between Hazardous and non-Hazardous would be commingled with municipal or household waste. Whether it is wise to concentrate Hazardous waste by preventing the previous practice of commingling remains a matter of doubt. It is feared that under the new Regulations, Hazardous landfill sites will be too expensive to operate and insure, if cover is available at all. The delays in defining the 91/689 HWD requirements and lack of clear Government details have made it difficult for industry to invest in infrastructure and new technology, even though it has been warning the Government of the impending Hazardous waste problem for many years.

As stated above, around 39% of Hazardous waste was landfilled in 2002. Thus if 90% of Hazardous landfill sites are no longer to accept Hazardous waste, then approximately 35% of the 5 million tonnes of Hazardous waste generated annually in England and Wales must find alternative disposal or recovery arrangements. If the estimates are correct, this means that 1.75 million tonnes of Hazardous waste will have to go somewhere. There are just two Hazardous waste incinerators in England and Wales with a combined capacity of 110,000 tonnes per year.

At present, the cost to business in the spring of 2004 of managing Hazardous waste is around £150 million per year in total, but likely costs from July 2004 will probably rise to more than three times that level. Under the EWC more wastes will be classified as Hazardous than were previously classed as Special under the Special Waste Regulations 1996. Items such as end of life vehicles and refrigerators are classed as Hazardous under the European system.

In April 2004 the EA expressed concern that illegal waste activity may result from the 16 July 2004 changes, but that they were being vigilant in tracking such waste disposal trails. The EA report is available online at www.environment-agency.gov.uk/subjects/waste/232021/232024/743177.

New guidance that explains the legislative framework for the definition of Hazardous waste under the 91/689 HWD has been published by the EA, the Scottish Environmental Protection Agency and the Northern Ireland

Box 3.4: Where will all the Hazardous waste go?

An alternative option for Hazardous waste is salt mines. ICI deposits Hazardous waste from its chemical works at the Holford Brine fields, Winsford, and Scottish power recently sought permission to store natural gas in a redundant salt mine near Middlewich. Plans to use a salt mine in Cheshire to store Hazardous waste were recently approved—the mine has a capacity of 2 million tonnes. Salt mines, however, have other uses: both national and Government documents are stored in the cool dry caverns of the Winsford mine.

Source: *The Guardian*, 8 January 2004.

Environment and Heritage Service. Technical Guidance WM2, *Interpretation of the Definition and Classification of Hazardous Waste*, is available from the EA website (www.environment-agency.gov.uk). Technical Guidance WM2 also provides an outline method for assessing wastes using the EWC 2002, and guidance on dangerous substances contained in waste. New Regulations to cover Hazardous Waste are expected, after consultation, to come into effect in July 2005.

3.5.4. The special tartan solution

Amended Regulations to bring Scotland in line with EU requirements will retain the term Special waste. Some wastes previously classified as Special are not included in the Hazardous wastes listed in the EWC. In Scotland it is proposed that wastes currently defined as Special, but not Hazardous by the EU, will remain Special waste.

The majority of the Special Waste Amendment (Scotland) Regulations 2004 SI 112 come into force on 1 July 2004. The Regulations:

- amend the definition of Special waste to ensure compliance with the 91/689 HWD
- extend, in certain circumstances, the application of the Special Waste Regulations 1996 to domestic asbestos waste
- make specific provision for the labelling and packaging requirements of Special waste
- provide that any waste consignment note must identify the waste by reference to the EWC
- require the producers of Special waste to keep a register that details the documents required to be kept
- require the Scottish Environment Protection Agency to carry out periodic inspections of the registers referred to within the 1996 Regulations

49

- impose an obligation to separate Special waste from other waste, as soon as reasonably practicable, where technically and economically feasible and necessary, before recovery or disposal of the waste
- provide for cross-border recognition of consignment notes (please see Chapter 11)
- amend the form of consignment notes.

For further information see www.scotland.gov.uk/library5/environment/sswswr.pdf and www.sepa.org.uk which are both very helpful.

3.6. Healthcare and clinical waste

Healthcare waste encompasses many different waste categories:

- Controlled waste (industrial and commercial)
- municipal waste
- Special (Hazardous) waste (e.g. prescription medicines, infectious or toxic waste)
- radioactive waste
- clinical waste.

A particularly difficult component of healthcare waste is clinical waste, defined in the Controlled Waste Regulations 1992 SI 588:

Any waste which consists wholly or partly of animal or human tissue, blood or other body fluids, excretions, drugs or other pharmaceutical products, swabs or dressing or syringes, needles or other sharp instruments being waste, which unless rendered safe, may prove hazardous to any person coming in contact with it; and any other waste arising from medical, nursing, dental, veterinary, pharmaceutical, investigation, treatment, care, teaching or research, or the collection of blood for transfusion being waste which may cause infection to any person coming in contact with it.

It is a definition which the Directors in Box 3.5 should have to recite before breakfast for 30 consecutive days.

Box 3.5: The company that left human body parts in a lorry park

Eurocare Environmental Services were fined £100,000 in 2003 for leaving trailers containing clinical waste in a lorry park. This was, at the time, the largest fine imposed by the EA for a waste offence. Shortly after the event the company was taken over by an Irish waste management firm called Sterile Technologies.

Source: *The Journal* (City Edition), 30 January 2004.

Table 3.3: The four Biological Hazard Groups

Group	Individual risk	Community risk	Example
1	Low	Low	Microorganisms unlikely to cause harm (non-infectious for carriage)
2	Moderate	Low	Pathogens causing human disease but not a serous hazard for which effective treatment exists
3	High	Low	Pathogens causing severe human disease but not easily transmitted for which prevention and remedy are readily available
4	High	High	Easily transmitted pathogens causing severe human disease for which treatment or preventative measures are not readily available

Source: SWEN 001

The management of clinical waste is governed by both waste management and health and safety legislation. England and Wales produces about 350,000 tonnes of clinical waste a year, approximately 100,000 tonnes of which presents a higher than normal risk of infection or harm.

The UK's clinical waste was traditionally incinerated on-site. This fulfilled the proximity principle, and reduced the need for the transportation of dangerous substances over long distances. However, under the plethora of regulatory changes over recent decades small-scale incinerators have been closed and alternative treatment and disposal options adopted. An interesting note on the impact of the 2000/76 Waste Incineration Directive on the NHS is available at www.nhsestates.gov.uk/download/ sustainable_development/WIDandNHS%20151003.doc). Under the 99/31 Landfill Directive, infectious waste is now banned from landfill.

Under the Approved Requirements and Test Methods for the Classification and Packaging of Dangerous Goods for Carriage, clinical waste is divided into four risk-based Biological Hazard Groups (Table 3.3). These are explained further in the EA Special Waste Explanatory Note on healthcare waste SWEN 001 (www.environment-agency.gov.uk/commondata/105385/swen001.pdf).

The changes to the Special Waste Regulations 1996 and adoption of the EWC explained earlier in this chapter will affect the classification of healthcare waste. For the latest position, consult www.environment-agency.gov.uk/netregs.

3.7. Waste covered by other legislation

3.7.1. Developments in the control of chemicals

There are approximately 100,000 different registered substances in the EU. Over 20,000 are manufactured or imported in quantities greater than 1 tonne, and only a small number of these have adequate environmental and health data. In October 2003 the EC adopted a proposal for a regulatory frame-work for the Registration, Evaluation and Authorisation of Chemicals (REACH) (europa.eu.int/comm/enterprise/chemicals/chempol/whitepaper/ reach.htm). REACH will affect an estimated 30,000 chemicals, including pesti-cides, cosmetics and pharmaceuticals,[5] while the existing regulatory system identifies only 140 chemicals of high concern. REACH will cover both existing and new chemicals, and will mean:

- a single data-gathering system for hazard information, risk assessment and classification and labelling
- all REACH substances manufactured or imported in quantities greater than 1 tonne annually must be registered on a central database
- the establishment of a European Chemicals Agency (ECA) to set up and manage the REACH database (to be funded mainly through registration and authorisation fees)
- the restriction of the marketing and application of particular chemicals
- industry must gain permission for particular uses, which have been demonstrated to be safe
- prohibition of certain uses.

The proposals have been delayed until autumn 2004, so that the Member States who joined the EU on 1 May 2004 can be involved in the consultation. The EU imports over €8 billion of chemicals per year from Eastern Europe.

EU Regulation 2076/2002 came into force on 1 April 2004, banning 81 chemical products, including ingredients used in many household brand name products. The active ingredients have been withdrawn, not the manufacturer's brand. A full list of withdrawn pesticides is available (www.tmbc.gov.uk/ assets/Environment/withdrawn_pesticides.pdf). The banned chemicals cannot be poured down drains or sinks, etc. Further information is available from the National Household Hazardous Waste Forum website (www.nhhwf.org.uk).

---

[5] Note that other EU laws also control these substances.

Box 3.6: Ban on household products

> Householders may unknowingly be in possession of illegal substances according to a new EU Regulation, and could face fines of up to £5000. Suffolk County Council has provided sites to allow householders to dispose of the banned chemicals safely. What happens when facilities are not provided? Please ask your MP or your local councillor. They are there to help you.
>
> Source: *Ipswich Evening Star*, 26 January 2004, and *South Shields Gazette*, 29 January 2004.

3.7.2. Animal by-products and catering waste

EU recycling targets and the implementation of the 99/31 Landfill Directive have increased the need for alternative treatments such as composting and biogas digestion. In order to reduce the risk of spreading diseases such as BSE and scrapie, animals must be prevented from consuming meat or products of animal origin. The Animal By-Products Order 1999 prevented all livestock (including wild birds) from having access to anything that contained meat or products of animal origin. From 1999 to 2003, park and garden waste could be composted but not catering waste. In May 2003 the 1774/2002 EC Animal By-Products Regulation became directly applicable to all Member States, except those temporarily exempted and was shortly followed by the UK Animal By-Products Regulations 2003 SI 1482 (ABPR 2003).[6] The new Regulations, revoking the 1999 Order, allow the composting and biogas treatment of catering waste and low-risk animal by-products. Specified standards are set for the treatment of higher-risk animal by-products.

Animal by-products are divided into three risk categories. Table 3.4 shows typical wastes in each of the three categories, and indicates the treatments permitted for each group. The 1774/2002 Regulation makes certain allowances for catering waste, which is a subgroup of animal by-products (some useful definitions are provided in Box 3.7).

3.7.3. Radioactive waste

Radioactive waste is not Controlled waste under s.75 EPA 1990. The use and disposal of radioactive material is covered by the Radioactive Substances Act 1993 (RSA 1993)[7], subject to the Secretary of State's provisions, and enforced by the EA. Section 2 of the RSA 1993 defines radioactive waste as waste which consists wholly or partly of a substance or article which:

---

[6] The ABPR 2003 can be viewed online at www.legislation.hmso.gov.uk/si/si2003/20031482.htm.

[7] The RSA 1993 can be viewed at www.hmso.gov.uk/acts/acts1993/Ukpga_19930012_en_1.htm.

Table 3.4: Summary of the ABPR 2003

Category	Risk	Typical material	Legal disposal method	Legal recycling or recovery methods
1	Highest-risk material	Carcasses and materials infected or suspected of being infected by transmissible spongiform encephalopathies[a] (please see Box 3.7)	Rendering in an approved plant followed by incineration or landfill	Material in this category cannot be recovered or recycled
		Carcasses of zoo and pet animals. Catering waste from international transport[b]	Catering waste from international transport must be landfilled at an authorised site	
2	High-risk material	Diseased animals, animals that die on farms and not containing specified risk material (SRM) at the point of disposal. Animals that are not slaughtered for human consumption	Incineration Rendering in an approved plant followed by incineration or landfill	Rendering in an approved plant followed by use as a fertiliser or treatment in a biogas or composting plant Fish: ensiling or composting (subject to rules yet to be established) Rendered fats: use in an oleochemical plant to produce tallow derivatives for technical use only

| 3 | Not specified | Material that is fit, but not intended, for human consumption, including catering waste | Incineration

Rendering followed by incineration or landfill | Rendering followed by use in feedingstuffs or fertiliser[c]

Use in petfood or in a technical plant

Treatment in a biogas or composting plant

Fish: ensiling or composting (subject to rules yet to be established)

Rendered fats: use in an oleochemical plant to produce tallow derivatives |

Source: www.environment-agency.gov.uk

[a] Under the Transmissible Spongiform Encephalopathies (TSE) Regulations (England) 2002, rendered mammalian material cannot be spread on agricultural land.

[b] Catering waste from international travel is classed as category 1 animal by-product. This includes all waste from international flights.

[c] Subject to the ban on feeding catering waste containing meat etc. to livestock and the restriction on the use of processed animal protein in feedingstuffs.

Box 3.7: Animal by-product definitions

Animal by-products are wastes containing animal meat or products, from whole carcasses to catering waste, including the following categories.

Catering waste is a category 3 animal by-product originating from:

- restaurants
- catering facilities
- kitchens
- household kitchens
- including cooking oil from the above premises.

Meat excluded catering waste is catering waste where the meat and non-meat fractions have been collected separately at source. The separation must be closely recorded and audited.

Former foodstuffs is food intended for human consumption, but not sold or used, usually exceeding its sell-by date (from food manufacturing premises and retail outlets). This category is not classed as catering waste. Until December 2005 former foodstuffs will be classed as catering waste as a transitional measure.

Specified risk material is material suspected of being infected by TSE, such as scrapie in sheep or BSE in cattle.

Green waste is biodegradable waste not containing animal by-products, e.g. grass cuttings or clippings, and does not come under the ABPR 2003.

(a) if it were not waste, would be radioactive material, or

(b) has been contaminated in the course of the production, keeping or use of radioactive material, or in proximity to other waste falling within (a) above.

The keeping, use, accumulation and disposal of radioactive waste must be registered and authorised by the EA. Authorisation is not needed for:

- radioactive waste accumulated while awaiting authorised disposal (e.g. in a radioactive waste receptacle in a science laboratory)
- radioactive waste accumulated on a premises situated on an authorised nuclear site
- disposal and accumulation of radioactive waste from clocks or watches
- activities covered by an Exemption Order issued as secondary legislation.[8]

---

[8] The EA registration and authorisation application pack includes a full list of Exemption Orders (except for Northern Ireland). To order a copy, contact the Stationery Office (0870 600 5522).

Box 3.8: Building a house without a WC

Japan's 53 nuclear reactors were built after the oil crisis, but there is no coherent strategy for disposing of spent nuclear fuel, which used to be reprocessed in the UK and France. The US would oppose shipping radioactive material half-way across the world on security grounds. Japan Nuclear Fuel Ltd (JNFL) hopes to reprocess in 2005, more likely 2010, when storage space will run out.

Registration certificates fall into three categories:

- open radioactive sources (material easily divided or diluted, e.g. radioactive powders, gases, solutions or solids)
- closed radioactive sources (the material is firmly bound in the source, e.g. foil or electro-deposited materials)
- mobile radioactive apparatus (portable or adapted to be transported).

Registration certificates must be displayed in a prominent position. Under the Nuclear Installations Act 1965, sites must prepare emergency plans. Further operational facts concerning the current Government position on radioactive waste are available from House of Commons DEFRA Select Committee, Session 2001–2002, 3rd Report, *Radioactive Waste: The Government's Consultation Process* (please see Appendix B). The Report is a damning indictment of successive Governments' ineptitude in radioactive waste management. It gives the reader a good picture of the lack of long-term solutions for most of the dangerous medium- and high-level radioactive wastes in the UK.

The UK has one of the largest stores of radioactive waste in the world, occupying the volume of approximately 300 detached houses. High-level radioactive waste (HLW) may be reprocessed to produce intermediate-level waste (ILW). Under an international requirement, nations sending their nuclear waste to British Nuclear Fuels Ltd (BNFL) for reprocessing must accept some of the resulting ILW in return. However, due to logistical difficulties, and the fact that many countries such as Japan do not have facilities for handling ILW, the Department for Trade and Industry has proposed a system of radioactive waste substitution: the UK could continue to store the ILW and instead send some of its own HLW back to its customer in exchange. The exchange would be radiologically equivalent. An estimated 225 shipments are needed to meet the contractual obligations to return ILW. The substitution proposal reduces this to just 38 (although this would be HLW and not ILW).

For further information see www.dti.gov.uk/nuclearcleanup, or type 'nuclear waste' into the www.environment-agency.gov.uk/netregs search facility. DEFRA has recently published a document intended to promote national debate about the issue of radioactive waste management: *Managing Solid*

Radioactive Waste Safely – Proposals for Developing a Policy for Managing Radioactive Waste in the UK (available from www.defra.gov.uk/environment/ index.htm).

3.7.4. Asbestos

Directive 87/217 covers the prevention and reduction of environmental pollution by asbestos. The following domestic regulations at present apply to work involving asbestos:

- The Asbestos (Licensing) (Amendment) Regulations 1998 SI 3233
- Control of Asbestos in Air Regulations 1990 SI 556
- Control of Asbestos at Work Regulations 2002 SI 2675 (CAWR 2002).

There are seven types of asbestos, which include amosite (brown), crocidolite (blue) and chrysotile (white). All types of asbestos are potentially harmful to health and the environment, but to varying degrees. Asbestos was used up to the 1980s for insulation and construction in industries such as shipbuilding and railway engineering. Today, an estimated 10 people per day die from asbestos-related diseases in the UK, and the Health and Safety Executive (HSE) predicts a rise in annual deaths. Removal operatives, re-fitters and building maintenance workers are most at risk, with 25% of deaths occurring in workers from the building and maintenance trade.

Under the Asbestos (Licensing) Regulations 1983 SI 3233 a licence is needed for working on asbestos

- insulation (usually in a soft and fibrous form)
- coating
- insulating board, or
- to erect a scaffold for an asbestos working area enclosure.

There are three types of licence: full, supervisory and ancillary. However, a licence is not needed for:

- working for a short duration
- air monitoring
- collecting samples for identification
- clearance inspections
- a householder's asbestos being handled by the householder.[9]

When removing asbestos:

- the material should be dampened with a water spray or sealant

---

[9] Householder's asbestos waste from domestic premises must be transported by the householder with great care (e.g. double-wrapping in thick plastic at least) to a civic amenity site.

Box 3.9: Twenty-first century ambulance chasing

UK insurers are facing increasing numbers of asbestos claims as solicitors use US-style scan vans. The vans, which contain X-ray screening equipment, are parked outside shopping and community centres in areas where there has been large-scale exposure to asbestos at work, such as at shipyards. The X-ray readers look for scarring on the lungs called pleural plaques. Treatment physicians claim it is a very good way to capture health information, not to mention clients.

Source: *Daily Telegraph Business*, 22 March 2004.

- it must not be broken up with machine tools
- the air should be monitored for fibre concentration before and after the removal work.
- operators must wear dust masks
- it is advisable to clear waste as it arises and avoid a pile building up.

The waste asbestos must be:

- double-wrapped
- clearly labelled as asbestos waste (usually in a red bag or sealed container)
- if stored in a skip, labelled, sealed and secured.

The sum of £2000 to have asbestos removed may seem a lot of money, and there are less then scrupulous builders who may charge at that level when not necessary. The Control of Asbestos at Work Regulations 2002 SI 2675 came into effect in May 2004 and introduced a specific Duty to Manage (but not necessarily to remove) for occupiers or owners (the Dutyholder) of non-domestic premises containing asbestos.

The Control of Asbestos at Work Regulations 2002 make no distinction between the genuinely dangerous amphibole asbestos and the white chrysotile asbestos. The latter is a wholly different mineral, chemically indistinguishable from talcum powder. The difficulty is that the EU and HSE claim that chrysotile is as dangerous as the amphibole form; however, there is a new study which shows that there is no mechanism whereby white asbestos cement and its use in textured plaster can be as dangerous as amphibole asbestos. It may therefore be that the costs of removing chrysotile are not justified. The costs of implementing the Control of Asbestos at Work Regulations 2002 were originally estimated by HSE to be £8 billion, making them the most expensive regulations placed on the statute books. Whilst the original estimate has been diminished, the cost to councils and householders is still extremely significant.

For further information on asbestos see the following websites: www.hse.gov.uk/pubns/manageasbestos.pdf, www.hse.gov.uk/campaigns/asbestos/duty.htm or www.hse.gov.uk/asbestos.

3.7.5. Explosive waste

Explosive waste is not Controlled waste under s.75 EPA 1990. Explosives are regulated under the Explosives Act 1875. If the waste contains explosives then its storage must be licensed by the local authority or HSE or registered with the local authority, as required by the Explosives Act 1875. The Classification and Labelling of Explosives Regulations 1983 SI 1140 and the Packaging of Explosives for Carriage Regulations 1991 SI 2097 may be relevant. The requirements are complex, and the Explosives Inspectorate of HSE (Rm 414, Merton House, Stanley Road, Bootle L20 3DL) should be contacted for advice.

To understand the markets for managing waste explosives reference should be made to the Hazardous Installations Directorate. The Land Division (LD2 Explosives Inspectorate) provides expert advice and guidance for the manufacture, storage, supply and carriage of explosives within Great Britain, and also for the formulation of new legislation. The Control of Major Accident Hazards (COMAH) Regulations 1999 SI 743 may also apply. For a comprehensive guide to explosive policy and legislation see www.hse.gov.uk/explosives/index.htm. Waste explosives can be even more potentially hazardous (such as in contaminated land remediation) than those securely under lock and key. So please take great care.

3.7.6. Contaminated land and historical waste management

Historically, the building regulation system provided building construction control, and the Building Regulations 1991 SI 2768 specifically addressed the need to consider potential hazards caused by substances on or in the ground. Section 29 of the Building Act 1984 enabled the local planning authority to reject plans where it was proposed to build on ground with offensive properties. However, in 1989–1990 a House of Commons All Party Environmental Committee Report decided that the UK should actively identify contaminated sites.[10]

The Environment Act 1995 amended the EPA 1990 by the addition of a new section (s.78A–78YC) on the identification and remediation of contaminated land, although the contaminated land provisions did not come into force until 1 April 2000. Further details for the designation, control of water pollution, remediation, compensation, appeals, notices and registers for contaminated

---

[10] Tromans S. and Turrall-Clarke R. (1994), *Contaminated Land*, Sweet & Maxwell, London, p. 16.

land are set out in the Contaminated Land (England) Regulations 2000 SI 227. Detailed statutory guidance is contained in DETR 02/2000. The complex regime is designed to identify land that, due to the presence of contaminants, poses a significant threat to human health, property or, in some cases, the natural environment.

The 1995 Act created a new system whereby local authorities must identify, and, if necessary, arrange for the remediation of contaminated sites in their own area, regardless of whether they are intended for redevelopment. Section 78A of the EPA 1990 defines contaminated land as any land which appears to the local authority in whose area it is situated, to be in such a condition, by reasons of substances in, on or under the land, that:

- significant harm is being caused, or
- there is a significant possibility of such harm being caused, or
- pollution of Controlled waters is being or likely to be caused (for a definition of Controlled Waters please see Chapter 12).[11]

'Harm' is defined as harm to the health of living organisms or interference with the ecological system of which they are part, and includes harm to property. Types of harm which are deemed significant are listed; for example, significant harm is that which causes serious injury or disease in humans, harm to protected ecosystems, a 20% loss of the value of livestock or crops, or damage to a building no longer capable of being used for its original purpose. In 1999 the EA estimated that there was approximately 300,000 hectares of contaminated land in the UK, constituting 1.2% of the total land area.

A significant possibility of significant harm will not exist unless three elements are present:

- one or more pollutants
- a receptor (i.e. a person, living organism or building which could be damaged by the pollutants)
- a pathway by which pollutants can reach the receptor, such as migration by dust or through groundwater.

Therefore, however unpleasant the substances present, the land would not be considered contaminated if the substances can cause no harm. Thus, there must be a pollution linkage. (See p. 75 of DETR Circular 02/2000.) The Waste Management Licensing Regulations 1994 SI 1056 Schedule 4 lists 'substances or objects which are waste when discarded', and paragraph 15 is more specific,

---

[11] The Water Act 2003 amends part of s.78A EPA 1990 on contaminated land, and the word 'significant' is added, e.g. the contamination must cause 'significant pollution' of Controlled waters.

Box 3.10: Pollution and contamination — what is the difference? Is not contaminated land in truth polluted?

> **Contamination** is the introduction by humans into the environment of potentially dangerous substances which do not necessarily constitute a risk to the environment, e.g. grass fertiliser, or chlorine to treat swimming-pool water. **Pollution** is the introduction by humans into the environment of potentially dangerous substances that constitute a risk to the environment.
>
> These definitions recognise that whilst environmental pollution is not acceptable, the prevention of environmental contamination is not possible, nor is it desirable. That was a bold attempt to distinguish the two words in a hope, probably forlorn, that one day the s.78A–78YC EPA 1990 contaminated land regime will be called polluted land. But as we have seen, many small and medium-sized waste disposal contractors do not use a dictionary as a nightly pillow.
>
> Source: R. G. P. Hawkins (1998), Lecture to Imperial College.

namely, 'contaminated materials, substances or products resulting from remedial action with respect to land'. Thus, the removal of such substances is subject to the waste management licensing regime (explained in Chapter 8).

Local authorities now have the responsibility of determining whether land in their area is contaminated, acting in accordance with the Secretary of State's guidance under s.78A(2) EPA 1990. The local authority has a duty to inspect its area from time to time to identify contaminated land, since the authority should have a good idea of what may have been historically deposited on its land. Inspections are the responsibility of environmental health officers. If a local authority identifies contaminated land it must give notice in writing, in accordance with s.78B(3) EPA 1990, to:

- the EA
- the owner of the land
- the person who appears to the authority to be in occupation of the whole or part of the land
- any other appropriate person.

Under the Town and Country Planning Act 1990 (TCPA 1990) local authorities can control the development of land which might be contaminated, in that a site investigation could be required before a planning application was determined. If an ensuing problem could not be solved by imposing a planning condition, the local authority and the developer could enter into a voluntary legal agreement under the TCPA 1990. The planning system is subject to significant reform in 2004, as explained in Chapter 7. For the latest situation visit the Office of the Deputy Prime Minister's website (www.odpm.gov.uk).

Special sites are defined in the Contaminated Land (England) Regulations 2000 SI 227, and are the sites which are likely to present the greatest threat to the environment, the enforcing authority for which is the EA. The local authority should consult with the EA when deciding whether or not a site is Special, and the EA may itself designate a Special site.

Foundries have been a considerable source of land contamination, particularly between 1950 and 1990, because of the nature of the raw materials and the lack of environmental controls. The use of scrap material increased significantly after 1945, with such contaminants as cadmium, chemical binders, lead, oil, petroleum products, plastics and zinc. Of the 2300 foundries in operation in the early 1960s, mainly in the west Midlands, Humberside, the North West, Yorkshire and central Scotland, only around 500 remain in operation.

Identifying former sites can be difficult, because foundries were not usually labelled as such on immediate postwar ordnance survey maps, unlike lunatic asylums. The report by Castings Technology International in Association with the consultancy Land Quality Management concluded that the highest contaminant concentrations resulted from associated non-foundry activities such as coking or former blast furnace production. The full project report is available at www.castingstechnology.com.

The Government's approach to cleaning up contaminated land according to s.78E EPA 1990 requires remedial action only when there are appropriate and cost-effective means available to carry out the clean-up, taking into account the suitable-for-use approach. The polluter pays principle also applies, in that the person responsible for the contamination meets the cost of remediation. Remediation is defined very broadly, and left to technical guidance documents.

Before serving a remediation notice the enforcing authority (i.e. either the local authority or EA) must reasonably endeavour to consult with the landowner or occupier. In deciding what is reasonable remediation, the enforcing authority must have regard to the guidance given by the secretary of State (s.78E(5) EPA 1990). The principle of 'suitable for use' lies behind the remediation package chosen, which must be reasonable, practicable, effective and durable.

Section 78L of the EPA 1990 gives the relevant procedures for appealing against a remediation notice. There are rules in the case of polluting substances migrating from a contaminated site onto adjoining land, and if the plume travels on further, then the owners of the first plot are only responsible for the clean-up of their own land. Unless they are the actual polluters they do not have to pay for the remediation of land affected downstream.

Much of the statutory guidance is concerned with assigning liability for remediation, with the basic principle that the polluter pays. But if the polluter cannot be found or no longer exists, liability passes to the current owner or occupier. The polluter is someone who has caused or knowingly permitted the pollution, with 'knowingly permitted' meaning that the site operator was well aware of the pollution and had the resources to deal with it but took no action. For further information see DETR Circular 02/2000, *Contaminated Land: Implementation of Part IIA of the Environmental Protection Act 1990* (www.defra.gov.uk/environment/landliability/circ2–2000).

The view of the EA is that contaminated soils are Controlled waste, and most likely to be, but not always, Special (Hazardous) waste, implying that the treatment of those soils requires a waste management licence (see the EA publication *Guidance on the Application of Waste Management Licensing to Remediation 2001* (www.environment-agency.gov.uk/commondata/105385/wmlrem.pdf). Waste from the clearing of contaminated land may in some cases be exempt from the landfill tax. Details are set out in the Landfill Tax (Contaminated Land) Order 1996 SI 1529 (www.legislation.hmso.gov.uk/si/si1996/Uksi_19961529_en_1.htm).

Installations and mobile plant used for the restoration of contaminated land will usually require a permit under the Pollution Prevention and Control Regulations 2000 SI 1973 or a licence under the Waste Management Licensing Regulations 1994 SI 1056. These systems are explained in Chapter 8.

Brownfield land is previously used land, which may or may not be contaminated. The contaminated land regime does not obviously apply to the cleaning up of brownfield sites for redevelopment which are not contaminated. Uncontaminated brownfield sites are dealt with by local authorities under specific planning legislation. However, in urban areas, particularly with the necessity to redevelop old docklands and industrial sites (e.g. the Greenwich Peninsular, the Newcastle and Southampton quayside developments, and Gosport's Royal Clarence Yard), many brownfield sites are contaminated. Remediation results inevitably in waste soils and materials, often hazardous, dispersed in varying concentrations in large soil volumes. Historical contamination can be poorly documented, and thus the contaminants unpredictable in their characteristics, location and migration.

In 1998 the Government said that by 2008 60% of all new homes must be built on brownfield land, which would be in fact, historical waste management. Lord Rogers' 1998 Urban Task Force aimed to improve the quality of urban environments in the UK,[12] and recommended:

- the redevelopment of vacant spaces and reduction of environmental pollution in cities, including remediation and use of contaminated land

---

[12] See www.odpm.gov.uk/stellent/groups/odpm_urbanpolicy/documents/page/odpm_urbpol_608466-04.hcsp.

- a single regeneration licence to cover all regulatory requirements for contaminated site remediation. (And about time too, would be the observation of many local councillors in England and Wales.)

These recommendations were taken forward by the Working Group on the Single Remediation Permit, comprising members from regulatory bodies, industry, landowners and developers technical suppliers and insurers. The working group reviewed the problems associated with brownfield site redevelopment and regulatory constraints, and the outcome is available in the Kirby report[13]. Kirby stated that 'It is hard enough to get developers to bring brownfield land back into use without putting up additional bureaucratic hurdles to regeneration ... this is not about deregulation, but it is about better regulation'. A consultation exercise on the Kirby and Rogers recommendations was recently undertaken by DEFRA. For information on the adoption of a single remediation permit see www.defra.gov.uk/corporate/consult/land-remediation/index.htm.

Although a streamlined permitting system may speed up permissions for development, the recent closure of around 90% of the UK's Hazardous waste landfill sites (with none remaining in Wales) presents a new barrier to achieving the Government's 60% brownfield target. The reduction in capacity will have a significant impact on contaminated land remediation projects (often containing Special waste), since these have traditionally relied upon Hazardous waste landfill for disposal. It is regrettable that the final disposal of waste material was not given due priority in either the Rogers or Kirby recommendations to speed up the redevelopment process—a scenario reminiscent of the Osborn approach of 1946 (please see Section 1.1.1), which omitted to consider waste disposal in its list of key town planning considerations. One day we may learn ....

3.7.7. Waste from ships

The London Convention 1972 (formerly the London Dumping Convention, amended 1996) controls the dumping of wastes at sea by a licensing system. Signatories are prohibited from dumping non-biodegradable materials from ships and other man-made offshore installations. The International Convention for the Prevention of Pollution from Ships 1973 (MARPOL 73/78) controls pollution by garbage[14] and sets minimum distances from land within which no waste can be disposed. Permitted wastes outside these limits are mostly foodstuffs. Disposal of all plastics is prohibited in the world's oceans. MARPOL 73/78 was implemented by the Merchant Shipping (Prevention of

---

[13] The Kirby Report, Remediation Permit — Towards a Single Regeneration Licence, prepared by Lowe, 2002 (www.claire.co.uk/pubframes.html).

[14] Waste in the context of shipping is sometimes known as garbage.

Pollution by Garbage) Regulations 1998 and Merchant Shipping (Port Waste Reception Facilities) Regulations 1997. The Regulations control dumping of garbage in UK waters and the provision of facilities at UK ports for appropriate disposal of waste generated by shipping.

For the protection of coastal waters around the UK a number of Acts exist, prominent amongst which is the Merchant Shipping and Fishing Vessels (Port Waste Reception Facilities) Regulations 2003 SI 1809 (MSFVR 2003),[15] derived from the 2000/59 Directive on the Implementation of the Strategy for Port Reception Facilities for Ship-generated Wastes and Associated Issues. Section 6 of the MSFVR 2003 requires harbour authorities to have a harbour waste management plan, which must be submitted to the Secretary of State for approval. The Secretary of State can, if necessary, provide direction on the waste plan and reception facilities. Under s.4 MSFVR 2003 all harbour and terminal operators must provide adequate reception facilities for port waste. Adequate means[16]

capable of receiving the types and quantities of prescribed wastes from ships normally using that harbour or terminal taking into account the operational needs of the users of the harbour or terminal, its size and geographical location, the types of ships calling there and any exemptions provided for under regulation 15.

For further information on waste management in ports and harbours see www.ukmarinesac.org.uk/activities/ports/ph6_1.htm.

Regulation 9 of the Special Waste Regulations 1996 sets out the arrangements for Special (Hazardous) waste removed from ships. These arrangements have recently been open to consultation and under review by the EA.

3.7.8. Batteries

The 91/157 Directive on Batteries and Accumulators (amended by the 98/101 Directive),[17] implemented by the Batteries and Accumulators (Containing Dangerous Substances) Regulations 1994 SI 232, as amended in 2001, requires batteries containing heavy metals to be marked so that consumers know that the batteries should not be discarded but recycled. In 1993, the Government proposed a recycling scheme for these batteries. Manufacturers have a choice of

---

[15] The Merchant Shipping (Port Waste Reception Facilities) Regulations 1997 3018 revoked.
[16] A ship is exempt if it is 'engaged in scheduled traffic with frequent and regular port calls and there is sufficient evidence of an arrangement ensuring the delivery of ship-generated waste and payment of charges in a port along the ship's route' (source: MSFVR 2003).
[17] Directive 93/86 harmonised the national laws of the EU Member States in the waste management of spent batteries and accumulators containing certain heavy metals.

two marks, both representing a crossed-out wheelie bin, accompanied by a chemical symbol indicating the heavy metal content, e.g. Hg for mercury.

There is currently no national collection and recycling scheme for batteries in the UK. All batteries that are collected (from ad hoc collections and civic amenity sites) are exported for recycling. In November 2003 the EC issued a proposal to revise the 1991 Batteries Directive. Measures under the new Directive could include:

- a national collection scheme
- specified recovery targets
- a ban on battery incineration
- a ban on landfilling of industrial vehicle batteries
- minimum recycling efficiencies (how on earth is that to be measured?) for collected batteries of different types
- rules on the financing of battery collection and recycling schemes.

The proposal originally specified a collection target of spent portable batteries of 160 g per head of population (about three to four batteries) per year to be met 4 years after the 2007 Directive becomes law, together with a subsidiary requirement for 80% of nickel–cadmium rechargeable batteries to be collected. However, 160 g is higher than the per capita battery consumption in some smaller EU Member States such as Estonia. The target has been changed to 50% of annual sales. This type of target is more appropriate since it also accounts for waste minimisation — if fewer batteries are consumed then fewer need to be recycled. The collection scheme is likely to be funded by manufacturers.

3.7.9. Tyres

The Landfill Regulations 2002 state that whole used tyres will not be accepted at landfill sites, except for:

- tyres used as an engineering material
- bicycle tyres
- tyres with an outside diameter greater than 1400 mm.

Until 16 July 2006, shredded tyres may be landfilled. After this date whole and shredded tyres will be banned (the above exceptions will still apply).

One might have expected alternative methods of treatment and disposal to have been found before the new Regulations came into force, or for preparations to have been made in the 3 years between the 99/31 Landfill Directive and its implementation in the Landfill Regulations 2002, as insufficient alternatives currently exist, and infrastructure is inadequate — a typical scenario for many waste streams brought under new legislation, in which the targets and rules have been agreed with little practical consideration given to how these will be met.

Box 3.11: Co-incineration trial under fire

About 40 million tyres are discarded annually in the UK. As of July 2006 all tyres will be banned from landfill. In 2003 the EA authorised Rugby Cement to conduct a 6-month trial using chipped tyres as a substitute for coal in its cement kiln. The aim of the trial was to determine the effect of tyre burning on emissions, smoke colour and odours, with an aim towards obtaining permission to burn tyres permanently. The trial was authorised under an Integrated Pollution Prevention and Control (IPPC) permit some 2 years after the original application was made. Baseline data were collected 12 months prior to the trial.

The statutory consultee, the Primary Care Trust (PCT), relied upon technical support from the Health Protection Agency (www.hpa.org.uk), which was established in April 2003 to protect the public from health impacts from, *inter alia*, industrial emissions. The PCT argued that bag filters should have been installed in addition to the existing electrostatic precipitators to control any increased dust emissions during the trial. According to the EA the filters, which would cost around £3 million to install, did not qualify as Best Available Techniques (BAT), and were not needed because the dust emissions would be environmentally insignificant. The PCT insisted that the technology should go beyond BAT.

Campaigners from Rugby In Plume felt that generally the public consultation had been inadequate. Consultations are continuing.

In May 2004 the results of the baseline survey (pre-trial, coal only) were announced by the EA. These results are promising, since they show that Rugby Cement have complied with the stringent permit conditions, although some improvements are required for dust levels. According to an EA spokesman the tyre-burning trial is set to go ahead once the EA is satisfied that the plant is 'running properly'.

Sources: www.rmc.co.uk, ENDS Reports 327 and 328, and www.environment-agency.gov.uk.

Chapter 4

The administration and management of waste

Under the European Communities Act 1972, EU Directives must be implemented into UK law, while EU Regulations apply directly to Member States. Over the past 20 years UK waste legislation has largely developed to comply with EU law. The regulatory regimes affecting waste management have five main purposes, namely to:

- protect public health and the environment
- protect employee and public health and safety
- promote waste reduction, recycling and reuse, while reducing landfill dependence
- ensure that responsible planning authorities develop and implement effective waste management plans
- establish the roles and responsibilities of regulatory and enforcement authorities, and provide statutory powers for the fulfilment of these roles.

Responsibility for Government policy is divided between specialist Government departments. For waste management these are the Department for Environment, Food and Rural Affairs (DEFRA), the Department for Trade and Industry (DTI), Department for Transport (DfT), and also the Office of the Deputy Prime Minister (ODPM). While these departments implement and provide guidance on Government policy and legislation, the regulation and enforcement are delegated to Government agencies (e.g. Customs and Excise (now part of the Treasury), the Highways Agency, the Food Standards Agency[1]

---

[1]Sir John Krebs, the Chairman of the Food Standards Agency, while commenting in a discussion on organic produce, whispered 'a single cup of coffee contains natural carcinogens equal to at least a year's worth of carcinogenic synthetic pesticides in the diet', *The Times*, 9 April 2004. A good illustration of placing a hazard in proper proportion.

and the Office of Fair Trading) and regional or local authorities. Planning, nuisance, air quality and public health matters are the remit of regional or local authorities, while regulation and enforcement of environmental law, applications for environmental permits or licences, remediation, and regulatory requirements such as monitoring and reporting are dealt with by the Environment Agency (EA).

The Environment Act 1995 established the EA, and represented a major step towards integrated environmental management and control. The Act made many amendments to the Environmental Protection Act 1990 (EPA 1990) and other environmental statutes relating to the powers of the regulators, who now have greater scope to take preventative as opposed to reactive action to the likelihood of pollution. It also made provisions applicable to National Parks, air quality, and producer responsibility.

4.1. The role of the Government

The Cabinet Office provides supporting services for the Government in carrying out its work and coordinating Government departments, agencies and regulators. The Regulatory Impact Unit (RIU) has published online guidance for policy makers such as *Better Policy Making: A Guide to Regulatory Impact Assessment* (www.cabinet-office.gov.uk/regulation/ria-guidance). An example of a draft Regulatory Impact Assessment is the *Interim Report of the Waste Permitting Review*, which discusses the updating of the waste management licensing system and phasing in of a permitting system (www.defra.gov.uk/ environment/waste/legislation/permitreview/pdf/interim.pdf). The aim of the Cabinet RIU is to 'ensure that regulations are fair and effective and that all new and existing regulation is necessary, meets the principles of better regulation, and imposes the minimum burden', and the website states that 'it is important that UK legislation implementing European legislation is simple, transparent and easily understood'.

Proposed regulation is usually open to consultation and public debate. When DEFRA has decided the final form of the legislation, the proposal is introduced either to the House of Lords or the House of Commons as a Bill. Once the Bill receives Royal Assent through the Privy Council it becomes an Act of Parliament. An Act is often supported by secondary legislation (Statutory Instruments or Orders), known as subordinate legislation in Scotland. Circulars, Codes of Practice and Guidance Notes are supplementary non-statutory guidance material provided by Government departments and the authorities under them, for example the EA, which is responsible to DEFRA.

As near an impartial opinion on Government policies and legislation as is possible can be obtained from the House of Commons and House of Lords all-party specialist committees, e.g. on the environment, transport and auditing.

Evidence is given in open committee, accessible to all, and recorded in printed summaries of evidence submitted. A list of some useful committee reports is given in Appendix B.

In the Preface to this practical guide the House of Commons All Party Committee February 2004 Report was quoted, commenting on whether DEFRA possessed enough of the specialist skills it needs to translate the End of Life Vehicles and Waste Electrical and Electronic Equipment (WEEE) Directives into UK law. The question of lack of resources and skills could be said to reflect the Government's allocation of funds to enable DEFRA and the EA to carry out their tasks, or a lack of consideration of available UK public and private sector management when the UK Government agreed to Directives in Brussels. It is well known that many in DEFRA and the EA work long hours, and that stress levels and staff turnover are high. Will the situation improve as more legislation comes in from Europe and ambitious targets set for the next decade are not met? Unlikely, unless Members of Parliament really bang the table. DEFRA deserves all the support it can get.

In order to give a proper perspective of the contemporary administration of waste management law, and therefore some reasons why delays in implementation of particularly EU laws seem to be commonplace, regard should be had to the observations of the House of Lords Select Committee on the EU 47th Report, Session 2002–2003, *European Waste Management Policy* (18 November 2003):

- The present Government approach to waste policy is apparently reactive.
- The Government should not agree to framework legislation without a full understanding of the practical implications.
- Without a clear idea of how EU policy should develop, the Government is at a severe disadvantage in representing the interests of the UK during negotiations.
- There is a lack of central Government leadership.
- There is a current split of waste management matters between Government departments, which results in a lack of responsibility and direction.
- Consultations on disparate websites are confusing.
- Relevant EU documents should be made available on the Stationary Office website.
- The level of transparency in agreeing the waste acceptance criteria and WEEE Directive is unacceptable and should be addressed.
- EA resources are lacking, and the EA should be involved earlier in the policy-making process.

In effect, UK policy making in waste management is not fair and effective, and legislation is late and impractical. The House of Lords all-party committee recommended that the Government should review the way that EU legislation is implemented, and that there should be a single waste policy unit for the UK.

71

Box 4.1: 'A sprawling mess of ill-matched responsibilities'

> This was how the now disbanded Department of Transport, Local Government and the Regions was recently described by a well-respected London-based international journal. Changes have been made since 2002, when Sir Richard Mottram, the then Permanent Secretary, described a tense situation in graphic, if not wholly quotable words to the effect of 'We're all miffed. I'm miffed. You're miffed. The whole Department is miffed. It's been the biggest mess-up ever and we're all completely miffed'. Not much room for doubt you may think. Things could only get better, and perhaps they have.
>
> Source: *The Economist*, 2 March 2002.

4.2. Impartial decision making in the English legal system

There has, in the past decade, arisen a tug–pull situation where, in the words of the then Home Secretary, 'Parliament debates issues, and the judges overturn them'.[2] There certainly has been a drift of power from the Government to the judiciary. Judicial review is a means whereby an application is made to the High Court to review the decision of a lower court or an inquiry, or even a dispute between members of a golf club. The court scrutinises the case to ensure that the law was followed in the decision-making process.

Over the past 30 years the number of judicial review cases has increased from around 100 per year to more than 4000. This lucrative growth industry for the lawyers received an extraordinary boost from the Government's decision to pass the Human Rights Act 1998, since it gave the judges power to declare Government policies incompatible with the European Convention on Human Rights. While ministers are not theoretically compelled to amend legislation, in practice the civil service tends to ensure that new laws are compatible with EU laws before they come to Parliament, and this will impact on the content of new environmental law.

If the Government fails to introduce an independent system of planning inspectors, it may in the future be forced to do so by the European Court of Human Rights, should a similar conclusion be reached to that of the High Court in December 2000.

Whilst few waste management cases reach the House of Lords (the Cambridge Water Company was a notable exception, please see Box 9.5 of Chapter 9), the Government proposes to institute a supreme court instead of the House of Lords, with the abolition of the office of Lord Chancellor. Part of the

---

[2] David Blunkett speaking about asylum seekers on the BBC Radio 4 *World at One* programme, 20 February 2003.

Box 4.2: Is the Secretary of State an impartial decision maker?

Alconbury Developments Ltd (AD) wanted to redevelop a Ministry of Defence airfield at Alconbury into a national distribution centre. AD made applications to Huntingdon District Council for planning permission for the overall scheme and infrastructure, and for various individual parts of the scheme. They also applied to Cambridge County Council (the local waste disposal authority) for planning permission for a temporary recycling depot on part of the site. After local opposition, an application for the commercial freight operations was withdrawn (March 1998). An application was made to the Secretary of State under section 1 of the Transport and Works Act for infrastructure developments. In August 1998 the Secretary of State refused a request to call in the planning application for his own determination, but later recovered the appeals for his own determination under paragraph 3 of Schedule 6 to the Town and Country Planning Act on the basis that the appeals related to proposals for a development of major importance, and were of more than local significance.

Dissatisfied local residents' groups challenged the planning system, contending that the proceedings were in contravention of Article 6 of the European Convention on the Protection of Human Rights and Fundamental Freedoms (1953) (Cmd 8969) (incorporated in the Human Rights Act 1998). In December 2000 Lord Justice Tuckey and Mr Justice Harrison concluded that the powers of the Environment Secretary to make planning decisions were incompatible with Article 6 of the Human Rights convention: 'everyone is entitled to a fair and public hearing ... by an independent and impartial tribunal'. As a policy maker, the Secretary of State was deemed not to be an impartial decision maker.

In the House of Lords, however, in May 2001 it was decided that the Secretary of State could be both a policy maker and a decision taker, because he was answerable to Parliament as regards the policy aspect of his decision and to the High Court as regards to the lawfulness and fairness of his decision-making process.

Sources: www.parliament.the-stationery-office.co.uk, www.odpm.gov.uk and www.telegraph.co.uk

constitutional reasoning behind this may well be that a new infrastructure will be more easily integrated with a potential new EU constitution, which may well be the subject of a referendum in 2004–2005.

4.3. European institutions

4.3.1. European Parliament

The European Parliament consists of elected Members of the European Parliament (MEPs) from EU individual Member States through varying forms of proportional representation.

Box 4.3: €24,600 per day for non-compliance with a ECJ ruling

In 1987 the EC received complaints that industrial waste, including waste from hospitals and slaughterhouses, was being deposited into a river mouth in Crete just 200 m from the sea. The EC brought a successful prosecution to the ECJ in 1992 against the Greek Government on the grounds that the waste disposal methods employed by the authorities did not comply with, *inter alia*, Article 4 of the 75/442 Waste Framework Directive, which states that 'Member States shall take the necessary measures to ensure that waste is disposed of without endangering human health and without harming the environment'.

When the offences continued and there was no apparent improvement, further legal proceedings followed, which resulted in a fine of €24,600 for each day that the breach of EU law persisted, and there were well over 50 days. This was the first EU fine for an offence of this nature, and it took into consideration the state's ability to pay, and the effect and severity of the pollution incident. Greece claimed in its defence that it could not build the necessary waste management facilities ear-marked in its plan owing to local opposition.

4.3.2. EU Council of Ministers

The Council of Ministers comprises the Foreign Minister from each Member State. If a particular issue is being discussed, then the minister from the relevant area from individual Member States will also attend the meeting.

4.3.3. European Commission

The European Commissioners are responsible to the European Parliament and are appointed by the Member States to act as the executive of the EU. From 2005 the European Commission (EC) will include one commissioner for each Member State.

4.3.4. European Court of Justice

The European Court of Justice (ECJ) exists to ensure that European law is observed. Many of the judges do not necessarily have a legal background or judicial experience of the courts in their own country, which will have a different legal system to that of the UK. The Attorney General to the Court always proffers to the ECJ his own opinion on the law, prior to the court considering the particular case. French is used as the ECJ working language.

4.3.5. The European Court of Auditors

The role of the European Court of Auditors (ECA) is to oversee large EC budgets. The ECA monitors all EC expenditure and revenue. Despite the resignation of all the commissioners in 1999 after whistle-blowing, the EC auditors have not been able to sign off the Commission's accounts for the last 9 years.[3] In this culture of financial indiscipline, it is perhaps not surprising that there is not even a simple estimate ascribed for each new individual EC environmental legislative initiative, either for the EU as a whole or for the individual 25 countries adopting the final result of the initiative.

4.4. Devolution and regional government

The national, regional and local organisational structure has recently been reformed under the:

- Government of Wales Act 1998
- Scotland Act 1998
- Regional Development Agency Act 1998
- Regional Assemblies (Preparations) Act 2003
- Planning and Compulsory Purchase Bill 2003 (to become an Act in 2004).

The Government of Wales Act 1998 established the National Assembly for Wales (Cynulliad Cenedlaethol Cymru), with powers to develop its own planning policies and secondary legislation. Section 53 of the Scotland Act 1998 (SA 1998) provided for a general transfer of planning functions from any UK Westminster Minister of the Crown to the Scottish Ministers.

The Regional Development Agency Act 1998 established eight English Regional Development Agencies to promote sustainable economic development in each of the regions. From late 2004 some, perhaps all, of the regions will hold referenda to decide whether or not to proceed with elected regional assemblies. The Regional Assemblies (Preparations) Act 2003 was passed to provide for such referenda and regional chambers have been established in all of the English regions. The Government is continuing to raise awareness of regional assemblies[4] throughout the UK. Prior to the referenda, regional assemblies exist in an informal way, and do not yet have development control powers. If and when they become statutory elected assemblies they will have such powers vested in them.

The regional assemblies will have between 35 and 40 members (elected under proportional representation), a leader and a cabinet of up to six people, which will be chosen by the elected members. They will have similar powers to the Greater London Authority. In some cases (Northumberland, Cumbria, Durham, North Yorkshire, Cheshire and Lancashire), district or county councils may be abolished depending on the outcome of a referendum vote.

---

[3] *The Times*, Business Section, 7 May 2004.
[4] The offices for England's eight regional assemblies are located in Brussels.

Box 4.4: The £5 million 2004 'Your Say' public information campaign

The ODPM is currently funding an information campaign to raise awareness of regional assemblies throughout the UK, which is intended to be objective and explanatory and not party political. Three referenda are to be held in late 2004 on the issue of regional assemblies in:

- Yorkshire and Humberside
- the North East
- the North West.

The Electoral Commission has decreed that 'yes' and 'no' campaigns may only spend between £665,000 and £940,000, according to the size of the region.

Source: *The Times*, 22 April 2004.

The regional assemblies have no direct power over taxation, but they can levy an additional council tax precept of approximately £25 per year. An additional amount of council tax can also be charged for special projects. Although unspecified, this amount will be capped by the Government. The regional assemblies will have limited legislative powers, but will be responsible for the region's planning and economic strategies, overseeing the regional development agencies. The regional assemblies will be subject to a limited number of national targets, but, in return, they will have the power to allocate large sums of money at their discretion. The general responsibilities for the new regional assemblies are to:

- initiate regional planning and economic strategies
- oversee regional development agencies.

Specific responsibilities are:

- environmental protection
- land use
- transport
- public health
- housing
- tourism
- culture
- sport
- economic development.

The powers of the regional assemblies are to:

- allocate funds as necessary
- levy an additional council tax precept (approximately £25)

- charge an additional capped amount for special projects
- pass a limited scope of legislation.

4.5. The national waste strategies

4.5.1. Reduction of landfill

The Waste Strategy 2000 sets out problems associated with landfill as a principal reason for the need to change waste management practice in England and Wales. Page 11 states that 'landfill is a major source of methane—a powerful gas contributing to climate change'. However, landfill engineers will know that landfill gas can be contained and collected and the emissions managed. The rational behind the strategy is not methane, to which landfill only makes a small contribution, it is because the EU passed the 99/31 Landfill Directive.[5] Landfill engineering practice varies widely across the EU, and individual Member States should have been allowed greater flexibility with respect to landfill. It is difficult to see how the new Accession States will be able to meet the same landfill requirements as the UK, where technology and practice are often significantly advanced. In practice, the EU rules will probably have to be different for each nation.

England, Ireland, Scotland and Wales have all developed individual strategies to set out how they will meet the EU waste management objectives.

4.5.2. The Waste Strategy 2000 (England and Wales)

Under s.44A EPA 1990 the Secretary of State must produce a waste strategy setting out waste disposal and recovery policies for England and Wales. The Waste Strategy 2000 (England and Wales) is available at www.defra.gov.uk/ environment/waste/strategy/. Legislation cited in the Waste Strategy 2000 is listed at www.defra.gov.uk/environment/waste/strategy/cm4693/17.htm.

4.5.3. A Way with Waste (Wales)

The Government of Wales Act 1998 established the National Assembly for Wales (Cynulliad Cenedlaethol Cymru). Primary legislation is still made by the UK Parliament in Westminster, but the Welsh Assembly has powers to make secondary legislation. It can also make policies in several areas including the environment, and is developing its own waste strategy separate to the Waste Strategy 2000 (England and Wales). The strategy, A Way with Waste, is

---

[5] On the BBC Radio 4 *Today* programme on 30 January 2004 a Dutch scientist stated that if all 4×4 drivers gave their vehicles to the local farmer and used a sensibly sized family saloon instead, it would save as much energy as recycling glass bottles for the next 400 years. The Minister of State recently said, in a change of emphasis, that the Government policy on recycling is not to reduce greenhouse gases but to reduce landfill and incineration.

Box 4.5: Climate change: global warming and global cooling

England's warming

Global warming can be ephemeral. In January 1660 apples were growing in London and the Home Counties.

January 8: proclamation issued for general fast in England.
January 16: prayers for the unreasonableness of the weather in London and Westminster
January 22: prayers for the rest of England.

Pepys recorded that he was asked by a breakfast companion

> whether we had not committed a fault in eating today, since it is a fast day ordered by Parliament to pray for more reasonable weather, having hitherto been summer weather. It does threaten the plague.

... but Italy's cooling

The Little Ice Age from 1450 to 1850 reached its coldest between 1645 and 1715. An unusual musical advantage came from its effect on the Cremonese spruce trees, with high-density wood produced during the cooler conditions, which contributed to the resonance in the renowned Stradivarius violins.

Sources: RGPH Hawkins European Parliament Group Address (March 1988) and *The Times*, 10 December 2003.

---

currently in draft form and is available at www.defra.gov.uk/environment/waste/strategy/.

4.5.4. The Scottish National Strategy for Waste

With effect from 1 July 1999 section 53 of the SA 1998 provided for a general transfer of functions from any UK Westminster Minister of the Crown to the Scottish Ministers. Almost all matters relating to the environment are within the legislative competence of the Scottish Parliament, but there are reserved matters in Schedule 5 of the SA 1998:

- coal
- marine transport
- nuclear energy
- oil and gas
- transport of radioactive materials.

The Scottish Executive first adopted the Scottish Environment Protection Agency's (SEPA) National Strategy for Waste in December 1999. It is not the same in style or content as the English/Welsh strategy. It is generally both more clearly written and realistic. In November 2003, the Scottish Parliament warned that a rush to meet the strategy's short-term targets could result in investments poorly fitted to achieve long-term targets.

4.5.5. The Waste Strategy for Northern Ireland

The 75/442 Waste Framework Directive was implemented in Northern Ireland by the Waste & Contaminated Land (Northern Ireland) Order 1997 SI 2778, which transfers responsibility for waste regulation from the 26 district councils to the Department of the Environment Northern Ireland and then the Northern Ireland Environment and Heritage Service (NI EHS), which is the competent authority for Northern Ireland. The 2000 strategy set targets to recover 25% of household waste by 2005 and 40% by 2010 (see www.ehsni.gov.uk/ environment/wastemanage/strategyni.shtml).

Northern Ireland waste management public and private sectors await the House of Commons report into Northern Ireland's waste strategy. The inquiry is to examine what action is being taken to reduce the amount of household waste destined for landfill, and the level of future and present landfill capacity. EU Landfill Directive Regulations introduced a permitting system for the Provinces in December 2003. Progress and potential development of the Northern Ireland recycling industry will be reported on, as well as alternative options such as incineration. Slow progress in Northern Ireland may be partly excused by the effect of the continuing Troubles, although this may not be the view of the EC.

The UK waste strategies and responsibility for regulation and enforcement of environmental legislation (competent authorities) are shown in Table 4.1.

4.6. The role and performance of local authorities

Before the 1972 Local Government Act the disposal of materials which seemingly had no further use was a localised service throughout the UK, and mainly the responsibility of under-resourced public but also private organisations. The deposit of industrial and other waste substances was often carried out by the manufacturer itself (an early form of producer responsibility), although the waste was often dumped within the factory's curtilage. Prior to local government reorganisation in 1974 (under the Local Government Act 1972), responsibility for refuse collection rested with the city, urban and rural district councils. Each small council tended to have its own landfill site or incinerator, very often administered to very basic standards and subject to the somewhat out-of-date Public Health Act 1936 (please see Chapter 1). Most waste disposal facilities were owned and operated by local authorities. There was no site licensing, let alone any rigorous development control or environmental impact assessment. The private waste management sector was only beginning to emerge, often as a result of wartime contract servicing work for aircraft and military bases.

Table 4.1: Summary of national waste strategies and competent authorities

Country	Regional government	Waste strategy	Competent authority	Useful websites
England	UK Parliament	The Waste Strategy 2000 (England and Wales)	Environment Agency	www.parliament.uk www.defra.gov.uk/ environment/waste/ strategy/ www.environment-agency.gov.uk
Wales	Welsh Assembly	A Way with Waste (in draft)	Environment Agency	www.defra.gov.uk/ environment/waste/ strategy/
Scotland	Scottish Parliament	The Scottish National Strategy for Waste 1999	Scottish Environment Protection Agency	www.scottish. parliament.uk www.sepa.org.uk
Northern Ireland	Devolution is currently suspended	The Waste Strategy for Northern Ireland 2000	Environment and Heritage Service	www.doeni.gov.uk www.ehsni.gov.uk/ pubs/publications/ NIWMS.pdf

After the Deposit of Poisonous Waste Act 1972, the Control of Pollution Act 1974 established the first regulatory framework for waste, together with the structure of the waste collection authorities (WCAs) and the waste disposal authorities (WDAs). The emergent site licensing regime was administered by the WDAs, some of which naturally lacked the experience and expertise necessary adequately to control their areas. However, the important fact was that the WDAs began to reflect the strategic aspects of the disposal function.

4.6.1. Waste collection and disposal

Today in England and Wales, arrangements for municipal waste collection and disposal are the responsibility of local authorities. Commercial and industrial wastes are largely controlled by market forces through the private sector. Waste planning is the responsibility of regional and local authorities, who must produce regional spatial strategies and a local development framework for the establishment of suitable waste management infrastructure. Under s.49 EPA 1990 waste recycling plans must be prepared by WCAs for the household and commercial waste arising in their area. Waste management planning has recently been subject to significant changes, and these are explained in Chapter 7.

Provisions for the collection and recycling of household waste are made in ss.45–63 EPA 1990, which were later in part amended by the Household Waste Recycling Act 2003. Under s.45 EPA 1990, waste collection authorities must arrange for (i.e. undertake itself or contract out) the collection of household waste in its area without making a charge, since the payment is included in the council tax. Waste need not be collected from isolated or inaccessible places where the cost of collection to the local authority would be unacceptably high, provided that comparable alternative arrangements are available. If requested, WCAs may also collect commercial waste, for which an appropriate and reasonable charge can be levied, and industrial waste may be collected provided that the WDA consents, again at a charge.

Since the 1992 EPA 1990 (Commencement No. 11) Order SI 260, under s.46 EPA 1990 a WCA may specify a reasonable number and the type of waste receptacles for household waste. Householders may be required by a waste collection authority to place household waste inside sacks or other receptacles, and to do this in a way that facilitates waste material selection for recycling. Section 47 of the EPA 1990 sets out rules concerning commercial and industrial waste. There is a right of appeal to the Crown Court (or in Scotland the Court of Session) within 21 days on the grounds that the requirements are unreasonable.

Section 48 of the EPA 1990 gives specific duties to WCAs to deliver collected waste for disposal under reasonable direction from the WDAs and having regard to the WCA's recycling plan. As a result of the Household Waste Recycling Act 2003, s.45A EPA 1990 gives power to WCAs to make arrangements for separate collection of at least two types of recyclable waste (this presently applies only in England, but will later apply to Wales).

Section 51 of the EPA 1990 outlines the duties of WDAs to manage the disposal of waste arising in their area at all reasonable times, and for the provision of neighbourhood sites (civic amenity sites), which must be free of charge for householders. Arrangements may be made with waste disposal contractors.

4.6.2. The role of local authority waste disposal companies

In June 1991, under s.32 EPA 1990, in an endeavour to raise the general operating standards through competition, the waste disposal operations of WDAs in England and Wales had to be transferred either to arms' length local authority companies or to waste disposal contractors in the private sector. The arms' length company element is defined in s.68 of the Local Government and Housing Act 1989. The Secretary of State had also to be satisfied that the local authority waste disposal companies, known as LAWDCs, had been properly constituted, which in some cases required reasonable scrutiny.

So there can now be several contracts for recycling, landfill disposal or incineration in one waste disposal catchment area, which soon may be on a regional basis (please see Chapter 7). There naturally has been a tendency in some areas for waste disposal authorities to prefer the work of their colleagues in the local authority WDAs, and this has occasionally raised some difficulties in the tendering procedures. The law here is quite complex: see *R* v. *Avon County Council* ex parte *Terry Adams Ltd* 1994 159 LG Review.[6]

The rules governing the tendering of waste disposal contracts and the accompanying procedures are set out in Part II of Schedule 2 of the EPA 1990, and are now subject to Regulations under the EU Public Procurement Directives (please see Chapter 10). The role of LAWDCs is complicated by the Best Value Performance Indicators (please see Section 4.6.5 below), and by the advent of the Private Finance Initiative.

4.6.3. Recycling credits

Section 52 of the EPA 1990 is concerned with the payment for waste which is recycled by a WCA, and which should be reimbursed by a WDA on the basis of the WDA's net saving in expenditure (recycling credits or payments). Likewise, payments will be made by a WCA to the WDA on the net saving on the waste which has not been collected. Net savings are determined by the Environmental Protection (Waste Recycling Payments) Regulations 1992 SI 462. Section 52A of the EPA 1990 is concerned with payments allowed for delivering pre-separated waste, and is complementary to s.31 of the Waste and Emissions Trading Act 2003 (WETA 2003), which should be in force at the end of 2004.

4.6.4. Other powers

Section 55 of the EPA 1990 gives wide powers to both WDAs and WCAs to secure the proper marketing of waste, for example for the WDAs to contract out for recycling, or the supply of heat or electricity. There are other similar powers for local authorities available under the EPA 1990, if not quite so prominent.

Over all these powers, the Secretary of State, through DEFRA, can, but only in writing, direct the holder of a waste management licence to accept, keep, treat, or retain Controlled waste at specified places on specified terms. Wide powers indeed, and they were used extensively in the 2001 foot-and-mouth disease crisis. Similar powers under s.59 EPA 1990 exist for a statutory authority to require an occupier of unlicensed land to remove or diminish the threat from any Controlled waste unlawfully deposited on his land. Likewise, s.60, entitled 'Interference with waste sites and receptacles for waste', is an attempt to stop the practice of totting, which can have considerable risks for example in the spread of AIDS, hepatitis and other drug-abuse-related infections.

Local authorities are also responsible, under byelaws, for controlling the fouling of land by dogs. This can be a slow process using valuable council time.

---

[6] *Garner's Environmental Law*, Binder I at Division II, p. 142, gives a coherent account, well worth reading.

Box 4.6: £50 fines unpopular

Local shopkeepers and residents were issued with £50 fines for leaving their bin bags out too early. They then retorted that the council did not collect rubbish for 5 days when refuse collectors did not turn up.

Source: *Birmingham Evening Mail* (City Edition), 3 February 2004.

A woman was fined £50 for putting rubbish out in non-council-issued black sacks. The woman refused to pay the on-the-spot fine and the matter will be taken to court.

Source: *Crewe Chronicle*, 21 January 2004.

Under the Dogs (Fouling of Land) Act 1996 local authorities may make their own designation, provided it follows DEFRA regulations. Abandoned motor vehicles can presently be removed and destroyed by district councils under the Refuse Disposal (Amenity) Act 1978, and other powers are given through the Road Traffic Regulation Act 1984 and Removal, Storage and Disposal of Vehicles Regulation 1989.

4.6.5. Measuring local authority performance with Best Value Indicators

Under the Local Government Act 1999 local authorities have a duty to monitor performance and continuously improve their services. The Local Government (Best Value) Performance Indicators and Standards Order 2003 SI 530 (BVIO 2003) sets out the criteria for assessing local authority performance in 2003–2004. These range from culture indicators to crime reduction, as well as planning and environmental performance. A full list of the indicators is given in the BVIO 2003 (www.legislation.hmso.gov.uk/si/si2003/20030530.htm). Environmental indicators, most of which are waste related, are given in Schedule 7. Waste performance standards are given in Schedule 8. Planning performance indicators are in Schedule 10, and include the percentage of new homes built on previously developed land. Performance levels, actions and future standards are reported annually in a Best Value Performance Plan.

The environmental indicators under Schedule 7 of the BVIO 2003 are:

- the percentage of the total tonnage of household waste arisings which have been sent by the authority for recycling
- the percentage of the total tonnage of household waste arisings which have been sent by the authority for composting
- the percentage of the total tonnage of household waste arisings which have been used to recover heat, power and other energy sources

- the percentage of the total tonnage of household waste arisings which have been land-filled
- the number of kilograms of household waste collected per head
- the cost of waste collection per household
- the cost of waste disposal per tonne for municipal waste
- the percentage of population resident in the authority's area who are served by a kerbside collection of recyclables or are within a 1 km radius of a recycling centre
- local street and environmental cleanliness
- satisfaction with waste collection, waste recycling facilities and waste disposal.

The April 2003 House of Commons Audit Committee Report stated in paragraph 35 that 'the Local Authority Recycling Advisory Committee (LARAC) told us that the statutory targets, together with the inclusion of performance targets within the Best Value regime, has been "a strong challenge to local authorities" and that "many will struggle to meet their own targets …"'.

DEFRA will be publishing a full report on the performance of English councils in meeting recycling and composting targets in the summer of 2004. Local authorities have a statutory target of increasing recycling and composting of household waste to 17% by 2003–2004, rising to 25% by 2005–2006. Early estimates, based on Best Value Performance Indicators, suggest that recycling levels in England were running at almost 15% in 2002–2003. There is concern, however, that 10% of local authorities have failed to improve their recycling rates over the year. There remains for the Government to consider using its powers under the Local Government Act 1999 to intervene in those authorities which do not meet the targets.

Box 4.7: A cost–benefit analysis jeopardises a career?

Dear Sir,

Your dig at the Chief Executive of the Royal Bank of Scotland for using a corporate jet (Business, April 16) reminds me of when the Chairman of HSBC in the early 1980s asked me to produce a cost/benefit analysis of acquiring such a vehicle for his use.

The most difficult item to factor into the analysis was the likely adverse effect on my future HSBC career of a negative result.

Yours sincerely,

Roy Munden TA3 7ST

Source: Letter to *The Times*, 13 April 2004.

Box 4.8: Another billion pounds?

> Although the allocation of landfill allowances under WETA 2003 may provide some incentive for action, it is not enough. A spokesman for the Environmental Services Association recently commented that 'The allocation of allowances itself will not address the problem ....We need much more: an additional £1 billion in funding for the management of the municipal waste stream, which international experience shows will be necessary, greater regulatory certainty and a quicker, more predictable planning system.'
>
> Source: *Resource Management and Recovery*, 31 October 2003.

To ensure that the targets are met, DEFRA established the Waste Implementation Programme (WIP) in May 2003, to provide initial backing for investment in recycling infrastructure and to support the development of new technologies for managing waste. A 3-year spending programme, based on income diverted away from environmental bodies established under the Landfill Tax Credit Scheme, has been set up.

4.6.6. The Waste and Emissions Trading Act 2003

The WETA 2003 has a new emphasis on local authorities working together as joint waste authorities. It introduces a new section on joint municipal waste management strategies, which requires local authorities in two-tier areas to prepare a statement on a joint waste management strategy for household waste. The Act brings in a regime of landfill allowances for councils that divert waste from landfill (please see Chapter 6), with possible discounts for householders who generate less waste and recycle. Variable charging for householders would involve infrastructure investment, and waste would need to be weighed.

The Act allows for disposal authorities to be fined. Although this provides incentives and controls for disposal authorities, they could well find themselves liable to fines because of failures outside of their control, i.e. because of problems originating from the collection authority.

4.7. Regulation and enforcement

Article 5 of the 75/442 Waste Framework Directive states that 'Member States shall establish or designate the competent authority (or Authorities) to be responsible, in a given zone, for the planning, organisation, authorisation and supervision of waste disposal operations'. The competent authorities in the UK are:

- England and Wales—Environment Agency (EA)
- Scotland—Scottish Environment Protection Agency (SEPA)
- Northern Ireland—Environment and Heritage Service (EHS).[7]

Prior to the Environment Act 1995, waste regulation was the responsibility of waste regulation authorities (WRAs). The Environment Act 1995 established the Environment Agency, which took over the duties of the:

- National Rivers Authority
- Her Majesty's Inspectorate of Pollution
- local WRAs.

The work of the EA encompasses:

- flood defence
- water quality and resources
- waste management
- process industry regulation
- fisheries
- radioactive substances
- contaminated land
- navigation
- biodiversity.

The EA has three main roles (Table 4.2):

- to set out how waste should be managed through guidance and advice, and setting conditions on licences or permits
- monitoring compliance with licences and the law
- solving problems, if necessary through prosecution and remediation.

The EA is empowered to:

- revoke or suspend permits or licences
- require illegally deposited waste to be removed or cleaned up
- require preventative measures to be taken against such tipping
- serve prohibition notices—prohibition could in the future be used for unregulated and non-permitted sites
- undertake prosecution proceedings in the Crown Court, and, if criminal proceedings for contempt are ineffectual, in the High Court
- order a person to remedy the harm caused
- issue fixed-penalty notices as alternatives to criminal proceedings.

---

[7] The Environment and Heritage Service (EHS) is an agency within the Department of the Environment, which advises on and enforces environmental legislation.

Table 4.2: Summary of the EA role

Communicating what is required	Monitoring	Solving problems
Advice and guidance	Inspections	Prosecutions
Regulations	Reports of incidents	Enforcement notices
Licences (or permits)	Self-reporting by operators	Licence amendments
Registration	Surveillance and investigations	Warnings and cautions

Source: National Audit Office Report, Session 2002–2003, *Environment Agency: Protecting the Public from Waste*

The EA's enforcement and prosecution policy is available from its website (www.environment-agency.gov.uk/commondata/105385/enfpolicy.pdf). The underlying principles are:

- proportionality—the balance of action against the risks and costs
- consistency—similar approaches and outcomes for similar cases
- transparency
- targeting—direct resources towards those who cause the most harm to the environment, and deliberate or organised crime.

The EA prosecution policy can be neatly paraphrased: the two circumstances that will not be tolerated are the cover-up and the shut-up. It is essential to report any possible breach of a licence or any environmental criminal offence to the nearest EA regional office as soon as possible, and certainly before it comes calling.

All the mitigating or contributory circumstances may not have become clear, but notification to the EA, even if it is not established then and there that an offence has been committed, must be prompt and on a 24-hour, 7 days a week basis. Waiting until Monday morning is just no excuse at all. And nor should it be. Fishes can die, irrespective of the hour or day. So have in your personal diary the local EA emergency number. This of course also applies to HGV driver/operators who have ditched, through no fault of their own driving, and may find that their load has leaked—their criminal liability is very real.

The EA will usually prosecute:

- when the activity has caused, or has the potential to cause, significant environmental harm
- when the activity is not, but should be, covered by a licence or permit
- when the activity is outside the terms and conditions of a licence or permit

- when the activity is in persistent breach
- when the activity fails to comply with remedial requirements
- when the activity demonstrates a reckless disregard for standards
- when there is sufficient evidence for a prosecution
- if it is in the public interest
- if anyone fails to supply information or provides false information
- if anyone impersonates, obstructs or assaults a member of EA staff.

The following factors are taken into account:

- environmental effect
- foreseeability
- intent
- history of offending
- attitude of the offender
- deterrent effect
- personal circumstances of the offender.

The EA may:

Box 4.9: £650,000 penalty to reflect public anguish and anger

In December 2003 a company was fined a record £250,000 for illegal waste activities and ordered to pay £400,000 costs in a prosecution brought by the EA. The Cleansing Service Group pleaded guilty to 15 offences, including health and safety breaches, which related to a fire at its Sandhurst plant in Gloucestershire. Offences included a fire in a Hazardous waste storage area which emitted fireballs and explosions and released noxious chemicals, resulting in the evacuation of local residents. Hazardous waste was illegally buried, radioactive waste was accepted without authorisation and there were breaches of waste management licence conditions. During the sentencing, His Honour Judge Jamie Tabor QC stated that 'It is not my job to break the company, but the sentence has to reflect the public's grave concern and disquiet.' The explosion and fire in 2000 devastated the company's site. The company cooperated with the EA throughout the 3-year investigation and pleaded guilty at the earliest opportunity. Although no conclusive cause of the fire was identified, much was learned. The company has implemented changes and improvements to its management systems and operations. As a result of consultation with local residents on the future of the site, the company decided not to continue with activities at Sandhurst, and sold the site for redevelopment.

Sources: *Wastes Management*, January 2004, the Cleansing Service Group website (www.csgwasteman.co.uk) and BBC News (www.news.bbc.co.uk).

Box 4.10: Small-time crook imprisoned for brazen act of contamination

In a recent case, a man was ordered to serve a 2-month prison sentence for dumping Hazardous waste. Bulk containers of oil, acid, alkali and charcoal, produced from diesel stripping (illegally blackening red diesel, which should only be used off-road), were dumped onto a pathway, which resulted in a £30,000 clean-up operation — courtesy of the tax payer.

Source: *Environment Business News Briefing*, 12 February 2004.

- issue a prohibition notice (work must cease until notified)
- issue an improvement notice (a timescale is set)
- prosecute for an illegal waste activity.

Individuals and company directors or managers may be prosecuted.

The EA will usually prosecute the person responsible, and where this is a company, the part played by individuals will be considered. Although often the company is usually prosecuted, there have been cases where individual directors, managers or the company secretary have been prosecuted for a criminal offence, especially when the offence has been a result of their consent, neglect or turning of a blind eye to the activities of employees under their supervision. Many think front-line managers and directors should be prosecuted more frequently. According to the EA, seven or eight directors have already received sentences; these tended to be in cases involving smaller companies.

The following points emerged from evidence given by the EA to a recent House of Commons Environmental Audit committee (EAC) inquiry into environmental crime:

- the number of cases against individual directors should be increased
- corporate probation should be introduced, whereby a company that re-offends during a probationary period is brought back to court
- companies should be made to list environmental offences in their Annual Report
- the fit and proper person criteria should be reassessed after court cases
- the Court of Appeal should produce sentencing guidelines for environmental cases
- consideration should be given to whether fines should be based on turnover, profitability or other factors.

For a copy of the EAC evidence see www.parliament.the-stationery-office.co.uk.

Unfortunately, the enforcement of the prosecution policy in 2004–2005 has been unacceptably curtailed because the EA has cut its routine inspections by up to a quarter. The EA has been unable to fulfil plans to do more to combat fly-tipping after having its grant-in-aid cut because of a cash squeeze on DEFRA.

DEFRA is trying to counterbalance this by setting higher supervisory charges for businesses. How much the DEFRA shortage of cash is due to its difficulties in conducting the controlling of the foot-and-mouth disease outbreak and accompanying compensation is difficult to ascertain, because of course, directly after the foot-and-mouth disease outbreak was brought more or less under control, the DETR became DEFRA.

The EA's difficulties have been compounded since the 2002 trend of increased fly-tipping (up that year by 19%), which continued in 2003; and of equal concern is the growing evidence of involvement by organised crime in more serious cases. Possible increases in illegal activity when the ban on landfill co-disposal of Hazardous waste takes effect in the summer of 2004, seem to be inevitable unless the EA can persuade local authorities to control more of the lesser incidents. In the spring of 2003 the House of Commons Environmental Audit Committee pressed DEFRA to give urgent consideration to an EA serious bid for a fly-tipping taskforce costing £40 million to start up and £1 million per year to run.

The basic difficulty with enforcement by regulators is that there are just not enough experienced enforcers in the UK. In broad terms there are 3 million regulated businesses, 20% of which are manufacturing based, with the total UK regulatory force being 10,000 plus, including environmental health officers. That of course does not take account of the adequacy of any financial budgets. It would therefore be not wholly correct to equate better regulation with more regulators. There can of course be targeted regulation based on an assessment of the process under enquiry and the general competence of the business in question. In addition, there are the controls exerted by financial pressures such as the climate change levy, the packaging recovery charges, the aggregate levy, the landfill tax and congestion and other highway and transportation charging.

In 2003 the first EA Financial Management and Policy Review stated that:

- no single statement exists to bring together the Government objectives for the EA
- there is no guidance for the EA contribution towards sustainable development (please see Section 1.3.2).

In 2003 DEFRA published statutory guidance on the role of the EA over the next 5 years. The guidance states that the EA should:

- take an integrated approach towards environmental protection and enhancement
- consider economic and social factors against the benefits of environmental enhancement
- provide wider policy-making advice to the Government on environmental matters.

To view the DEFRA guidance visit www.defra.gov.uk/environment/ea/sustain.

The National Audit Office Report, Session 2002–2003, *Environment Agency: Protecting the Public from Waste* provides an informative summary of the role of the EA, and is available online (www.nao.gov.uk/publications/index.htm).

In 2004 Scotland developed a network of specialist environmental prosecutors throughout its 11 regions in order to integrate the Crown Office, Procurator Fiscal Service and SEPA. The prosecutors will provide specialist knowledge and expertise for others involved with enforcing environmental crimes. For further information see www.scotland.gov.uk/pages/news/2004/02/SECO191.aspx. For further information on SEPA see www.sepa.gov.uk, and for the EHS see www.ehsni.gov.uk.

4.8. Other organisations

4.8.1. The Health and Safety Executive

The Health and Safety Commission (HSC) and the Health and Safety Executive (HSE) regulate risks to health and safety arising from work activity in the UK and enforce health and safety legislation (www.hse.gov.uk/aboutus/index.htm). The Hazardous Installations Directorate (HID), a part of HSE, regulates and promotes improvements in health and safety in order to reduce and control major risks in high-hazard industries. These industries include diving, chemical manufacture and storage, explosives, gas storage and transportation, mining, and offshore oil and gas extraction (www.hse.gov.uk/hid/index.htm).

4.8.2. The National Audit Office

The National Audit Office (NAO) is an independent organisation that scrutinises public spending on behalf of Parliament (see www.nao.gov.uk). The NAO audits the accounts of all Government departments (e.g. DEFRA) and agencies (e.g. the EA) and other public bodies.

4.8.3. Environmental health officers

Environmental health officers (EHOs) are usually employed by local authorities, although there are some private consultants, to assist in controlling risks to human health and the environment. EHOs have responsibility for monitoring and enforcing standards of environmental and public health. Their remit covers, for example:

- health and safety
- nuisance
- industrial waste
- food safety
- fly-tipping
- contaminated land.

91

EHOs have statutory powers to enforce environmental health standards and implement public health policies, as well as enforce legislation including the EPA 1990 and Health and Safety Regulations. EHOs are responsible for investigating public health complaints such as illegal fly-tipping, odour or noise, and inspecting contaminated land.

4.8.4. The Health Protection Agency
The Health Protection Agency (HPA) was set up by the Department of Health in 2003 to provide coordinated advice on public health issues. Support is available in areas such as emergency planning, the control of incinerator emissions and communicable disease control. The agency management does not at present convey legal powers or responsibilities, but may well do so in the future if amended by the Secretary of State.

4.8.5. The British Standards Institution
The British Standards Institution (BSI) is responsible for implementing the Eurocodes, which will eventually replace the British Standards used for the design of civil engineering buildings structures (see www.bsi-global.com).

4.8.5. Customs and Excise
The landfill tax is under the care and management of Her Majesty's Commissioners of Customs and Excise (HMCCE), under Part III of the Finance Act 1996. Customs and Excise is now part of the Treasury, as announced in the 2004 Budget.

4.8.6. The United Kingdom Accreditation Service
The United Kingdom Accreditation Service (UKAS) is the Government-recognised accreditation body that assesses organisations that provide certification, testing, inspection or calibration by the Government against international standards (see www.ukas.com).

4.8.7. Waste Transporters and Brokers
Anyone transporting Controlled waste must be a registered carrier with the EA (for details and exemptions please see Chapter 11). A waste broker is anyone who is a:

- trader or dealer of scrap metal or other recyclate
- waste management contractor or carrier who makes disposal arrangements for waste they cannot accept at their own sites
- broker or environmental consultant who arranges for the disposal of waste on behalf of clients.

Box 4.11: Awareness campaign fails to make a real impact

In January 2004 it was announced that WRAP will stop funding the Waste Awareness Campaign. According to an independent assessment, although engaging many stakeholders, the campaign failed to make a real impact on consumer trends, which is required to curb growing waste generation. WRAP will take over and launch its own National Awareness Campaign in June 2004. For further information visit www.wrap.org.uk.

Source: CIWM News Online, 20 February 2004.

Table 4.3: UK compost market outlets 2001–2002

Market section	Tonnage
Landfill engineering (site restoration)	330,000 (181,000)
Agriculture	287,000
Amateur gardening	127,000
Landscape	106,000
Ground maintenance	78,000
Horticulture	51,000
Land restoration	19,000
Total	998,000

Source: The Composting Association (www.compost.org.uk)

4.8.8. Charities, not-for-profit and non-governmental organisations

The Waste and Resources Action Programme (WRAP) is a not-for-profit organisation, which aims to create stable markets for recycled materials and products. It is funded jointly by the Government (DEFRA and the DTI) and the devolved administrations of Scotland, Wales and Northern Ireland. In 2003 the DEFRA Waste Implementation Programme provided £30 million to WRAP to fund its communications and awareness campaign. WRAP will allocate the funding in three stages, focusing on projects to promote recycling and waste minimisation. For further information visit www.wrap.org.uk.

Composting is an example where market forces have often led to the successful marketing of the end-product. Typical composting market outlets are shown in Table 4.3.

Another Government agency involved in implementing the Government's waste minimisation and recycling programme is Envirowise, which has been in business since 1994, providing free services to businesses, including a helpline and consultancy advice to identify waste minimisation opportunities. Envirowise is managed by AEA Technology Transfer and Information, and is funded jointly by DEFRA and the DTI, with an annual budget of some £5 million plus. The Envirowise business plan incorporates a target to deliver savings worth 10 times its own expenditure, and its contract can be ended if this is not met, which in the past it very nearly wasn't. A recent report on the efficacy of Envirowise has expressed some reservations about the Envirowise presentation of data, and apparent gaps and inconsistencies in the reports to its sponsor Government departments. It would appear that Envirowise will in the future need to justify its claims as to its effectiveness in a somewhat more detailed and rigorous approach than in the past. There is no reason to think that it cannot achieve that object.

4.9. Education and training

The Waste Management Industry Training and Advisory Board (WAMITAB) was established in 1989 to provide advice on education policy and standards for the waste management industry. WAMITAB is responsible for issuing the Certificate of Technical Competence, which is a statutory requirement for managers of waste facilities under the Waste Management Licensing Regulations 1994. Government funding has been allocated to encourage the uptake of level 2 and level 3 National Vocational Qualifications (NVQs) in England. The money is available from the Learning and Skills Council, which has an agreed contract with WAMITAB. The initiative is intended for people employed in the waste management industry, and is sponsored by industry. For further information contact WAMITAB on 01604 231 950 or visit www.wamitab.org.uk.

The Waste Industry National Training Organisation (WINTO) was recently established with backing from the Environmental Services Association, the Chartered Institution of Wastes Management (CIWM) and WAMITAB. It is intended to be the UK's national training organisation for the waste management industry. An office has been established in Coventry, and WINTO has been working on a strategy for an NVQ/SVQ awards framework. Further details are available from the WAMITAB website (www.wamitab.org.uk).

The Institution of Wastes Management achieved chartered status in 2003, to become the CIWM. One of the key aims of the CIWM is to 'achieve and maintain the highest standards of practice, competence and conduct by all its members'. In 2004 the CIWM launched a new training initiative to make employees of all waste producing businesses aware of waste. For further information on this contact the Waste Awareness Certificate Team on 01604 620426 or e-mail wac@ciwm.co.uk. Several CIWM-accredited modular postgraduate training courses exist, many of which cover a range of topics including legislation. For further information visit www.ciwm.co.uk.

94

Chapter 5

Waste minimisation, recycling, bioprocessing and recovery

5.1. The waste hierarchy

Under the Town and Country Planning (Development Plans) (England) Regulations 1999 SI 3280, planning authorities must take into consideration the national waste strategy when producing development plans. Under the Integrated Pollution Prevention and Control regulatory regime and the Office of the Deputy Prime Minister Planning Policy Guidance there is an obligation to select the Best Practicable Environmental Option (BPEO).[1] According to the Waste Strategy 2000 (p. 28) the waste hierarchy should be used as a guide when carrying out a BPEO assessment.

In the waste hierarchy, consideration must first be given to whether the waste needs to be generated at all. Much of industry for decades will have looked at, if not scrutinised, minimisation to save both production costs and waste disposal fees. If the waste cannot be minimised at source, then the options for reuse must be considered. Next, there is recycling (including composting), followed by incineration with energy recovery and then, as a final resort, disposal through incineration or landfill (Figure 5.1).

The definitions of disposal and recovery are explained in Chapter 2. Part III of Schedule 4 of the Waste Management Licensing Regulations 1994 SI 1056 (WMLR 1994) lists disposal operations, while recovery operations are listed in Part IV of Schedule 4 of the WMLR 1994. Disposal includes landfill, discharge to water, incineration, long-term storage, and any pretreatment activity in preparation for final disposal. Recovery includes, *inter alia*, recycling, materials reclamation, the use of waste as energy, and the spreading on land for beneficial use. Most statutory waste management targets, ironically enough, relate to landfill and recycling, at the lower end of the hierarchy. There are no direct statutory targets for waste minimisation, almost certainly because it is very difficult to measure.

---

[1] BPEO is the waste management option which provides the most benefit or least damage to the environment as a whole, at acceptable cost, in the long and short term.

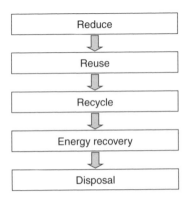

Figure 5.1: The waste hierarchy

Materials recycling is, after all, first and foremost a manufacturing issue. It has less to do with waste management than most people imagine, notwithstanding the importance of upstream waste analysis, contracting and management. The recycling loop is not closed until a manufacturer has contracted to use the particular recyclate as feedstock to make a product and it has been successfully marketed and sold with customer satisfaction. In the past it had been thought that there was little point in converting one form of rubbish into another, such as using construction rubbish to produce building blocks as expensive as veined Carrera marble. Economic competitiveness and markets remain key weaknesses in the recycling loop. There is unfortunately no gold in refuse, in that despite all the past and present design and development efforts there is no known process to recover resources from solid waste in which the proceeds from the sale of the recovered product is sufficient to offset the cost of obtaining it.

However, the perspective from Westminster and Whitehall is that a lack of markets should not be an obstacle to collecting materials for recycling. The March 2001 House of Commons All Party Select Committee on Environment, Transport and Regional Affairs, 5th Report, *Delivering Sustainable Waste Management*, paragraph 41, states that

> the problem of markets for recycled materials is a challenge for innovation, it is not an argument against the broad strategy proposal [to expand recycling]. Nevertheless, there are problems with markets and in our previous Report on Sustainable Waste Management, we concluded that the Government would need to intervene in markets to secure stability.

It would appear from this policy that even if the recycled materials cannot find a market, their production must be subsidised by the tax and/or rate payer until (hopefully) markets become established.

5.2. Waste minimisation and zero waste

Rising economic prosperity in the West over the last half of the 20th century has increased waste generation. This has been accompanied by a distinct apathy by some, but by no means all, producers, and a low value attributed to recyclable or reusable materials. At the other extreme, campaigners have been lobbying for a zero-waste society, with proposals for targets to reduce municipal waste by 50% in 2010, 33% in 2015 and to zero by 2020. However well intentioned, those targets are unlikely to be met, although there is certainly much scope for reduction and improved residuals' management. Despite waste minimisation being at the top of the waste hierarchy, most of the statutory targets have been for recycling as a means of tackling the rising waste tonnages across Europe. Of course, recycling does not decrease waste generation, and there has been in the EU no calculation of recycling rates by reference to useable outputs from recyclable materials.

Waste costs money through decreased productivity, more raw materials, transportation, staff time and the direct costs of disposal. Waste generation also costs local authorities money and loss of amenity through the need for more treatment facilities. Article 3 of the 75/442 Waste Framework Directive requires Members States to take appropriate action to encourage the prevention or reduction of waste production, in particular by:

- the development of clean technologies
- reducing the use of natural resources
- the technical development and marketing of products that minimise the amount and harmfulness of waste.

The Waste Minimisation Act 1998 empowers waste collection and disposal authorities to make arrangements to minimise Controlled waste, that is, household industrial and commercial waste, generated in their area. There is still no duty on individuals to reduce waste, and no targets are set (probably too difficult) for waste minimisation at source. Local authorities cannot impose any restrictions or requirements on businesses or individuals, but they can set up initiatives as part of waste management strategies and waste plans, such as:

- public information about alternatives to wasteful products
- waste reduction targets in waste contracts
- repair schemes for household appliances.

Waste minimisation is incorporated into the Environmental Protection Act 1990 (EPA 1990) under s.63A. However, according to the House of Commons All Party Environmental Audit Committee, 5th Report, *Waste — An Audit*, 'UK measures to encourage waste minimisation are very weak'(www.defra.gov.uk/ environment/waste/management/guidance/mwms/12.htm). Financial incentives such as deposit schemes have in practice been far more effective than legislation for promoting waste minimisation and reuse.

The Pollution Prevention and Control Regulations 2000 SI 1973 (please see Chapter 8) introduced a requirement for industrial activities and installations to reduce waste emissions. However, these Regulations apply only to certain specified installations or mobile plant, with a focus on overall emissions' control for notoriously polluting activities. A broad range of manufacturing industries produce large amounts of waste in the production process; the manufacture of a mobile phone, for example, generates an estimated 75 kg of waste, whilst a computer generates 1.5 tonnes.

5.3. Reduction and recovery targets

Most of the statutory recycling targets specified in UK law emanate from EU legislation. The Department for Environment, Food and Rural Affairs (DEFRA) 2003–2006 Corporate Strategy, Chapter 6, entitled 'Less waste and more recycling', focuses on targets relating to:

- the Landfill Directive (namely for biodegradable municipal waste)
- other EU Directives and future EU targets under the 6th Environmental Action Programme
- waste recovery, recycling and composting targets
- the reduction of commercial and industrial waste landfill
- radioactive substances.

Table 5.1 shows a timetable of some key current and forthcoming EU waste management targets and deadlines.

The UK recycling targets are set out in the Waste Strategy 2000. These are summarised in Table 5.2.

The above are currently not all statutory targets, in that if they are not attained there will not generally be a criminal sanction imposed on the local authority in the form of a fine. However, the UK Government does have powers to intervene, and under the Waste Emissions Trading Act 2003, upper limits for landfill can be imposed, and local authorities could be liable to a £200 fine for every tonne above the imposed limit. If certain EU targets are not nationally met, then the European Commission (EC) has power to impose fines on the UK.[2] Average recycling rates in the UK are currently (perhaps optimistically) at 13.5%, and society takes little or no notice of the annual 3% increase in waste

---

[2] The imposition of fines for not achieving EU targets for recycling or diminishing biodegradable waste is in practice subject to proof. If Germany and France, and at least potentially two or three other EU countries, can be seriously in breach of the Stability and Growth Pact, contrary to the pact terms and not be fined, it is easy to anticipate the argument against a fine for failing to meet a recyclate growth target.

Table 5.1: Some key EU waste management deadlines and targets

Date	Objective	Legislation
July 2003	Whole tyres banned from landfill	99/31 Landfill Directive
August 2004	Implementation of producer responsibility for waste electrical and electronic equipment (WEEE)	2002/96 Waste Electrical and Electronic Equipment Directive
August 2005	WEEE collection systems must be operational	2002/96 Waste Electrical and Electronic Equipment Directive
December 2005	Requirement to establish markets for biofuels and renewable energy (estimated to be 2%)	2003/30 Biofuels Directive
January 2006	85% of end of life vehicles must be recycled	2000/53 End of Life Vehicle Directive
July 2006	Ban on shredded tyres to landfill	99/31 Landfill Directive
July 2006	New WEEE can no longer contain hazardous substances	2002/95 Restrictions of Hazardous Substances Directive
December 2006	4 kg of WEEE per head of population to be collected	2002/96 Waste Electrical and Electronic Equipment Directive
January 2007	The last owner of an end of life vehicle can have the vehicle treated and recovered free of charge	2000/53 End of Life Vehicle Directive
December 2008	Overall packaging recovery target 70%	94/62 Packaging and Packaging Waste Directive
2010	Biodegradable waste going to landfill must be reduced to 75% of 1995 levels. (The target date includes a 4-year extension to the dates set out in the 99/31 Directive)	99/31 Landfill Directive
January 2015	Some 95% of end of life vehicles to be recycled	2000/53 End of Life Vehicle Directive
2020	Biodegradable waste going to landfill must be reduced to 35% of 1995 levels (the target date includes a 4-year extension to the dates set out in the 99/31 Directive)	99/31 Landfill Directive

Table 5.2: Local authority waste strategy targets for waste reduction and recovery

Targets	Target date
Industrial and commercial waste	
Reduction of the amount sent to landfill to 85% of the amount landfilled in 1998	2005
Municipal waste	
Reduction of the amount of biodegradable municipal waste landfilled to 75% of that produced in 1995	2010
Reduction of the amount of biodegradable municipal waste landfilled to 50% of that produced in 1995	2013
Reduction of the amount of biodegradable municipal waste landfilled to 35% of that produced in 1995	2020
Recover value from 40% of municipal waste	2005
Recover value from 45% of municipal waste	2010
Recover value from 67% of municipal waste	2020
Household waste	
Recycle or compost at least 25% of household waste	2005
Recycle or compost at least 30% of household waste	2010
Recycle or compost at least 33% of household waste	2015
Waste disposal authorities	
Authorities with a recycling and composting rate of under 5% in 1998–1999 must increase this to at least 10%	2003
Authorities with a recycling and composting rate between 5 and 15% in 1998–1999 must double their recycling rate	2003
All others authorities must recycle at least one-third of household waste	2003

Source: House of Commons All Party Environmental Audit Committee, 5th Report, *Waste—An Audit*

generation. Under present trends the household waste recycling targets are likely to be missed by a wide margin.[3]

London ReMaDe estimates that the average recycling rate in London is just 9%. In a few European countries, recycling/composting rates of 50% or more are being achieved, but these are in small areas with low population densities, high levels of composting and access to funds. Daventry and Litchfield are the closest UK examples, with rates of just less than 45%. In Austria, a small country with a total population of 8 million, where the landfill tax is at €55 (£45) per tonne and the gate fee is about £100 per tonne the national recycling and composting rate is about 50%, with 39% in Vienna. The total cost of waste

---

[3] Source: *Recovered Fibre News*, **14**, No. 12.

Box 5.1: 'Wider still and wider'[4]

The House of Commons All Party Environmental Audit Committee, 5th Report, *Waste—An Audit*, states in paragraph 37 that

Projections based on the current rates of performance improvement indicate that we will not come close to meeting any of the national targets set for recycling or recovery. Under the current set of policies, the targets set for 2015 and 2020 in particular will be missed by a wide margin.

Paragraph 48 states that

Inadequate funding and a lack of clear Government guidance have made it harder for local authorities to reach the targets they have been set. We are extremely concerned that the measures taken to date do not reflect the urgency of the need for improvement.

management in Austria is about €500 (£350) per tonne. In contrast, the average UK taxpayer spends more on the telephone bill than on all the utilities and waste combined. UK householders pay about £600 per year for water, which is 10 times the average £60 per annum spent on waste disposal services. The average family home discards around 1 tonne of waste per year.

Meeting the collection targets is only half—probably even less than half—of the problem. Infrastructure is needed to separate, treat and reprocess the recyclate, and end markets are needed to purchase the new recycled products. In today's affluent society, with the abundant supply of often imported resources, recyclate is perceived to be of little value. Establishing markets is very, very difficult. Despite lacking market opportunities, many quasi-statutory targets focus on just the collection of recyclable materials, leaving the stimulation of markets to government organisations and non-governmental organisations with no statutory powers and often limited resources. In the past, a material was not accepted to be recycled until it had been made into a useful product and sold to a satisfied customer, who may well have returned for another, or recommended that product at that price to a friend. This makes today's real recycling rates difficult to quantify. Sadly, dutifully collected recyclate often has no UK outlet, and is often exported to developing countries such as Indonesia, China and India for recycling (or disposal). Difficulties lie in the disparities between health and safety standards, working conditions, and environmental regulation and enforcement in the UK and the countries receiving the recyclate. It is very difficult for the Environment Agency (EA) to monitor the fate of the materials down any form of economic or environmental audit trail, and so to enforce the UK law.

---

[4] Last Night of the Proms, Edward Elgar (1857–1934), remember when you were younger …?

In 2001 the Government asked the Strategy Unit to carry out a review of the waste strategy, and investigate how the UK can improve municipal waste reduction, reuse and recycling. The Strategy Unit Report, *Waste Not Want Not*, was published in November 2003 (available at www.number-10.gov.uk/su/waste/report/downloads/wastenot.pdf). The report concluded that the economic and regulatory framework must:

- provide freedom for local authorities to introduce household incentive schemes to encourage waste reduction and recycling (notably variable charging based on the weight of waste collected)
- extend voluntary producer responsibility for waste reduction and recycling.

The key recommendations were for:

- incentives for the reuse of goods
- economic instruments to encourage environmentally friendly products
- reducing hazardous and non-recyclable waste
- promoting the use of secondary resources
- raising the landfill tax to £35 a tonne in the medium term (please see Section 6.3.3 of Chapter 6)
- making space in new housing developments for storage for recycling
- increasing government green procurement
- setting new targets for waste minimisation/disposal
- reviewing the case for banning the use of landfill/incineration for some materials in 2006–2007

Box 5.2: Accident exposes waste destination

On 22 March 2003 RMS *Mulheim* ran aground off the coast of Cornwall. The cargo ship was carrying 2200 tonnes of shredded scrap car plastic from Cork in the Republic of Ireland to Lubeck in Eastern Germany — for landfilling. After a difficult salvage operation, in which a pump and conveyor belt were used to recover the material from the unstable wreckage, the material was eventually landfilled in Devon. The 1846 tonne ship itself has been left on the seabed. It was later reported that the ship had hit the rocky seabed between Land's End and Sennen Cove after the Captain had been knocked unconscious, having caught his trousers on a control lever and fallen on the ship's bridge.

To what extent are EU Member States exporting similar wastes for landfilling or recycling in Eastern Europe, and how many other similar wrecks lie quietly on the European seabed while the Able UK US navy ship debate rages on (please see Box 11.1)?

Source: www.news.bbc.co.uk.

Box 5.3: EU grant funding for an urban gold mine

An organisation known as Urban Mines is facilitating the development of large recycling centres, which incorporate recyclate sorting facilities and small manufacturing units, to use the recyclate as a raw material all on one site. EU grant funding is available for projects that provide employment for the long-term unemployed. The projects fulfil the proximity principle, and provide local employment and opportunities often in deprived areas for new businesses and innovation. Consultants work closely with the planning system to secure suitable sites and attractive lease rates for prospective businesses.

For further information see www.urbanmines.org.uk.

- imposing higher fines and more rigorous enforcement of fines for fly-tipping
- keeping the case for an incineration tax under review
- DEFRA to have overall long-term responsibility for the implementation of the strategy.

Many of these recommendations, some of which will certainly be implemented, will have to be implemented either through statutory law or part of a package of fiscal measures.

In December 2003, under the third round of DEFRA funding (2004–2006), 14 partnership projects were established for waste minimisation and recycling partnerships with waste disposal authorities. Over 2 years these will expand the infrastructure available for recycling and composting. Under the category of more general funding, 170 applications were received, totalling £146 million. Of these, a total of 51 projects were selected, and are expected to divert 306,000 tonnes of municipal waste. Twenty-three of these projects will be supported with the condition that they work in partnership with the Waste and Resources Action Programme (WRAP). DEFRA has also set up a £30 million funding programme which is intended to stimulate take-up of new technologies to handle biodegradable municipal waste. The funding is intended to support pilot plants investigating the viability of new technologies. Allied to these new funding schemes the Government expects that the £3 per tonne annual rise in landfill tax beginning in 2005 will create additional incentives to cut the amount of waste being sent to landfill.

5.4. Recycling

Annex IIB of the 75/442 Waste Framework Directive gives a list of operations which may lead to recovery. Article 3(7) of the 94/62 Packaging and Packaging Waste Directive defines recycling as 'the reprocessing in a production process of the waste materials for the original purpose or for other purposes including organic recycling but excluding energy recovery.' A waste is recycled when it is:

- worked in order to produce a new material or make a new product
- transformed into its original state to be usable, and where appropriate for its original application
- transformed for any other purposes, provided that purpose is not energy recovery
- transformed into a new material or product that has the same properties as the material from which it was made.

5.4.1. Waste recycling plans

Under s.49 EPA1990 waste recycling plans must be prepared by waste collection authorities (WCAs) for the household and commercial waste arising in their area. A WCA must:

- investigate the best arrangements for waste separation, bailing and packing for the purpose of recycling
- decide on the best arrangements to fulfil the above, including contractual arrangements and equipment
- prepare a statement of the arrangements
- consider the impact on local amenities and cost savings
- periodically review the plan and modify it as needed
- send a copy of the statement to the Secretary of State for approval.

The plans do not have to be approved by the Secretary of State, but must be sent to the Secretary of State in draft form before it is adopted.

5.4.2. Household waste recycling

Provisions for the collection and recycling of household waste are made in ss.45–63 EPA 1990 (please see Chapter 4). Under s.46 EPA 1990, householders may be required by a waste collection authority to place household waste inside sacks or other receptacles, and to do this in a way that facilitates waste materials collection for recycling. The containers may be provided free of charge or on payment, or the householders must provide them themselves. Under Part II of Schedule 2 of the EPA 1990, the terms of a local waste disposal contract must, among other requirements, aim to maximise recycling of the Controlled waste collected by the local authority.

The EPA 1990 was amended by the Household Waste Recycling Act 2003 (HWRA 2003), which stipulates that:

- councils must provide domestic properties in England and Wales with a doorstep collection for a minimum of two recyclable materials
- by 31 October 2004 the Secretary of State has a duty to report on the performance of each English waste authority in meeting its recycling and composting standards arrangements for separate collection of recyclable waste.

Box 5.4: Waste not want not

The Southampton City and Region Action to Combat Hardship (SCRATCH) collects household furniture, surplus supermarket food and excess paint stocks to ameliorate local poverty. SCRATCH operates 10 projects which provide clothing, bedding, electronic goods and other services (the project reuses an estimated 4000 m³ of equipment and furniture, including approximately 1000 beds per year), and employs warehouse tradesmen to carry out refurbishment and electronic testing.

Unfortunately, this recovery work does not contribute to the local authority recycling figures because the goods are not considered to be waste. However, if any goods are found to be unusable during refurbishment, then SCRATCH must pay for their collection and disposal costs as a waste.

Organisations such as SCRATCH already have the infrastructure established for collection and reuse services. Perhaps other organisations could join in order to diminish the costs of WEEE recycling.

Source: Southampton City and Region Action to Combat Hardship (Tel. 02380 773 123).

Recyclable waste is defined as waste that is capable of being recycled or composted. Section 3 of the HWRA 2003 stipulates that recycling and composting must be carried out to standards set out by the waste authority in an Order to be made under the Local Government Act 1999. There is no legislative requirement for the recycling process to change the chemical properties of the waste.

Local authorities must implement the doorstep recycling requirements by 2010, or 2015, at the Government's discretion. Currently, approximately half of the 273 waste collection authorities in England provide a doorstep collection of household recyclables.

According to the Local Authority Recycling Advisory Committee (LARAC) chairman, most local authorities will meet the 2010 target (but please see Box 5.1), and many would proceed to include more than two material streams for separate collection. The need for modernisation of the method of waste collection charging (i.e. the need for direct waste charging) has arisen in light of the HWRA 2003. Resources for implementation remain insecure while local authority waste managers compete with libraries and leisure facilities for tax payers' income. The HWRA 2003 is available at www.hmso.gov.uk/acts/acts2003/20030029.htm.

5.4.3. Recycling payments

Under s.52 EPA 1990, recycling credits are payments made by waste disposal authorities to their waste collection authorities. Payments equate to those disposal costs avoided by recycling, and support the waste collection authority's recycling activities. The Environmental Protection (Waste Recycling Payments) (England) Regulations 2004 SI 639 came into force on 1 April 2004. Further details can be found at www.legislation.hmso.gov.uk/si/si2004/20040639.htm.

5.4.4. Variable charging

Environmental control practices should determine a policy and then ascertain whether or not the national tax or local rate payers can afford the cost of implementation preferably in relation to other priorities such as education, health, highways and recreation, etc. In the case of achieving the Waste Strategy 2000 recycling targets, which were set for a 20-year period to 2020, cost estimates given to the House of Commons in 2004 range from £3.4 billion to £7.7 billion, which is a very wide range indeed. The Government is still considering whether it can offset some of these very high costs by allowing local authorities to introduce a direct or variable household charging scheme, which should provide an incentive for waste minimisation and recycling.

Charging householders directly for waste services occurs elsewhere in the EU. Variable or direct charging, unit pricing, and pay-as-you-throw are all terms used with the following characteristics:

- revenue raised is for the cost of the service provision and upgrading
- waste services charge is related to the extent of use of the service (the variable element)
- the charge is differentiated across the collection service.

Three main benefits can accrue:

- deeper householder awareness and responsibility
- weight-based schemes have the strongest impact on resource reduction (in the US, pay-after bag schemes had an average effect on reduction at source of 6%)
- in line with the differential nature of the charging scheme there can be increases of source separated materials for recycling.

Monitoring and enforcement actions can forestall fly-tipping, and indeed have achieved this in practice. The barriers to direct charging may well disappear in the next 5 years. Remember the London Mayor's success with congestion charging. For further information see *Waste Collection: To Charge or Not to Charge* (Eunomia Research and Consulting for CIWM, www.ciwm.co.uk/iwm-eb).

5.4.5. The aggregates levy

A typical fiscal measure to reduce the consumption of virgin materials, which can in their production result in waste, is the aggregates levy, which was implemented under the Finance Act 2001. The aggregates levy:

- is charged at £1.60 per tonne
- applies to sand, gravel and rock subjected to commercial exploitation in the UK — this includes aggregate dredged from the seabed within UK territorial waters (12 miles from the shoreline)
- is payable in one stage and is non-deductible.

For further information see www.hmce.gov.uk/business/othertaxes/agg-levy.htm.

5.4.6. Environmental management systems

An environmental management system (EMS) is a method for identifying and controlling the environmental impacts of an organisation. The main requirements of an EMS are to:

- comply with all relevant legislation
- prevent pollution
- determine which environmental impacts are significant and put systems in place to manage and reduce these.

An EMS comprises five stages:

- an initial environmental review to identify the significant environmental impacts of the organisation's activities
- publication of an environmental policy, demonstrating commitment to the EMS
- establishment of objectives and targets for improvement
- production of an environmental management manual, implementation and operation
- audits, reviews and improvements.

During the environmental review, all legislative and regulatory requirements must be identified and considered. Criteria can be assigned to identify significant aspects and impacts, but if a particular activity is required by law to be controlled, then it will always be classed as significant.

The two formally recognised EMS schemes are:

- British Standard EN ISO 14001
- the Eco-Management Audit Scheme (EMAS).

Guidance for how to compile a register of legislation for an EMS is provided by Envirowise on www.envirowise.gov.uk. The website also provides a list of relevant legislation.

5.4.7. Ecolabels

EC Regulation/92 originally set out arrangements for a community ecolabelling scheme. This required Member States to appoint a competent authority to specify ecolabelling performance criteria and administer applications. This role was, for a while, carried out by the Ecolabelling Board. The Ecolabelling Board was abolished under the UK Ecolabelling Board (Abolition) Regulation 1999 SI 931, after which the Department of the Environment, Transport and the Regions (now DEFRA) took over its duties. All had run into the sand since there was no agreement on the common criteria. It is possible that a revised ecolabel awards scheme may be resurrected in the future, and the 2002/18 Commission Decision put forward an EC ecolabel working plan. In 2000 EC Regulation 1980/2000 extended the scheme to include services. The Government Green Paper on Integrated Product Policy (IPP) proposes a new strategy to refocus product-related policies and to develop the market for greener products. This is one of the innovations of the EU 6th Environmental Action Programme, *Our Future, Our Choice*, COM (2002)31.

For further details see www.defra.gov.uk/environment/consumerprod/ecolabel/history.htm.

5.5. Bioprocessing

A draft EU Biowaste Directive was published in January 2004, which, along with the 86/278 Sewage Sludge Directive, is part of the EU Soil Protection Thematic Strategy. The Directive focuses on biodegradable municipal waste to complement the biodegradable municipal waste diversion targets set out in the Landfill Directive. The draft Biowaste Directive aims to promote the production of high-quality compost to replenish organic matter in impoverished soils, particularly in southern Europe. The EC has suggested that the Directive should contain provision for the mandatory separate collection of biowaste and recycling targets.

5.5.1. Composting and anaerobic digestion

The Composting Association estimates that approximately 40% of municipal waste is suitable for composting. Schedule 3 of the Waste Management Licensing Regulations 1994 SI 1056 defines composting as any biological transformation process that results in materials which may be spread on land for the benefit of agriculture or ecological improvement. Annex IIB of the 75/442 Waste Framework Directive lists 'Spreading of waste on land resulting in benefit to agriculture or ecological improvement' as a recovery activity.

Composting activities include:

- biological treatment pending disposal
- recycling or reclamation of organic substances
- storage pending disposal or recovery
- spreading of waste on land resulting in benefit to agricultural or ecological improvement.

Composting facilities using Controlled waste (household, commercial or industrial waste) are regulated by the EA, and require a waste management licence (please see Chapter 8). Certain activities may be exempt from licensing; for example, activities are exempt if the amount being composted at any one time does not exceed

- 10,000 m^3 for the purpose of cultivating mushrooms
- 1000 m^3 for all other purposes.

Biodegradable waste may also be stored without a licence if kept at the site where the waste is produced or is to be composted (further details on exemptions are available from the EA, www.environment-agency.gov.uk/commondata/105385/ld3_exemptions_ta_627862ble, and Chapter 8 of this guide).

Composting facility operators should consider that:

- for new facilities the planning system must be navigated, and public resistance can be strong (please see Chapter 7)
- the EPA 1990 Duty of Care requirements apply with important implications for the quality control of waste deliveries (please see Chapter 10)
- statutory nuisance and nuisance in the law of tort apply in the context of dust, odours and noise (e.g. from shredding or chipping equipment)—nuisance (explained in Chapter 9) is important, particularly when centralised facilities are located close to houses
- the Health and Safety at Work etc. Act 1974 is also an important area for composting facilities, since it is concerned with the general health of not only local residents but the employees themselves (please see Chapter 10)
- the integrity, control and public confidence in the composting site is ultimately due to the care and time available of the EA assigned officer.

The EA has recently issued draft guidance for the monitoring of bioaerosols (airborne disease-causing organisms) and other particulate matter around centralised composting facilities. The guidelines are also applicable to other activities, such as waste transfer and landfill, but will be of particular interest to compost site operators. The guidelines (*Technical Guidance Document M17*) are available from the EA website.

There is no law to say that waste must be composted at home. Nor are the materials so composted included in the local authority recycling statistics. Domestic households can compost their own kitchen waste, and are exempt from the Animal By-Product Regulations 2003 SI 1482 (ABPR 2003) (see below), provided that they do not keep livestock. Kitchen scraps must not be composted if pigs and ruminants are kept, but may be composted in a closed container if chickens are kept.

The House of Commons All Party Environmental Audit Committee, in its 5th Report (April 2003), states in paragraph 47 that:

There is a lack of coherence for instance between the operation of the BPEO principle, which does not take targets into account, and local authorities' statutory obligations. The methods of measuring performance under the Best Value regime can also have unintended effects. Following a consultation that closed on 21 November 2003, DEFRA has concluded that anaerobic digestion of municipal waste is to be included as 'composting' in the local authority best value performance standards.

The full consultation response document is available at www.defra.gov.uk/corporate/consult/anaerobic-digestion/response.pdf.

The same operation principles discussed above apply in general terms to the integrity of anaerobic digestion (AD) plants. Regulations for the treatment processes depend on the plant feedstock. Statutory technical requirements for composting and AD plants depend on the source of the feedstock. These are explained below. Definitions of the terms used for different types of biodegradable waste are given in Section 3.7.2.

5.5.2. Bioprocessing of catering waste, foodstuffs and animal by-products

Typical animal by-product processes include composting, biogas (anaerobic digestion), incineration, pet food manufacture and rendering. Until recently, restrictions under the Animal By-Products Order 1999 (ABPO 1999) limited the end-use of composted or digested waste, and meant in practice that local authorities could only collect and compost green waste (garden clippings, etc.) The ABPO 1999 has now been superseded by the Animal By-Product Regulation (ABPR) 2003 SI 1482, which has relaxed the rules for composting biodegradable waste (please see Chapter 3).

The EC/2002 Animal By-Product Regulation specifies European standards for the treatment of animal by-products. It allows Member States to set their own national standards for catering waste. These are set out in the ABPR 2003. A summary of treatment standards is shown in Table 5.3.

The EC 1774/2002 Regulation was amended by the EC 808/2003 Regulation, which clarifies that composting must take place in a closed vessel or contained area. For example, open windrows (a windrow is a ridge of composting material) inside an enclosed building (subject to design requirements) are permitted.

Transitional measures have been implemented to allow industry to adapt to the changes under the ABPR 2003 (please see Chapter 3)

- small (less than 50 kg/h) incinerators can be used for animal by-products (but not Specified Risk Material) until 31 December 2004
- cooking oils can continue to be used as animal feedstock until 31 October 2004
- mammalian blood may be rendered at atmospheric pressure until 31 December 2004
- former foodstuffs will be classed as catering waste until 31 December 2005.

Table 5.3: Treatment standards for animal by-products

Waste[a]	Standard	Specified pretreatment 1	Specified pretreatment 2
All animal by-products except catering waste	EU	Rendered in an approved plant to 133°C at 3 bar pressure for 20 minutes	70°C for 1 hour in a closed vessel. Maximum feedstock particle size 12 mm[b] (in one plane)
			If composted, the temperature must principally be achieved as part of the composting process (some energy input is allowed)
Catering waste	National	First stage of a two-stage composting process (in a closed vessel or enclosed building)	Second stage of a two-stage composting process (can be an open site)
			The premises must treat only catering waste
Meat excluded catering waste	National	–	If one stage is used, it must be a closed system. Storage for 18 days is required at the end of the process
			The premises must treat only catering waste[c]
Former foodstuffs	Until December 2005: as for catering waste		
	After December 2005: to EU standard		

[a] For definitions of these waste types please see Section 3.7.2
[b] In practice, 12 mm is too large for a composting process, so this standard is usually applied to biogas facilities
[c] If a site treats catering waste and other animal by-products, then both must be treated to the EU standard

Box 5.5: Health warning on DEFRA survey results

Margaret Beckett, the DEFRA Secretary of State, in a written House of Commons reply following a DEFRA consultation survey stated (*Hansard*, 22 July 2002):

> The majority of respondents were in favour of a ban on the feeding of catering waste containing meat or meat product as swill to livestock.

Not much hogwash about that you might think. But, alas, her Minister of State a year or so later confirmed that the actual result had been only 32% for and 37% against (*Hansard*, 30 March 2004). Undaunted, DEFRA in April 2004 explained:

> The use of the majority was not simply a matter of numerical counting of letters, but that those in favour of a ban included major organisations representing widespread interests.

So next time conclusions are drawn from a DEFRA survey, make certain beforehand how DEFRA, rightly or wrongly, weight the results, and from which end they are opening the bowling.

The Government Statistics Commission is calling for statutory regulation of official figures, which is an acknowledgement of the imperfections that currently exist (source: *The Times*, Business News, 6 May 2004).

Anyone transporting or receiving animal by-products must keep records on an EA prescribed form (excluding manure transported between two points on the same farm, or locally between farms and users in the same country). Plants for the processing, storage and, in some cases, disposal (such as small-scale incineration) of animal by-products must be approved by the State Veterinary Service, which operates throughout the UK on behalf of DEFRA. Application forms for the approval of animal by-product collection, storage or treatment activities are available at www.defra.gov.uk/corporate/regulat/forms/Ahealth/by-products/index.htm. Completed forms must be sent to the local Animal Health Office (for the nearest office see www.defra.gov.uk/corporate/contacts/ahdo.htm).

Draft DEFRA guidance on the treatment in approved composting or biogas plants of animal by-products and catering waste is available at www.defra.gov.uk/animalh/by-prods/publicat/compost_guidance.pdf.

This is a new and complex subject in the lexicon of waste management, but the law is the result of some particularly traumatic operational occurrences in the farming industry such as BSE and foot-and-mouth disease. These crises have resulted somewhat naturally in closer scrutiny by central Government of the waste materials arising from the unfortunate stock which were the victims of those diseases.

5.5.3. Mechanical and biological treatment

A mechanical and biological treatment (MBT) facility contains a combination of technologies for recovering materials from mixed waste streams. It is effectively a materials recovery facility for non-segregated waste containing a biodegradable fraction. The two key stages are a mechanical separation step followed by anaerobic digestion or composting, in varying degrees of complexity. The MBT process residuals may be used as a soil improver, stabilised for landfill, or used as a fuel. Greenpeace claimed in a 2003 report, *Cool Waste Management*, that MBT combined with kerbside collection could lead to an 85% landfill diversion rate. Although these rates are unlikely to become a reality, the EC recognises that MBT can help meet the Landfill Directive targets, and that there are potential uses for the residuals. Local authorities are looking into the use of MBT as part of the integrated waste management strategy, and consideration is being given to the development of treatment standards.

5.6. The recovery of specific types of waste

5.6.1. Packaging

The 94/62 Packaging and Packaging Waste Directive sets the following targets for the recycling and recovery of packaging waste. Recovery encompasses recycling, energy recovery, composting and the spreading of waste on agricultural land as defined in the 75/442 Waste Framework Directive. The 94/62 Directive was implemented into UK law by the Department for Trade and Industry (DTI) under the Environment Act 1995 by the:

- Producer Responsibility Obligations (Packaging Waste) Regulations 1997 SI 648 (PWR 1997)[5]
- Packaging (Essential Requirements) Regulations 1998 SI 1941.

These Regulations apply to all in the packaging chain:

- manufacturers of packaging materials, e.g. cardboard or plastic granules.
- converters, i.e. those who convert materials into cans and boxes
- packers/fillers who package the goods
- retailers who sell the packaged goods.

Producers are exempt from the Regulation if they

- handle less than 50 tonnes of packaging per year
- have a financial turnover of less than £2 million.

---

[5] As amended by 1999 SI 1361, 1999 SI 3447, 2000 SI 3375, 2002 SI 732 and 2003 SI 3294.

Parts

Box 5.6: Cheese firm fined for packaging offences

The Meadow Cheese company in December 2003 pleaded guilty to 13 offences under the PWR 1997. Since it had a £2 million annual turnover, and handled more than 50 tonnes per year of packaging, the company was subject to the Regulations, but failed to:

- register for the last 4 years to buy packaging waste recovery notes
- take reasonable steps to recycle or recover packaging waste
- register in time in 2003.

The company was fined £19,000 and £1206 in costs.

Source: *ENDS Report 347.*

The Packaging (Essential Requirements) Regulations 1998 require that packaging (which eventually may become waste) must:

- be kept to a minimum, subject to the safety, hygiene and acceptance criteria for the product and consumer
- contain minimal noxious or Hazardous substances
- be recoverable through either material recycling, incineration with energy recovery, and/or composting
- be designed to specified product design standards.

These must be adhered to when placing packaging on the market.

The PWR 1997 qualifying organisations must:

- register with the EA or SEPA, providing them with packaging information[6]
- take reasonable steps to recover and recycle packaging waste
- provide evidence (usually in the form of a Packaging Recovery Note (PRN), see below) that the necessary recovery and recycling has been carried out.

Under Regulation 34 PWR 1997, it is an offence to fail to fulfil the above requirements.

Unlike other recycling targets the packaging recovery targets are given in terms of tonnes as well as a percentage. Therefore, the targets can be met by reducing the overall amount of packaging produced in the first place. Packaging recovery targets are revised every 5 years, and the latest revision came into force on 1 January 2004. The targets for 2004–2008 are shown in Table 5.4.

---

[6] Registration for an individual producer is currently £768 if registering directly with the EA, or £558 if joining a scheme.

Table 5.4: UK packaging business recovery and recycling targets 2004–2008

Material	2004		2005		2006		2007		2008	
	%	mtpa	%	mtpa	%	mtpa	%	mtpa	%	mtpa
Paper	65.0	3.215	66.0	3.218	68.0	3.219	69.0	3.219	70.0	3.219
Glass	49.0	2.040	55.0	2.040	61.0	2.040	66.0	2.040	71.0	2.040
Aluminium	26.0	0.128	28.0	0.128	30.5	0.128	33.0	0.128	35.5	0.128
Steel	52.5	0.601	55.0	0.601	58.0	0.596	60.0	0.592	61.5	0.587
Plastic	21.5	1.660	22.0	1.850	22.5	1.900	23.0	1.960	23.5	2.020
Wood	18.0	0.982	19.0	1.030	20.0	1.030	20.5	1.030	21.0	1.030
Overall recovery	63.0	8.650	65.0	8.890	67.0	8.940	69.0	8.990	70.0	9.050
The minimum % of recovery through materials recycling (not energy recovery)	94.0	–	94.0	–	94.0	–	95.0	–	95.0	–

mtpa, million tonnes per annum

Source: DEFRA

115

Producers may join a compliance scheme that can arrange for the reprocessing of packaging waste. The reprocessor will supply the customer with a Packaging Recovery Note (PRN) or Packaging Export Recovery Note (PERN) as proof of compliance with the regulatory target. There are about 15 compliance schemes in the UK, which play an important part in achieving the overall EU packaging targets. To issue PRNs the compliance scheme must be approved by the Secretary of State and meet competition standards, and must be accredited with the EA. A list of accredited compliance schemes is available at www.defra.gov.uk/environment/waste/topics/packaging/compliance-schemes.pdf.

An estimated £400 million is needed to fund the necessary infrastructure to meet the 94/62 Directive 2008 packaging waste recycling targets. According to some the deadline is feasible, but the only way that the target will be met will be through 'doorstep collections for every household in the country, if not for every local authority',[7] although it is hoped that companies will reduce the amount of packaging produced in the first place.

Under s.75 EPA 1990 packaging is Controlled waste, and the Duty of Care and other regulations apply to its transportation (please see Chapters 10 and 11).

A Directive to amend Directive 94/62 was proposed in April 2002. Negotiations to agree revisions came to a halt in mid-October 2003 due to inconsistencies in the outcome of European Court of Justice cases (see the Mayer Parry Recycling Ltd case in Chapter 2). The meaning of the term 'recycling' determines the point at which a material ceases to become waste, and for a PRN to be issued the recycling process must be complete.

DEFRA's document *The Producer Responsibility Obligations (Packaging Waste) Regulations 1997 (as amended), The User's Guide* is available online at www.defra.gov.uk/environment/waste/topics/packaging/pdf/userguide.pdf. For further information see www.letsrecycle.com. The position in Scotland is regulated under the Producer Responsibility (Packaging Waste) Amendment (Scotland) Regulations 2002 SSI 147.

5.6.2. Waste electrical and electronic equipment and the RoHS Directives

The 2002/96 Waste Electrical and Electronic Equipment (WEEE) Directive and 2002/95 Restriction of the Use of Certain Hazardous Substances in Electrical and Electronic Equipment (RoHS) Directive control the manufacture, retail, import, collection and recovery of electronic and electrical goods. A summary of the WEEE implementation timetable is given in Table 5.5.

Products covered by the 2002/96 WEEE and 2002/95 RoHS Directives are:

---

[7] Quote from Labour MEP David Bowe (source: www.guardian.co.uk).

Table 5.5: Summary of WEEE implementation

Date	Action
February 2003	2002/96 WEEE Directive published
August 2004	Deadline for implementation. End of consultation
August 2005	Collection systems to be operational
December 2006	The first WEEE recycling and recovery targets for materials and components (e.g. 4 kg WEEE per head of population to be collected per year)
2008	Recycling and recovery targets to be revised

- large and small household appliances
- IT and telecommunication equipment
- consumer equipment (e.g. televisions or videos)
- lighting (e.g. bulbs)
- electrical and electronic tools (with the exception of large stationary industrial tools)
- toys, leisure and sports equipment containing WEEE
- medical devices (exempt from the RoHS Directive and reuse and recovery targets under the WEEE Directive), monitoring and control instruments (exempt from RoHS) and automatic dispensers.

The 2002/95 RoHS Directive also has a transposition deadline of August 2004. RoHS restricts the use of hazardous substances in the manufacture of electrical and electronic products. From July 2006 lead, mercury, cadmium, hexavalent chromium, poly-brominated biphenyls (PBBs) and other flame retardants used in plastics will be banned. The use of these chemicals will be allowed however, for a limited number of applications until alternatives are available.

In summer 2004, around 25,000 WEEE producers face an uncertain future:

- a form of national clearing house is proposed for WEEE recycling
- there will be a possible domestic collection from civic amenity sites by local authorities and delivery to clearing houses and treatment facilities
- treatment facilities will come under compliance schemes.

The clearing house concept may be restricted to:

- registration of producers
- collection of market share data, and
- calculation of producer's recovery and recycling obligations.

Unlike vehicle dismantling (see below), WEEE does not benefit from a network of facilities, and those that do exist are often small independent shop outlets or charities (please see Box 5.4). Large producers (e.g. Philips and SMEG), with assistance from the Association of Manufacturers of Domestic Electric Appliances (AMDEA) have grouped together to form the Recycling Electrical Producers Industry Consortium (REPIC). REPIC will manage the WEEE recycling obligations on behalf of the companies. Other similar consortiums are likely to develop, and other large producers, and small and medium-sized enterprises, will be able to join the established schemes. The Industry Council for Electronic Equipment Recycling (ICER) may well succeed in establishing a WEEE accreditation scheme.

The Environmental Services Association (ESA) envisages:

- a WEEE carriers' registration system allied to the clearing house including a database of accredited waste carriers to which the clearing house would allocate collections
- a clear audit trail to ensure that equipment is delivered to authorised treatment facilities.

A sensible protocol.

The treating, keeping, disposal and retailer take-back of household appliances are currently exempt from waste management licensing under Schedule 3 of the Waste Management Licensing Regulations 1994 SI 1056. It is likely that the WEEE Regulations will follow these exemptions. Under the WEEE Regulations, householders can return WEEE to retail outlets free of charge. Retailers can alternatively set up a collection system.

For the latest position visit www.dti.gov.uk/sustainability/weee.

5.6.3. End of life vehicles

The 2000/53 End of Life Vehicles (ELV) Directive came into force in October 2000. Its main objectives are:

- that manufacturers must consider their product disposal at the design and manufacturing stages
- that manufacturers must assume a significant part of the free take-back costs
- to set vehicle recovery and recycling targets for 1 January 2006 and 2015
- to achieve higher environmental standards through an end of life vehicle permitting system.

The DTI leads on the implementation on the majority of the ELV Directive, while DEFRA is responsible for the permitting system and the EA for its enforcement. The End of Life Vehicles Regulations 2003 SI 2635 (ELVR 2003) partly implement the 2000/53 Directive, and further secondary legislation is expected to follow.[8] A summary of the implementation timetable is shown in Table 5.6.

Table 5.6: Summary of end of life vehicle legislation implementation

Date	Action
2000	The 2000/53 Directive came into force
April 2002	The UK missed the April 2002 transposition deadline
March 2003	Consultation documents were issued in March 2003
November 2003	In November 2003 the ELVR 2003 came into force
2004	Permits to be issued to authorised treatment facilities
2006	85% of all ELVs must be reused or recycled
2007	Producer responsibility and free take-back scheme fully implemented
2015	95% must be reused and 85% recycled

The EU Hazardous Waste List classifies end of life vehicles as Hazardous waste. The ELVR 2003 introduced significant and expensive changes to the way in which vehicles are manufactured and scrapped. Under the 2000/53 Directive manufacturers of new vehicles must:

- stop using certain heavy metals in new vehicles
- limit the use of certain hazardous materials
- increase the quantity of recycled material used in the manufacture of new vehicles
- design vehicles for easy recycling by marking vehicle components and providing dismantling information (coding standards)
- provide a free take-back for vehicles put on the market from 1 July 2002 (if such vehicles have a negative value when scrapped).

The ELVR 2003 require producers to meet the component coding standards set out in the 2000/53 Directive, and provide reports on the recoverability and recyclability of vehicle components, which are made available to customers. Technical compliance documents must be kept by the manufacturer for 4 years. Compliance notices will be served on producers suspected of not meeting the design and reporting requirements set out in the ELVR 2003, and they will be fined if convicted of non-compliance.

Around 2 million vehicles are scrapped every year in the UK. Under the 2000/53 Directive the scrapping of old vehicles will be funded by the manufacturer. However, the new funding mechanism has not taken immediate effect. Between now and 2007:

---

[8] The EC originally agreed that details for compliance control and a database would be provided in October 2002. These are now expected in 2004. When the EC misses its promised target dates it makes the task of the EA, local authorities and industry to plan plant mobilisation and proper compliance training for managers so very difficult.

- the 2000/53 Directive gives flexibility to Member States in deciding how to fund take-back and treatment between 2002 and 2007
- under s.28 ELVR 2003 'an authorised treatment facility shall not impose any charge on the last holder or owner of an end of life vehicle for the issue of a certificate of destruction'
- according to DEFRA, the manufacturers and importers must fund the take-back and treatment of vehicles sold after 1 July 2002. It is still not wholly certain who will fund the vehicle take-back between now and 2007 of vehicles manufactured before 2002.

After 2007 the last owner can have his vehicle treated (scrapped) under a free take-back scheme, funded by the vehicle manufacturers and importers.

The DTI recently proposed an own-marque system, under which importers and manufacturers can establish a network of authorised treatment facilities (ATFs). Contracts under the system, which has been met with industry approval, would be negotiated between the ATFs and the manufacturers. The Society of Motor Manufacturers and Traders (SMMT) is urging the Government to reconsider its intention to impose a maximum 10 mile journey for the transportation of end of life vehicles to ATFs, since allowances will have to be made for low-density areas. Recent estimates from industry suggest that the cost of collection and treatment will be between £15 and £30 per end of life vehicle. The DTI estimates that the total annual cost to industry will be between £24 million and £60 million.

Under the 2000/53 Directive any treatment (scrapping) facility must:

- be authorised under a permitting or licensing system
- meet specified environmental standards for treatment (scrapping)
- provide a certificate of destruction for all vehicles scrapped in compliance with the ELV regulatory regime (Part V, s. 27 ELVR 2003)
- comply with minimum technical requirements.

For information on site licensing please see Chapter 8. For further ELV information see www.defra.gov.uk/environment/waste/topics/elvehicledir.htm.

5.6.4. Scrap metal

The Scrap Metal Dealers Act 1964 showed that the Government recognised that scrap metal recovery should be encouraged and controlled. The 1964 Act obliged scrap metal dealers to keep records, since proceeds of theft can often find their way onto the scrap metal market, even with the most vigilant of scrap metal dealers. So, in respect of all scrap metal received, there must be a record of:

- date and time of receipt
- description and weight

- price payable, or estimated metal value
- registration vehicle number
- date of processing or dispatch and process used
- name and address of the purchaser and price.

These records can be used as a basis for the s.34 EPA 1990 Duty of Care Note (please see Chapter 10).

In general, a metal recycling site waste management licence must be issued by the EA for:

- scrap metal yards
- waste metal storage sites
- scrap metal dismantling and processing sites.

Some activities such as sorting and baling are exempt (but still subject to restrictions). The exemption depends on the type and quantity of scrap metal being handled. Exempt activities are listed in Schedule 3 of the Waste Management Licensing Regulations 1994 SI 1056, a useful summary of which is given in the EA publication *Exemptions from Needing a Waste Management Licence* (www.environment-agency.gov.uk/commondata/105385/ld3_exemptions_ta_ 627862ble). Some of the more polluting industrial metal processing activities are covered by the Integrated Pollution Prevention and Control permitting regime (please see Chapter 8).

Of course, metal recycling can, *inter alia*, cover the following business areas:

- appliances, parts and components
- vehicle dismantling
- recovery of metal packaging
- lighting
- battery recycling.

For example, vehicle dismantling is now subject to the End of Life Vehicle Regulations (ELVR) 2003 SI 2635, and lighting and appliances are subject to the Waste Electrical and Electronic Equipment Regulations (due to be passed in August 2004). There are significant exports of scrap metal from the UK to the EU and other countries, and this topic is covered by Regulations discussed in Chapter 11. This is not an exhaustive list.

5.6.5. Recovery of components containing ozone-depleting substances

Under Article 16 of the 2037/2000 EC Regulation on ozone-depleting substances the recovery of certain substances (CFCs and HCFCs) contained in refrigeration, air-conditioning and heat pump equipment, domestic refrigerators and freezers, equipment containing solvents and fire protection systems can

Box 5.7: Delivery firms fined for subtle oversight

Two companies delivered fridges to Industrial Plastics Recyclers (IPR). IPR held a waste management licence to process waste plastic and foam from fridges, but their licence did not allow them to accept, store or process whole fridges. Evans Logistics and Carr Brothers Ltd (the companies who delivered the fridges) were prosecuted and fined a total £18,000 for depositing waste on land in a manner that was not in accordance with the waste management licence.

Source: *Brecon and Radnor Express*, 5 February 2004.

only be carried out using approved destruction technologies. Recovery facilities must be licensed under the Waste Management Licensing Regulations and are subject to the s.34 EPA 1990 Duty of Care. Under the EU Hazardous Waste List refrigerators are classified as Hazardous waste.

Under the Montreal Protocol (signed in 1987 and amended in 1990 and 1992) all signatories agreed to a rigorous programme of Halon phase-out. Halon is a gaseous suppressing agent used, for example, as an extinguisher in electrical installations, and has a high ozone-depleting potential. The deadline for decommissioning all halons (except critical users, e.g. defence sites, the channel tunnel and the military) was 31 December 2003.

Chapter 6

Energy recovery, incineration and landfill

6.1. Incineration and energy recovery

Incineration includes treatment techniques such as pyrolysis, gasification or plasma processes, the use of waste as a fuel or for energy recovery, and disposal through incineration. Incineration is defined in Annex IIA of the 75/442 Waste Framework Directive Waste (as amended by 91/156) as a disposal operation. But under Annex IIB 75/442 if a waste is used 'principally as a fuel or other means to generate energy' it is defined as an 'Operation which may lead to recovery'.

Although incineration residuals (e.g. incinerator bottom ash) can be dense and contaminated, and often Hazardous, incineration has the advantage of reducing the volume of waste by approximately 10 times. Incinerators are an essential part of the integrated waste management system, particularly in the South of England where the population density is high and landfill space is increasingly limited. In Scotland, apart from the few densely populated urban areas, the dispersed population makes centralised incineration uneconomic. There are around 7000 incinerators in England and Wales, with 12 burning municipal waste, 60 burning chemicals, clinical waste and sewage sludge, 10 co-incineration plants, 1700 burning waste oil, and some 3000 small farm incinerators.[1] France has 16 incinerators able to handle 770,000 tonnes of waste annually. Germany has 30 waste incinerators with a capacity of 1 million tonnes per annum.

The general public are apprehensive of incineration, so waste management companies often face considerable opposition and expensive delay in the planning process. Non-governmental organisations (NGOs) and some local authorities consider that alternative means of recovery are preferable. However, many in industry, as well as the Department for Environment, Food and Rural Affairs

---

[1] Source: the Environment Agency (www.environment-agency.gov.uk).

(DEFRA) and the Environment Agency (EA), believe that new incinerator construction is inevitable if the biodegradable municipal waste targets in the 99/31 Landfill Directive are to be achieved.[2] It is unlikely that domestic and municipal waste incinerators burning rubbish will be given planning permission unless they incorporate energy recovery.

The Government recognises that incineration is an area where limited scientific data continue to cast doubt on environmental and health impacts. The House of Commons Report (May 2003) *The Future of Waste Management*[3] recommended that the Government should:

- commission new scientific research into areas where there is still significant doubt concerning the health impacts, particularly from incineration
- clarify its position on incineration and the associated environmental and heath impacts.

6.1.1. Incineration of waste

The 2000/76 Waste Incineration Directive was adopted in December 2000. It merged the 94/67 Hazardous Waste Incineration Directive and the (non-hazardous) 89/369 and 89/429 Incineration Directives. The Waste Incineration Directive came into effect for all existing UK incinerators from December 2002, and will apply to new incinerators from December 2005. It covers virtually all[4] waste incineration and co-incineration plants.

The main aims of the Waste Incineration Directive are to:

- prevent, or where that is not practicable reduce as far as possible the detrimental environmental effects of waste incineration
- reduce the risks to human health and land and aquatic ecosystems by reducing pollution caused by emissions into the air, soil, surface water and groundwater.

The Waste Incineration Directive sets out

- stringent operational conditions and technical requirements
- emission limit values

---

[2] A letter on 17 May 2004 from Dr David Davies to *The Times* put the dilemma fairly and squarely in front of its readers: 'For too long we have given in to the headline-hitting scaremongering of so-called environmental campaign groups and zero-waste enthusiasts. This has led to near-paralysis in the development and implementation of rational waste management strategies, which affect every household throughout Britain.'

[3] The House of Commons Environment, Food and Rural Affairs Committee, 8th Report, Session 2002–2003, *The Future of Waste Management*, May 2003.

[4] There are exemptions for vegetable waste, radioactive waste and animal carcasses (the latter is covered by the 1774/2002 EC Animal By-Products Regulation).

After full implementation in 2005, the Waste Incineration Directive aims to have reduced emissions of dioxins and furans from non-Hazardous waste incinerators across Europe from 2400 g per annum in 1995 to only 10 g per annum. Other emission limits are set for dust, sulphur dioxide, nitrogen oxides and heavy metals. For the first time, the legislation includes emissions limits to water bodies to reduce impacts on marine and freshwater ecosystems. Under the Waste Incineration Directive, operators must publish annual reports which include emissions data. The public may have access to information on all incineration plants with a capacity greater than 2 tonnes per hour.

The Waste Incineration Directive makes a clear distinction between incineration and co-incineration. Co-incineration is the burning of waste mixed with conventional fuel or the thermal treatment of waste for the purpose of disposal in a plant whose main purpose is to generate energy for power stations or manufacture a product, such as cement kilns.

The Waste Incineration Directive was implemented under the Waste Incineration (England and Wales) Regulations 2002 SI 2980. Guidance on the Waste Incineration Directive is available from DEFRA at www.defra.gov.uk/environment/ppc/wasteincin/, and further information is available at europa.eu.int/comm/environment/wasteinc/.

Larger facilities, which are Part A prescribed processes under the Integrated Pollution Prevention and Control (IPPC) regime (see examples given in Table 8.2 of this guide):

- are subject to the stiff permitting regime under the Pollution Prevention and Control Act 1999
- must use the Best Available Techniques (BAT)
- are regulated by the EA.

Smaller facilities are subject to the Local Air Pollution Prevention and Control (LAPPC) regime, and are regulated by local authorities.

Specific details for IPPC and waste incineration are set out in the:

- Pollution Prevention and Control Regulations 2002 SI 1973
- Pollution Prevention and Control (Designation of Council Directives on Large Combustion Plants, Incineration of Waste and National Emission Ceilings) Order 2002 SI 2528
- Waste Incineration (England and Wales) Regulations 2002, SI 2980.

The IPPC and LAPPC regulatory regimes are explained in Chapter 8.

6.1.2. Hazardous waste incineration

As already stated, the 2000/76 Waste Incineration Directive merged the 94/67 Hazardous Waste Incineration Directive and the non-hazardous 89/369 and 89/429 Incineration Directives. Hazardous waste incinerators are also subject to the Integrated Pollution Prevention and Control permitting regime under the

Pollution Prevention and Control Act 1999, which is explained in Chapter 8. Care and control provisions for transporting Hazardous waste, such as safe containment and labelling regulations, training and equipment for personnel, health and safety, documentation, record-keeping systems and risk assessment, are all important for considerations, and add to the cost of these facilities. Transportation requirements for Hazardous waste are explained in Chapters 10 and 11.

Approximately 5% of the 5 million tonnes of Hazardous waste generated in 2002 were incinerated, and 39% landfilled. However, pending the closure of an estimated 90% of landfill sites accepting Hazardous waste in July 2004, Hazardous waste incineration may well increase unless other alternatives can be found (please see Chapter 3). However, with only two merchant Hazardous waste incinerators in England and Wales, with a combined capacity of 110,000 tonnes per year, it is unlikely that Hazardous waste incineration will provide a solution in the short term. There are around 60 specialist incinerators designed for burning clinical waste, chemicals and sewage sludge.

Highly toxic wastes such as pharmaceuticals and pesticides, including flammable waste, require incineration. Costs for Hazardous waste incineration are dependent upon the chlorine content of the waste and its physical form, since liquids are easier to incinerate than sludges or solids. Due to the limited network of facilities, transportation costs can be significant, although transfer stations can provide a means of reducing overall disposal costs. Costs vary between £100 and £200 per tonne. Draft guidance for the operation of low-capacity animal carcass incinerators is now available at www.defra.gov.uk/animalh/by-prods/DraftGuidance/Low_Capacity_030204.pdf.

6.1.3. Incineration and the Emissions Trading Scheme

The Emissions Trading Scheme (ETS) is one of the policing instruments that DEFRA intends will reduce greenhouse gas emissions according to its 2003 Energy White Paper. The Greenhouse Gas Emissions Trading Scheme Regulations 2003 SI 3311 came into force on 31 December 2003. On 1 January 2005 about 1300 UK installations and 12,000–20,000 European installations will have to operate under the 2003/87 Emissions Trading Directive, and limit carbon dioxide emissions. The domestic goal under the 2000 UK Climate Change Programme is to reduce carbon dioxide emissions by 20% of 1990 levels by 2010.

To emit carbon dioxide after 1 January 2005, installation operators must hold a permit (issued by the EA). The permit sets out monitoring and reporting requirements, and enables allowances to be allocated to an installation covered by the scheme. A permit does not determine the allowance allocated, but provides a means of quantification.

The ETS limit values for carbon dioxide apply to installations which fall under the Pollution Prevention Control (PPC) Regulations. Some key waste management activities covered by the PPC regime are listed in Table 8.2 of this guide. Environment Agency guidance on the *Emissions Trading Scheme* is available at www.defra.gov.uk/environment/climatechange/ trading/ukets.htm, www.environment-agency.gov.uk/commondata/105385/ operatorguidedrft1_624857.pdf and www.defra.gov.uk/environment/airquality/ lapc/aqnotes/aq01(04).htm.

6.2. Landfill

Under the Landfill (England and Wales) Regulations 2002 SI 1559 (LFR 2002) the statutory definition of a landfill is a waste disposal site for the deposit of waste onto or into land, including sites on which waste has been temporarily stored for more than 12 months, and internal disposal sites. The definition excludes transfer stations and the storage of waste for up to 3 years prior to recovery. Around 60 million tonnes of waste per year are landfilled in the UK. Although landfill as a final disposal method lies at the bottom of the waste hierarchy, it is by far the most widely used disposal route in the UK, particularly in Scotland and Northern Ireland. Approximately 75% of municipal waste is currently sent to landfill.

The 99/31 Landfill Directive imposed significant changes to EU and UK waste management practice. Under the 99/31 Directive:

- the quantity of biodegradable municipal solid waste (BMW) sent to landfill must be reduced to 35% of 1995 levels by 2016 (it is not apparent whether any financial, energy, or environmental cost appreciation has been made)
- the disposal to landfill of certain types of waste are banned (infectious, liquid (excluding sludge), explosive, corrosive, oxidising, flammable, highly flammable waste,[5] and new or unidentified substances, e.g. from laboratories, whose effects on humans and the environment are unknown)
- the landfilling of whole tyres is currently banned, and all tyres, whole or shredded, will be banned from 16 July 2006
- landfill sites must be classified as suitable for accepting Hazardous, non-Hazardous or inert waste
- waste acceptance criteria (WAC) and procedures (please see Section 6.2.2) are being phased in
- engineering standards are more prescriptive
- Hazardous wastes can be accepted only at sites specifically designed to accept them

---

[5] These terms are defined in Regulation 9 of the LFR 2002.

- the disposal of Hazardous and non-Hazardous wastes together (co-disposal) is banned
- most Hazardous waste requires pre-treatment before it can be disposed of to landfill.

The term Hazardous means Hazardous waste as defined in the 91/689 Hazardous Waste Directive, which in the context of landfill replaces the previous term Special waste. The definition of Hazardous waste is explained in Chapter 3. A non-Hazardous waste can become Hazardous by reacting with other waste after placement in the landfill site. Other wastes may react with water or oxygen to emit Hazardous gases.

6.2.1. The Landfill (England and Wales) Regulations 2002

The 99/31 Directive was implemented under the Landfill (England and Wales) Regulations 2002 SI 1559 (LFR 2002) (available at www.hmso.gov.uk/si/si2002/20021559.htm). The LFR 2002:

- introduce a system of landfill permitting under the Integrated Pollution Prevention Control (IPPC) regime (please see Chapter 8)
- stipulate a list of landfill siting requirements to be considered before planning permission can be granted under the Town and Country Planning Act 1990; these requirements are given in Schedule 2(1)
- require that landfills are classified as Hazardous, non-Hazardous or inert according to the class of waste accepted (using the 91/689 Hazardous Waste Directive definition of Hazardous, which is given in the European Waste Catalogue)
- specify waste acceptance criteria (WAC) and waste acceptance procedures (WAP) for the different classes of landfill site
- specify monitoring and post-closure care requirements
- amend the Environmental Protection (Duty of Care) Regulations 1991 so that waste is identified on the Waste Transfer Note by reference to the European Waste Catalogue six-digit code — this allows waste at the gate to be identified using a classification system that conforms to the terminology used in the Landfill Regulations and the Landfill Directive.

The Regulations do not apply to:

- sludge spreading for soil fertilisation
- the use of inert waste for redevelopment, restoration, infilling or construction
- certain dredging activities
- landfills that ceased accepting waste before 16 July 2001.

Schedule 1 of the LFR 2002 prohibits the landfilling of any waste that would:

Box 6.1: Judge rules on unacceptable risks

The 91/156 Directive states in Article 4 that 'Member States shall take the necessary measures to ensure that waste is recovered or disposed of… in particular without risk to water, air, soil and plants and animals'. In a 2001 case Mr Justice Collins considered whether the 'without risk' objective of the 91/156 Directive is any stricter than the requirement to apply BATNEEC:[6] 'That seems to me an impossible construction. The purpose of the "without risk" provision is to enjoin the competent authorities to ensure that positively harmful techniques are not used.'

To an outsider this seems a very pragmatic view of the wording of the 91/156 Directive. It remains to be seen whether judges in the other 24 EU countries will take the same view. Hopefully so, lest harmonisation of the law is put at risk.

Source: *R* v. *Daventry DC* ex parte *Thornby Farms* 2001 EHLR 94, p. 106.

- endanger human health
- jeopardise landfill environmental protection systems
- threaten waste stabilisation processes such as degradation
- result in unacceptable emissions to the environment including groundwater.

Under the LFR 2002 and the ban on co-disposal in July 2004, an estimated 90% of landfill sites previously accepting Hazardous waste are no longer accepting Hazardous waste (please see also Chapter 3). The Government set up the Hazardous Waste Forum to discuss the issue of Hazardous waste, and to ensure that it continues to be managed appropriately.

The EA has a statutory responsibility for the regulation of landfill sites, and the Scottish Environment Protection Agency has responsibility for administering the complementary Scottish Regulations. In preparing for full implementation of the 99/31 Directive, the EA is proposing to review and update existing technical guidance on landfill development and operation. The Landfill (England and Wales) (Amendment) Regulations are expected to be passed in late 2004, and should come into force on 16 July 2005.

6.2.2. Waste acceptance criteria

The 2003/33 Decision on WAC clarified the standards to be met for waste to qualify for each of the three 99/31 Landfill Directive classes (Hazardous, non-Hazardous or inert). The 2003/33 Decision sets out the WAC together with the testing procedures, and lists:

---

[6] Best Available Techniques Not Entailing Excessive Cost, now shortened to Best Available Techniques. These terms are explained in Chapter 8.

- contaminant limit values
- procedures for characterising waste, waste compliance checks (against the WAC) and the on-site verification that the waste actually is the documented waste arriving at the landfill
- acceptance criteria for inert waste, certain non-Hazardous wastes, stable non-reactive Hazardous waste accepted at landfills, non-Hazardous waste, Hazardous waste and for underground storage
- test methods
- a risk assessment alternative approach.

Interim arrangements have been made to implement WAC under the LFR 2002. The LFR 2002 set out the WAC and WAP by which an operator can determine which waste can be accepted at the landfill site according to its classification. Under the LFR 2002, when a waste delivery arrives the operator must inspect the waste at the gate to ensure that the consignment matches the description given in the documentation, taking samples for analysis if necessary (for waste transfer documentation please see Chapters 10 and 11). When the information is obtained it must be entered into a register. If the waste is Special/ Hazardous, the exact location of deposit on the site must also be recorded. The above data must be made available to the EA on request, and written receipts must be given to the delivery person. If a waste consignment is rejected at the gate the EA should be informed.

DEFRA launched the WAC consultation outcome in March 2004. Consultation documents for the new Regulations are available from DEFRA (www.defra.gov.uk/corporate/consult/landfill-regs/index.htm). The Hazardous Waste Forum has published a comprehensive WAC action plan with a clear communication strategy and decision-making procedure for Hazardous waste (www.defra.gov.uk/environment/waste/hazforum/index.htm). For further information visit www.defra.gov.uk/corporate/consult/landfill-regs/index.htm.

In April 2004 the DEFRA Minister of State advised that:

- the implementation date for the 2003/33 Decision on WAC will be 16 July 2005
- during the interim year (July 2004 to July 2005) landfills will be managed using a site-specific approach, based on loading rates of new wastes, the types of new waste, and on the nature of waste already in the landfill
- this site-specific approach will continue after 2005, and certain rules will govern specific materials such as gypsum, cadmium and mercury
- the option of opening separate cells in Hazardous sites for waste deposited after July 2005 will not be pursued.

For full details see www.defra.gov.uk/corporate/consult/landfill-regs/summary_responses.pdf. Interim EA guidance on WAC is available from the EA (www.environment-agency.gov.uk). Full implementation is anticipated on 16 July 2005 under the Landfill (England and Wales) (Amendment) Regulations 2004.

6.2.3. Design, monitoring and aftercare

Schedule 2 of the LFR 2002 specifies that landfills must be designed and situated so as to prevent pollution of the soil, groundwater or surface water. Protection must be provided by means of a base liner during operation and a top liner following closure, and a geological barrier, which must meet specified requirements.

Schedule 3 of the LFR 2002 sets out the minimum monitoring procedures that apply from the start of operation until the EA defined closure date. The procedures aim to check that the:

- waste accepted conforms to the WAC
- landfill processes are proceeding as intended
- environmental protection systems are functioning properly
- permit conditions are met.

Typical procedures include leachate sampling and landfill gas monitoring, which can be technical and difficult in practice. For detailed procedures and requirements Schedule 3 can been viewed online at www.legislation.hmso.gov.uk/si/si2002/20021559.htm.

The EA can serve a closure notice, or the operator may request to initiate closure. Post-closure conditions are specified in the landfill permit, and closure must be approved by the EA through a system of rigorous inspections and reporting. The operator is responsible for post-closure monitoring, which is less frequent than during the operational phase. The duration of post-closure monitoring depends on the length of time that the landfill could pose a threat to the environment or human health. Financial provisions must be made for at least 30 years from closure.

Landfills are also subject to the s.34 EPA 1990 Duty of Care and the law on nuisance (please see Chapters 9 and 10). Under Schedule 2 of the LFR 2002 measures must be taken to minimise nuisances, which include litter, traffic, noise, vermin, odours, dust, fires and aerosol formation. Measures such as odour suppressors, vermin control (e.g. hawks) and fencing to trap windblown litter can be effective controls.

EA Landfill Regulatory Guidance Notes are available at www.environment-agency.gov.uk. *Landfill Regulatory Guidance Note 6* provides guidance on the interpretation of the engineering requirements of Annex 1 of the 99/31 Landfill Directive. Waste Management Paper 27 on *The Management of Landfill Gas* may also provide some useful technical guidance. This has recently been updated by the EA. In May 2004 the EA launched a consultation on the assessment of risks from landfill sites, guidance for which is available at www.environment-agency.gov.uk/commondata/105385/ risk_a_landfills_v1_768278.pdf.

6.2.4. Municipal waste landfill reduction targets and tradeable landfill permits

The 99/31 Landfill Directive targets have been fundamental to the UK's municipal waste management strategies in the past decade. Biodegradable municipal waste (BMW) must be reduced to:

- 75% of 1995 levels by July 2006
- 50% of 1995 levels by July 2009
- 35% of 1995 levels by July 2016.

The UK is eligible for 4-year extensions to these dates, which it intends to use, making the target dates 2010, 2013 and 2020, respectively.

The Waste and Emissions Trading Act 2003 introduced a system of tradeable allowances to help the UK meet the 99/31 BMW requirements. The Secretary of State has set gradually reducing BMW landfill limits for England, Wales, Scotland and Northern Ireland, and can set specific targets for any year (target years), and for any individual country.

Regional governments (the Scottish Minister, the National Assembly for Wales and the Department of the Environment for Northern Ireland and, in the future, regional assemblies) share out the total BMW landfill allowance for their regions between the local disposal authorities. The total regional allowance cannot be exceeded, but individual disposal authorities can:

- bank any unused allowance for later use
- in addition, councils may borrow up to 5% of their own allocations from future years as well as banking allowances for future use
- transfer any unused allowance by trading with another disposal authority who wishes to landfill more than its allowance
- buy allowances from another disposal authority if needed
- councils will be fined about £200 per tonne, almost four times the average cost of landfill, if they do not take reasonable steps (*sic*) to secure sufficient landfill allowances for the amount of waste they need to landfill.

Regulations for the Landfill Allowance Trading Scheme (LATS) have been delayed until 2005. On 14 May 2004 the Government announced that the LATS will begin for English (*sic*) county and unitary council authorities on 1 April 2005. For further information visit www.defra.gov.uk/corporate/consult/land-fill/faqs.htm or www.hm-treasury.gov.uk.

Box 6.2: April 2004 HM Customs and Excise change in waste definition

HM Customs and Excise, following recent EU trends (see the Palin Granit case in Chapter 2 and ARCO Chemie case in Box 6.5) has accepted that for landfill tax purposes, material is disposed of as waste if, when disposing of it, the producer intends to discard or throw it away. The fact that someone else uses it or intends to use it, or would have done so is irrelevant. It is the original producer's intention that determines whether the material is waste. Only when the material is recycled is the original producer's intention no longer relevant.

Until April 2004 guidance by Customs and Excise had been that material had to undergo a chemical change to have been recycled. However, Customs and Excise will now accept that if a material is processed, changing it to a usable material, the process does not have to change the material's chemical properties in order for it to be considered to have been recycled. The tax liability will now hinge on the intention of the recycler, as evidenced by the nature of the transaction. Therefore, if a landfill site operator can demonstrate to the satisfaction of Customs and Excise that, for example, the material used in site engineering is not discarded by its producer, it will not be subject to the tax.

Further information is available from the Customs and Excise website (www.hmce.gov.uk).

6.3. Landfill tax

The landfill tax was introduced in order to encourage waste reduction and recycling, and to promote alternative means of waste management. The primary law for landfill tax is the Finance Act 1996 (FA 1996), and the detail is set out in the Landfill Tax Regulations 1996 SI 1527, as amended by the Landfill Tax (Amendment) (No. 2) Regulation 2003 SI 2313.

6.3.1. When is a material liable for landfill tax?

Part III of the FA 1996 sets out the basic provisions and exemptions. A disposal under s.40 FA 1996 is subject to the landfill tax if all the following criteria apply:

(a) the material is disposed of as waste
(b) the disposal is made by way of a landfill at a landfill site.

The interpretation of (a) depends on the definition of waste, as discussed in Chapter 2. The scope of the landfill tax covers all sites authorised for the disposal of waste on or in land. The landfill operator is liable to pay the tax (a cost which is passed onto the disposer via the site gate fee).

133

Box 6.3: Who pays landfill tax?

Parkwood Recycling (a wholly owned subsidiary of Parkwood Landfill) received waste from Sheffield City Council. The material was divided into waste and material for recycling, the latter being processed to produce a soil substitute, which a landfill operator bought and used (instead of virgin materials) for road making and landscaping within the landfill site curtilage.

The Commissioners of Customs and Excise contended that the recycled material used on the landfill site was liable for landfill tax under Part III of the Finance Act 1996. However, the landfill company won an appeal before a Finance and Tax Tribunal: although the material used for the landfill site landscaping was deemed to have been deposited by way of landfill, the material was not discarded as useless and was therefore not subject to landfill tax. The conclusion stated that 'it was not the intention of the legislature to tax recycled material…even when disposed of to a landfill site.' The appeal was allowed.

This ruling was later overturned by the High Court, on the basis that the material had been disposed of as a waste. However, this ruling meant that the landfill operator would have to have paid landfill tax if he had used the recycled material for the landscaping but not if he had used virgin material, effectively penalising recycling. Given that this could not have been the Government's intention when it introduced the landfill tax in 1996, the site operator's appeal was accordingly allowed.

Source: *Parkwood Landfill* v. *Commissioners for Customs and Excise* Manchester Tribunal Centre April 2001 (MAN/00/9502); 1 AER 2002 at page 579 November. The case is also reported in its earlier stages at EWCA Civ 1707 2002.

6.3.2. Exemptions

The following are exempt from landfill tax:

- dredged material from natural or artificial watercourses
- mining and quarrying waste
- pet cemeteries
- waste from the clearing of contaminated land may in some cases also be exempt, for example waste soil from contaminated sites which are undergoing reclamation—details are set out in the Landfill Tax (Contaminated Land) Order 1996 SI 1529.

A restoration exemption may also apply to inert waste used for restoring a landfill site or part of a site. The work must comply with the planning consent and licence conditions. Prior notification to Customs and Excise of intention to restore is needed. Further details are set out in the Landfill Tax (Site Restoration and Quarries) Order 1999 SI 2075. The exemption does not apply to material used for daily cover.

6.3.3. The situation following the 2003 Budget

There are two rates of landfill tax, depending on whether the waste is inert or active. The lower rate for inert waste (e.g. bricks, soil and mineral dust) is £2 per tonne. Materials qualifying for the lower rate are detailed in the Landfill Tax (Qualifying Material) Order 1996 SI 1528. To qualify for the lower rate, evidence is needed in the form of a Waste Transfer Note (please see Chapters 10 and 11) to substantiate any application. For in-house disposal, evidence is still needed that the waste qualifies. A reasonable amount of active waste contamination is acceptable.

The standard rate for all other waste (active waste) started at £7 per tonne from 6 April 1996 to 5 April 1997, and increased at a rate of £1 per year. From 6 April 2003 to 5 April 2004 the rate was £15. The April 2003 Budget announced reforms to improve waste management, which included, *inter alia*:

- an increase in landfill tax to £18 per tonne in 2005–2006
- an increase in the landfill tax rate of £3 per year from 2005–2006 onwards
- a projected medium- to long-term rate of £35 per tonne.

For mixed loads (inert and active), standard tax must be paid on the whole load. The Commissioners for Customs and Excise will not advise on whether a load is inert or active, since it is for the site operator to decide. Decisions must be justified to the landfill tax officer.

6.3.4. Registration and accounting

Requirements for registration and accounting are set out in the Landfill Tax Regulations 1996 SI 1527. Landfill tax is payable quarterly, and the tax point is either the date when the waste was disposed of to landfill, or the date on which a landfill invoice was issued. If an operator pays tax on a consignment of waste but the customer subsequently reneges on the debt, the tax can be reclaimed. If the EA requires landfill waste to be removed to another site or for recycling, the tax can be reclaimed.

Landfill site operators can claim credit against their annual landfill tax liability. The maximum credit increased in the 2004 Budget from 6.5 to 6.8%. For further Budget information visit www.hm-treasury.gov.uk and www.hmce.go.uk. For further information see www.hmce.gov.uk/business/othertaxes/landfill-tax.htm. The Customs and Excise telephone advice line is 0845 010 900.

6.4. The Landfill Tax Credit Scheme

If a landfill operator pays a voluntary contribution to an environmental body, up to 90% of the contribution can be claimed as a landfill tax credit against the landfill tax payment. The total amount of credit claimed during the year must

Box 6.4: Skateboarders benefit from landfill tax

Revenue generated from the Landfill Tax Credit Scheme (LTCS) is awarded via a charitable trust (e.g. Entrust). For example, in Oxfordshire, money recently was awarded under the LTCS to create additional exhibition space and disabled toilets at a bus museum, and also to help build a local skateboard park.

Source: *Whitney and West Oxfordshire Gazette*, 22 October 2003.

not exceed 6.5% of the total landfill tax bill, and the contribution must be used for an approved purpose, e.g.:

- restoration of contaminated industrial sites
- closed landfills
- creation of conservation areas near landfill sites
- conservation or promotion of biological diversity
- maintenance or restoration of historic buildings, churches, etc., near landfill sites.

From April 2003 two-thirds of the landfill tax revenue has been used to promote sustainable waste management by increasing recycling and recovery of municipal waste.

A recent HM Treasury report examined 11 ways for using landfill tax revenue to assist businesses in reducing the amounts of waste they produce and send to landfill, including:

- interest-free loans and tax credits for investment in sustainable waste management
- support for research into recycling options
- rebates
- tradeable permits
- incentive schemes.

6.5. Energy recovery and the renewables obligation

Waste energy recovery plants are subject to the 2000/76 Waste Incineration Directive (please see Section 6.1 of this guide). Recent European Court of Justice rulings have meant that by-products destined for energy recovery are still classified as waste, as shown by the ARCO Chemie case described in Box 6.5.

Under the Renewables Obligation Order 2002 SI 914 and the Renewables Obligation (Scotland) Order 2002 SI 163 (both amended in 2004) all licensed electricity suppliers are obliged to produce evidence, in the form of a Renewables Obligation Certificate (ROC), that they have sourced a specified

Box 6.5: A 2002 definition of incineration waste fuel

> ARCO Chemie Netherland Ltd produced, in the course of manufacturing, industrial by-products which could be used as incinerator fuel. Were these by-products classified as waste under the 75/442 Waste Framework Directive (as amended by the 91/156 Directive)? Annex IIB of the 91/156 Directive lists 'operations which may lead to recovery' and includes the entry 'use principally as a fuel or other means to generate energy'.
>
> Despite this apparently clear distinction, the European Court of Justice (ECJ) held that the concept of waste could not in this case be interpreted restrictively. The term waste depended on the meaning attributed to the word 'discard', which included the disposal or recovery of an object. Both Directives' aims were to protect human health and the environment. The fuel substance was a residue of a manufacturing process, and no other use for that substance other than fuel could be envisaged. Special precautions had to be deployed when it was being burnt. All these reasons (and some others) suggested that the by-products used as a fuel were waste, which the ECJ found that they were.
>
> Source: *ARCO Chemie Netherland Ltd (ACN)* v. *Minister van Volkshulsvesting, Ruimtellike Ordening en Milieubaheer (MVROM)* 2002, case

Box 6.6: Less waste from energy policy

> On 24 February 2003 the Government's Energy White Paper *Our Energy Future — Creating a Low Carbon Economy* was published, with four goals:
>
> - to cut the UK's carbon dioxide emissions by 60% by about (*sic*) 2050, preferably by 2020
> - to maintain reliability of energy suppliers
> - to promote competitive markets
> - to ensure all homes are adequately and affordably heated.
>
> Source: www.dti.gov.uk/energy/whitepaper/ourenergyfuture.pdf.

proportion of their electricity supplies from renewable energy sources. Landfill gas, co-firing of biomass and sewage gas are all sources of renewable energy that qualify for ROCs. Suppliers who do not meet the obligation must pay a fee to the Office of Gas and Electricity Markets (OFGEM).

Under the 2001/77 Electricity from Renewable Sources Directive, energy produced from biomass is classified as a renewable resource. Energy produced from the incineration of the biodegradable fraction of waste qualifies as renewable energy, and is exempt from the climate change levy. The tax break is calculated on the proportion of energy derived from biodegradable wastes only (approximately 50%), and administered by OFGEM. ROCs can be issued for the energy recovered from the biodegradable proportion. Several waste-to-energy facilities are accredited with OFGEM for the purpose of the Renewables Obligation and the Climate Change Levy. For further information visit www.ofgem.gov.uk.

Chapter 7

The planning system and structural reform

It is estimated that around 500 new waste management facilities are needed to meet the recycling and landfill diversion targets set out in the Waste Strategy 2000, the equivalent to the construction of one new facility processing 40,000 tonnes per year each week for the next 10 years. The implications for the emergent development control law and structure of planning as envisaged by the Government are considerable and possibly surmountable. Just meeting the targets set out in the 2002/96 Waste Electrical and Electronic Equipment Directive alone would cost London an estimated £15 million in infrastructure and facilities. In addition, technicians, trained operators and support services are needed to operate these facilities. Failure to establish the necessary infrastructure will not only have direct effects, such as EU fines and loss of Brussels confidence, but can also result in transportation over large distances between approved facilities.

Typical contemporary waste management development control situations include:

- a local authority wishing to construct waste management facilities to implement the waste plan
- a public or private company undertaking a project on behalf of, or in partnership with, the local authority, or on its own account after a successful tendering procedure
- existing facilities needing a change of location or enlargement
- smaller firms wishing to extend or change the use of a site, or increase waste storage (e.g. an old vehicle scrapyard needs to invest and redevelop the site to meet the specifications of the End of Life Vehicles Regulations 2003 in order to become an authorised treatment facility).

Planning permission is required for any new development or building operation (e.g. structural alterations), and may be required for a change in use of a property. Permission will be refused, *inter alia*, if the proposed development is

139

considered to result in unacceptable levels of pollution or contamination. Typical infrastructure, facilities and systems necessary for the recovery, treatment and disposal of waste, include:

- source separation and collection systems
- materials recovery facilities
- centralised composting sites
- anaerobic digestion facilities
- mechanical and biological treatment (MBT)
- thermal treatment facilities for energy recovery and/or district heating
- incinerators
- effluent discharge and land application systems
- landfill sites
- structures to house the equipment
- transport infrastructure
- specialist vehicles and professional transportation services.

A project director or local authority planner, in order to construct and operate a waste management facility, must, *inter alia*, in simple terms:

- obtain funding for the scheme, perhaps through a Private Finance Initiative (PFI) rate or tax payers' money or a bank loan
- identify and minimise, through formal or informal environmental impact assessment (EIA), the potential effects of the proposal, not least on the neighbouring communities
- ensure legal compliance of all activities by identifying which regulatory regimes apply, if not already identified in the EIA
- research and apply the Best Available Techniques,[1] processes or management systems necessary for compliance
- justify the need for the proposal, and identify the Best Practicable Environmental Option
- ensure that the proposal is in line with the Office of the Deputy Prime Minister, the Department for Environment, Food and Rural Affairs, and the Department of Transport published policies and guidelines
- after consultation with the local planning department and local communities, apply for and obtain planning permission
- obtain the necessary permits or licences to operate the facility
- manage the available resources, e.g. the skills base and financial provisions.

---

[1] This is a statutory requirement for installations coming under the Integrated Pollution Prevention and Control Regime (please see Chapter 8).

Box 7.1: Some public attitudes

> In October 2003, residents staged a protest against plans for a waste
> incinerator in Newhaven on the grounds that it may jeopardise the health of
> future generations.
>
> Source: *The Argus* [Brighton], 21/22 October 2003.
>
> In December 2003, every resident on an inner-city street signed a petition
> against council plans for communal rubbish bins, a commonly accepted system
> in many European cities.
>
> Source: *The Argus* [Brighton], 23 December 2003.

The markets or final disposal options for the facility output must be identified or developed at the very early planning stages. Not only will planning
inquiry inspectors will be interested, but banks can be reluctant to lend money
for waste management projects, since the risks are not easy to identify and costs
sometimes unquantifiable.[2] New waste management technologies are considered to be high-risk, and markets immature and slow to establish. Planning
appeals present one of the greatest risks to investors since the decisions of individual inspectors can be, but are not always, unpredictable.

Before the waste management facilities and infrastructure in the waste planning authority's local plan can be built, there must be a long and often arduous
planning process. If planning permission is refused, the project manager must
count the cost so far, reconsider his options, return to his project management
committee, and perhaps, after further consultation with the planning authorities
and the local community, lodge a second amended application.

The planning process is separate to the waste management licensing or
permitting process. A planning application must be submitted to the local planning authority, while permits to operate the installation or mobile plant must be
obtained from the Environment Agency (EA). Planning permission must be
obtained before a waste management licence can be issued by the EA (this is not
the case for permits), and the waste manager should not assume that because the
planning permission is in place a site licence or permit will follow. Even if an
activity is exempt from licensing, planning permission, if none exists, will
almost certainly be required. Local planning officers are very careful with their

---

[2] Barclays Bank has taken initiatives in the past on waste management market analysis, and has
begun to identify market characteristics and funding opportunities. For further information on
services for the waste management industry visit www.barclays.co.uk/wastemgt.

advice to their council's local planning committee, since planning permission once approved cannot generally be revoked without serious compensation.

7.1. Legislative background and recent changes to the planning system

The present primary statutory provisions for planning are in the Town and Country Planning Act 1990 (TCPA 1990), the Planning (Hazardous Substances) Act 1990, the Planning (Listed Buildings and Conservation Areas) Act 1990 and the Planning and Compensation Act 1991 (PCA 1991). Planning applications are made to the local authority under the Town and Country Planning (Applications) Regulations 1988 SI 1812. The Town and Country Planning (Use Classes) Order 1987 SI 764 allows a change of use within certain specified classes, such as light industrial, office, and research and development uses. Under the Town and Country Planning (Development Plans) (England) Regulations 1999 SI 3280, planning authorities must take into consideration the national waste strategy when producing development plans.

The Planning and Compulsory Purchase Bill is due to receive the Royal Assent in 2004, and will have a considerable effect on the local and regional planning structure, local authority planning policies and procedures concerning the location and type of new developments. The key changes under this Act are described in this chapter.

The PCA 1991 introduced a plan-led system, stronger enforcement powers and more formalised arrangements for securing planning benefits through planning obligations. The PCA 1991 requires local authorities to produce waste local plans. In most areas these have traditionally been produced in tandem due to the link between mineral extraction and landfill. There are now considerable doubts about the plan-led system, and the new Planning and Compulsory Purchase Act 2004 intends to reform this to make it a regional strategy-led system to which the local plans conform. Local plans will be subject to a different structural framework, which is explained in the following section. In the past, the waste and minerals local plans served the following roles under the PCA 1991:

Waste local plan
- Identifying existing waste disposal sites and their remaining capacity.
- Evaluating waste disposal requirements for different waste streams.
- Identifying the number and location of waste management facilities needed to meet the requirements.
- Prioritising waste management options included in the waste disposal management plan in the formulation of land-use planning.
- Specifying criteria against which planning applications for waste management will be assessed.

Box 7.2: A view from the heavens: planning practice in other EU countries

Italy is smothered with illegal construction, even in protected areas, perhaps 326,000 buildings that should never have gone up. An amnesty by Italy's Prime Minister is proposed, which should raise €1.5 billion in fines. Rome's public works department will use a satellite to spot non-licensed building work from space. Yet what will the expense be of laying on public services for the newly legalised buildings?

Source: *The Economist*, December 2003.

Mineral local plan

- Providing a policy framework for the assessment of mineral workings.
- Protecting resources.
- Promoting recycling initiatives.
- Encouraging the bulk transportation of minerals.
- Making provisions for the winning and working of minerals for local, regional and national needs.
- Protecting the environment and local amenity.
- Ensuring the beneficial restoration and after-use of mineral workings.

It is likely that plans under the new local planning framework, although arranged in a different organisational structure, will carry out a similar role, albeit within a more integrated regional framework.

The Planning and Compulsory Purchase Act 2004 (PCPA 2004) will, for the first time, provide a statutory basis for regional planning. The Bill was introduced to reform a planning system which the Government Regulatory Impact Assessment stated 'has become too inflexible and bureaucratic', and to speed up the planning system and improve community involvement. But views on the planning system vary, and many advocate that the planning system is remarkably effective when compared with practices in other countries.

The 85/337 Environmental Impact Assessment Directive, implemented by the Town and Country Planning (Environmental Impact Assessment) Regulations 1999 SI 293 (as amended), requires that environmental effects are assessed at the planning stage. Where significant effects exist these must be reported in the form of an environmental statement (ES), which is submitted with the application. Applications may be submitted without an ES, but full reasons must be given for the omission. Local planning consultations are imperative. Transposition of the 2001/42 Directive on the Assessment of the Effects of Certain Plans and Programmes on the Environment, referred to as the Strategic Environmental Assessment (SEA) Directive, began in July 2004 (see europa.eu.int/eur-lex/pri/en/oj/dat/2001/l_197/l_19720010721en00300037.pdf). The development framework is underpinned by Strategic Environmental Assessments (SEAs), which assess the environmental aspects of a programme and plans at a strategic level, and

Sustainability Appraisals, which balance social, economic and environmental factors. Annual monitoring reports will be used to follow efficacy of policies. The regulatory impact assessment for the national waste strategy is given in Annex C of the Waste Strategy 2000.

7.2. The new organisational structure

7.2.1. Regional and local authorities

The restructuring of local and regional government is explained in Chapter 4. Referenda are to be held over the next 2 years on whether to appoint elected regional assemblies. If elected, these bodies will have development control powers. The local government structure of the 25 EU Member States is now based on regions.

Regional development agencies (RDAs) have been set up to promote sustainable economic development in each of the regions. Regional development agencies are answerable to the regional assemblies. Regional technical advisory bodies provide officers to advise regional development agencies on matters such as the Environment Agency statistics, waste management information (e.g. collection contracts), planning of facilities, monitoring and the adequacy of arrangements in relation to capacity requirements. The Planning Inspectorate processes planning appeals, inquiries and other casework (www.planning-inspectorate.gov.uk).

In summary, the authorities involved in planning, from a strategic level to individual facilities, are the:

- regional coordination unit
- regional assemblies
- regional development agencies (RDAs)
- regional planning bodies (RPBs)
- unitary authorities
- regional technical advisory bodies (RTABs)
- Planning Inspectorate
- waste planning authorities (WPAs)
- waste collection authorities (WCAs)
- waste disposal authorities (WDAs).

Until recently, county councils had to prepare a county structure plan setting out the policies and general proposals for the development and use of land in the county. Under the PCPA 2004, structure plans will have been abolished, and the former regional planning guidance replaced by regional spatial strategies. Regional development agencies are now required by the Government to review regional policies and develop regional strategies for issues such as transport, tourism, renewable energy and waste. These regional strategies are then incorporated in the new regional spatial strategies, and form a framework for local planning.

In summary, under the PCPA 2004:

- regional spatial strategies (RSSs) now replace regional planning guidance (RPG)
- county structure plans have been abolished
- regional strategies provide the framework for local plans.

Further information is available in *Planning Policy Guidance Note 11 (PPG 11) on Regional Planning*, which is accompanied by an interim Regional Spatial Strategy guidance note.

7.2.2. The local development framework

Under the PCPA 2004 the new local development framework (LDF) comprises:

- development plan documents (DPDs)
- supplementary planning documents (SPDs)
- a statement of community involvement (SCI)
- a local development scheme (LDS).

It is proposed that the local development framework will replace the old framework of Borough Local Plans (borough councils), County Minerals and Waste Plans (county council) and Borough Council Development Briefs and Supplementary Planning Guidance. However, for an interim period existing council plans will remain in place even after the 2004 Act has been passed, until the new plans have been developed. The new local development plan documents will include waste and minerals plans, and these will be subject to the regional spatial strategy. Regional and local strategies are coordinated through the Government's Regional Coordination Unit (RCU).

The statement of community involvement sets out the local authority's policy on community involvement, and is subject to independent approval by the Planning Inspectorate. A local authority can request direction from the Secretary of State on a planning application, and the Secretary of State can call in applications for his own determination. For the latest information visit the ODPM website (www.odpm.gov.uk).

Local development documents will include:

- core policies
- core strategies
- proposal maps
- action area plans
- site-specific information.

The new organisation framework is illustrated in Figure 7.1. In practice, the adoption of the new planning framework has been a contentious and time-consuming process for local authorities. It has proven very difficult indeed to develop a strategy or a plan that both elected members and the public will adopt.

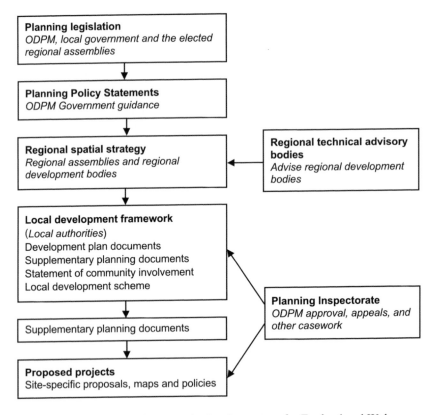

Figure 7.1: The new planning organisational structure for England and Wales

The Scottish system differs from the above framework. The Scottish National Waste Plan includes 11 area plans and was launched in February 2003 (for further information visit www.sepa.org.uk/nws/). The Scottish Executive established the Strategic Waste Fund in order to provide grants for implementation of the national waste strategy. The grants can help local authorities implement the area plans individually as joint bids covering several areas. Details are available at www.scotland.gov.uk/library5/environment/stwf.pdf.

7.3. Planning Policy Statements (formerly Planning Policy Guidance)

There are 25 Planning Policy Guidance Notes (PPGs), many of which will have some relevance to waste management planning. These documents are important for successful waste management proposals, since applications will be rejected if they do not conform to Government policy. PPGs are currently being revised and reformed into Planning Policy Statements (PPSs). All 25 PPGs/PPSs are listed in Table 7.1. They are available online at www.odpm.gov.uk.

The most relevant PPGs for waste management are PPG10, *Planning and Waste Management*, and PPG 23, *Planning and Pollution Control*. They give guidance to local authorities, the EA, industry, the media, non-governmental organisations and local communities. They should be more widely distributed and read than they are in 2004. PPG10 sets out the planning policy relating to the management of Controlled waste, reducing waste generation, and controlling and managing waste, taking into account social, economic and environmental factors. In summary, it:

- sets out the waste planning framework
- explains how the provision of waste management facilities and infrastructure is regulated
- explains the authorities and their roles, monitoring and enforcement

Table 7.1: List of PPGs and PPSs

PPG/*PPS*	Title
PPS1	*Creating Sustainable Communities*
PPG2	*Green Belts*
PPG3	*Housing*
PPG4	*Industrial, Commercial Development and Small Firms*
PPG5	*Simplified Planning Zones*
PPG6	*Town Centres and Retail Development*
PPG7	*Countryside*
PPG8	*Telecommunications*
PPG9	*Nature Conservation*
PPG10	*Planning and Waste Management*
PPG11	*Regional Planning*
PPS12	*Development Plans*
PPG13	*Transport*
PPG14	*Development on Unstable Land*
PPG15	*Planning and the Historic Environment*
PPG16	*Archaeology and Planning*
PPG17	*Planning for Open Space, Sport and Recreation*
PPG18	*Enforcing Planning Control*
PPG19	*Outdoor Advertisement Control*
PPG20	*Coastal Planning*
PPG21	*Tourism*
PPS22	*Renewable Energy*
PPG23	*Planning and Pollution Control*
PPG24	*Planning and Noise*
PPG25	*Development and Flood Risks*

- provides criteria for siting waste management facilities, planning consider-ations and planning conditions
- explains the relationship between the planning and licensing regimes
- assists waste planning authorities in the preparation of waste develop-ment plans
- explains the determination of waste management facility planning applications
- sets out the role of the regional technical advisory bodies.

According to PPG10, waste management decisions must be based on:

- the waste hierarchy
- the proximity principle
- the Best Practicable Environmental Option (BPEO) for each waste stream
- regional self-sufficiency (waste should be treated or disposed of within the region in which it is produced).

BPEO is the option which provides the most benefit or least damage to the environment as a whole, at acceptable cost, in the long and short term. These terms are all explained in PPG10 which is available online at www.odpm.gov.uk. PPGs should be read in conjunction with the Waste Strategy 2000. PPG10 does not take account of the new Pollution Prevention and Control Permitting regime and some other recent changes in waste management law. It will be revised.

PPG23, *Planning and Pollution Control*, provides guidance on the relationship between the planning regime and the pollution prevention and control regime under the EPA 1990, in particular the coordination between the planning authorities and the EA. The document provides planning authorities with information on implementation of the 75/442 Waste Framework Directive. Part of this PPG has been overtaken by events, e.g. the Integrated Pollution Prevention and Control Regime, and it also will be revised (please see Chapter 8).

Box 7.3: Plans did not follow Government recycling policy

An application for an integrated waste management facility in Ridham, Kent, which incorporated an energy from waste plant, was recently turned down, with one of the principal reasons being that the proposal did not meet the Waste Strategy 2000 recycling targets for 2010 and beyond.

Source: Evans D. (2003), *Examples of Actual Planning Inquiries with their Procedures and Findings and the Lessons to be Learned*, Addleshaw Goddard, Lecture for the University of Southampton, September 2003.

Box 7.4: Government puts up cash for new waste management infrastructure

> In December 2003 Lancashire County Council was awarded £75 million
> to fund a scheme to build nine waste management facilities to process
> 900,000 tonnes of waste per year, with the aim of reducing by 80% the amount
> of waste going to landfill. Despite advanced Government funding, the scheme
> will be subject to the new planning system, and it may be some time before the
> infrastructure and landfill diversion become a reality.
>
> Source: *Rossendale Free Press*, 12 December 2003.

A supplementary note on regional spatial strategies is provided with PPG11 as interim guidance to help regional planning bodies prepare for the changes. The supplementary guidance note advises regional planning bodies, *inter alia*, of:

- the style and content of the regional spatial strategies
- coordination with other strategies
- delivery, monitoring and implementation
- how local development documents can conform to the regional strategy.

An outline of proposed regional spatial strategy arrangements is given in Annex A of the PPG11 supplement regional spatial strategy guidance note, and the transitional arrangements are set out in Annex B.

Several other PPG/PPSs are of interest:

- PPS1, *Creating Sustainable Communities* (previously PPG1, *Planning Policy and Principles*). This statement discusses the concept of sustainable development, and describes the broad Government planning policies as an introduction to the other PPGs and PPSs.
- PPG2, *Green Belt*. A planning application for a facility on green belt land will most probably be refused if there is a non-green belt alternative.
- PPS12, *Development Plans*. This provides information on local development frameworks, to which the waste local plans must conform.
- PPG22, *Renewable Energy*. The introduction states that 'combustible or digestible industrial, agricultural and domestic waste materials are also regarded as renewable sources of energy'.

Most of the remaining PPGs may contain peripheral guidance of some relevance to waste management planning. A proposed facility must have regard for its surrounding environment, so, for example, PPG15, *Planning and the Historic Environment*, may be of relevance in some cases.

Chapter 8

Integrated Pollution Prevention and Control and the permitting regime

8.1. A licence or a permit?

Licensing and permitting are a means of preventing and controlling pollution from activities that may harm the environment or human health. Both enable the relevant regulatory authorities to obtain important information on potentially harmful activities, sometimes in advance of possible damage, and to impose conditions and requirements to reduce risks and emissions to an acceptable level. Conditions imposed are based on the principles of the Best Available Techniques and the Best Practicable Environmental Option, explained in this chapter.

The licensing of activities concerning the treatment, keeping or disposal of Controlled waste[1] is regulated under Part II of the Environmental Protection Act 1990 and the Waste Management Licensing Regulations 1994 SI 1056. Other processes that may cause harm to the environment are controlled under Part I of the Environmental Protection Act 1990. Part I of the Environmental Protection Act 1990 has been modified as a result of the Pollution Prevention and Control Act 1999.[2] The Pollution Prevention and Control Act 1999 introduced the Integrated Pollution Prevention and Control permitting regime largely to implement the 96/61 Integrated Pollution Prevention and Control Directive. The Integrated Pollution Prevention and Control permitting regime (as opposed to licensing) is currently replacing Part I of the Environmental Protection Act 1990 and will eventually replace the waste management licensing system.

---

[1] Controlled waste is a particular class of waste controlled under s.75 EPA 1990. Please see Chapter 2 for further information.

[2] The general practice throughout this guide is to begin a chapter with the full title of an Act or an agency, and then for the rest of the chapter to use the abbreviation or acronym. This rule has been waived in respect of this chapter because of the potential real confusion in using the abbreviations too early for the reader's textual understanding and general comfort.

Integrated Pollution Prevention and Control permits now apply to landfill sites under the Landfill Regulations 2002 SI 1559, but, for the present, waste management licensing Regulations still apply to other waste management activities. Integrated Pollution Prevention and Control permitting will be fully implemented by 31 March 2007.

This chapter explains both the Integrated Pollution Prevention and Control regime and the waste management licensing system, and clarifies the sometimes confusing terminology and abbreviations. In this interregnum where permitting is replacing licensing, it is necessary for the public and private sector responsible officers and managers to keep themselves absolutely up to date.

For the very latest Government position and guidelines please refer to the Environment Agency (EA), Scottish Environment Protection Agency (SEPA) and the Department for Environment, Food and Rural Affairs (DEFRA) websites.[3] In March 2004 DEFRA published *Integrated Pollution Prevention and Control: a Practical Guide*, 3rd edition (www.defra.gov.uk/environment/ ppc/ippcguide/ippc_ed3.htm). Integrated Pollution Prevention and Control background information is also available from the EU website (europa.eu.int/ comm/environment/ippc/index.htm).

8.2. Integrated Pollution Prevention Control and Local Air Pollution Prevention and Control

Integrated pollution control means the assessment and then the control, with a view to reduction, of all pollution—to the air, water and land—under one regulatory regime. This concept of integrated control was first introduced under Part I of the Environmental Protection Act 1990, entitled Integrated Pollution Control (IPC) and Air Pollution Control by Local Authorities (LAPC). Part I of the Environmental Protection Act 1990 refers to the prescribed processes (i.e. those processes set out in the Regulations) that must have a licence before they can operate. Its principles and structure were later adopted by the EU and formed the basis of the 96/61 Integrated Pollution Prevention and Control (IPPC) Directive. The aim of the 96/61 IPPC Directive in its Preamble is partly to achieve 'a high level of protection of the environment taken as a whole by, in particular, preventing or, where that is not practical, reducing emissions into the air, water and land.'

---

[3] Also, a detailed commentary of the Integrated Pollution Prevention and Control regime is available in Kellett P., Farthing J. and Marshall B., *Pollution Prevention and Control—The New Regime*, Butterworths LexisNexis, London.

Box 8.1: Abbreviations made simple

- IPC or *Integrated Pollution Control* under Part I of the EPA 1990 will progressively become the IPPC or *Integrated Pollution Prevention and Control* regime by 31 March 2007.
- LAPC or *Local Air Pollution Control* under Part I of the EPA 1990 will progressively become the LAPPC or *Local Air Pollution Prevention and Control* regime by 31 March 2007.
- IPPC and LAPPC under the Pollution Prevention and Control Act 1999 are progressively becoming UK law through the Pollution Prevention and Control Regulations 2000 SI 1973 (PPCR 2000).
- The transitional process will be complete by 2007, after which Part I of the EPA 1990 should be repealed.

The 96/61 IPPC Directive is being implemented in the UK under the Pollution Prevention and Control Act 1999 (PPCA 1999).[4] The old Part I Environmental Protection Act 1990 IPC and LAPC systems are progressively being replaced, between 2000 and 2007, by the new IPPC regime under the Pollution Prevention and Control Act 1999. The details of the new regime are being implemented under the Pollution Prevention and Control (England and Wales) Regulations 2000 SI 1973 and for north of the Border, the Pollution Prevention and Control (Scotland) Regulations 2000 SI 323. Existing authorisations granted under Part I of the Environmental Protection Act 1990 will remain in force during the transitional period. In Scotland, however, new permits are to be granted for all activities covered by the Regulations.

The IPPC regime is broader in scope than IPC and includes the release of pollutants, waste production, energy efficiency and site restoration. The new regime introduces wide protection measures for most industrial sectors, and makes extensive changes to the system of waste regulation. It more than doubles the processes subject to the regime that were previously covered by IPC. The new regime now covers over 5000 processes, and applies to over 3000 landfill sites.

---

[4] For the sake of clarity, Integrated Pollution Prevention and Control is the name of the 96/61 Directive, but the UK Act derived from this Directive is the Pollution Prevention and Control Act 1999, which introduces what is known colloquially as the IPPC regime. Perhaps the reason why the Government did not follow a logical course and call the Pollution Prevention and Control Act 1999 the *Integrated* Pollution Prevention and Control Act 1999 was to avoid confusion with the superseded Part 1 of the EPA 1990, which was entitled 'Integrated Pollution Control and Air Pollution Control by Local Authorities'.

Table 8.1: Overview of the pollution control regimes

Old regime		New regime		Process category	Regulator	Typical waste activities subject to the regime
Integrated Pollution Control	IPC	Integrated Pollution Prevention and Control		A1	EA	Larger incinerators Larger landfills Some disposal and recovery operations
Integrated Pollution Control	IPC	Integrated Pollution Prevention and Control		A2	LA	None
Local Air Pollution Control	LAPC	Local Air Pollution Prevention and Control	LAPPC	B	LA	Smaller incinerators

Processes subject to IPPC permitting are set out in the PPCR 2000. A group of activities forming a technical unit is referred to as an installation. Activities, installations and mobile plant are grouped into three process categories, A(1), A(2) and B (Table 8.1). In very broad terms, IPPC currently applies to:

- incinerators
- larger landfills
- disposal and recovery operations usually involving biological or physico-chemical processing.

Waste activities predominantly fall under IPPC, with LAPPC applying, in the context of waste, to small-scale incinerators. This is summarised in Table 8.1.

The new regime is from now on in this text referred to as IPPC permitting. In practice it is often abbreviated to PPC permitting. For the present, the waste management licensing system will remain applicable to all waste management activities not yet covered by the IPPC regime. Planning Policy Guidance Note 23 (PPG23) provides Government guidance on planning and pollution control. The planning system is explained in Chapter 7.

8.3. Integrated Pollution Prevention and Control permitting

Article 9(a) of the 75/442 Waste Framework Directive states that all companies operating a waste disposal or recovery operation must have a permit from the competent authority:

- the EA for England and Wales
- the SEPA for Scotland
- the Environment and Heritage Service for Northern Ireland.

The new IPPC regime is partly being introduced to implement and unify the permitting requirements of this and other Directives. During this transitional period, waste management activities currently fall between the new IPPC permitting regime and the old waste management licensing system. This section explains the activities that are covered by the new IPPC regime.

8.3.1. To whom does Integrated Pollution Prevention and Control apply?

The waste management activities that are subject to IPPC permitting are listed in Schedule 1, Chapter 5 of the PPCR 2000. Activities, installations and mobile plant are grouped into three process categories, A(1), A(2) and B, and there are no specific waste management activities under category A2. Table 8.2 provides a summary of some key waste management activities, installations and plant subject to the IPPC permitting regime. For full details the reader should refer to

155

Table 8.2: Some key waste management activities listed under Schedule 1, Chapter 5 of the PPCR 2000

Type	Incineration	Landfill	Other disposal	Recovery	Fuel production
Part A(1) (EA responsibility)	The incineration of any waste chemical or waste plastic arising from the manufacture of these materials	Landfill receiving > 10 tonnes of waste in any day, or landfill with a total capacity > 25,000 tonnes (excluding inert only landfills)	Disposal of Hazardous waste in a facility with a capacity > 10 tonnes per day	Recovering by distillation of any oil or organic solvent	Making solid fuel (other than charcoal) from waste by any process involving the use of heat
	The incineration, other than incidentally in the course of burning other waste, of any waste chemical		The disposal of waste oils in a facility with a capacity > 10 tonnes per day	Cleaning or regenerating carbon, charcoal or ion exchange resins	
	Unless falling within Part B of this Section, the incineration of Hazardous waste in an incineration plant (except for specified Hazardous waste in an exempt incineration plant)		Disposal of non-Hazardous waste in a facility with a capacity > 50 tonnes per day by biological or physicochemical treatment (as specified in the PPCR 2000)	Unless carried out as part of any other Part A activity, recovering Hazardous waste in plant with a capacity > 10 tonnes per day for energy recovery, and other reclamation activities specified in the PPCR 2000	
	The incineration of municipal waste in an incineration plant with a capacity > 3 tonnes per hour				
	The incineration of any waste, including animal remains, otherwise than as part of a Part B activity, in an incineration plant with a capacity of ≥ 1 tonne per hour				

The cleaning for reuse of metal containers used for the transport or storage of a chemical by burning out their residual content —

Part A(2) —

Part B (local authority responsibility)

The incineration of specified Hazardous waste in an incineration plant with a capacity of ≤10 tonnes per day and <1 tonne per hour, unless the plant is an exempt incineration plant

The incineration of any non-Hazardous waste in an incineration plant, other than an exempt incineration plant, with a capacity of <1 tonne per hour

The cremation of human remains

157

Schedule 1 of the PPCR 2000. The food and drinks sector came under IPPC Regulations in 2004. Contaminated land restoration activities are also subject to the IPPC permitting regime. The European Commission (EC) provides a practical explanation of the implications of IPPC for each sector covered by the BREF Notes, which are prepared in Seville. The last BREF Note was on the surface treatment of metals and plastics, published in August 2003.

8.3.2. Applying for an Integrated Pollution Prevention and Control permit

The new IPPC regime has several permit variations, namely:

- registered exemptions
- simple permit codes of practice
- lighter permitting procedures for waste electrical and electronic equipment (WEEE), end of life vehicle (ELV) and agricultural waste sites (e.g. generic, non site-specific permits).

The permit application must consider the:

- types and quantities of wastes covered
- facility technical requirements
- security precautions
- disposal site
- treatment method.

The grant of permits under the PPCR 2000 are covered in Schedule 4 of the PPC Regulations. Applications must be made in writing, and include:

- full contact and company details, address of the site, with a plan and name of relevant local authority
- details of considerations such as energy use, wastes and emissions
- a site report on any substances in or on the land that may present a pollution risk
- the proposed technology or techniques for preventing emissions where practicable, or failing that reducing emissions
- conclusions from the Environmental Impact Assessment
- any information to take into account when considering whether the applicant is a fit and proper person
- a non-technical summary of the above.

The application form must be sent to the EA (with the relevant fee), and must demonstrate that the option meets:

- all relevant legislation and EU law
- the BAT (see below)
- the BPEO (see below).

158

The application form is placed on the EA and the county and the district council public registers (regional where appropriate). It is then sent to statutory consultees, including the Health and Safety Executive and the Food Standards Agency, and the local health authority and local environmental health department for comment. The application will be advertised in the local press, and subject to a technical review. After all the public and consultant comments are considered, and a decision is made, a permit may be:

- granted for a specified period of time, but is renewable and
- subject to conditions and obligations, or
- refused.

A permit will be refused if the proposed method of disposal is unacceptable in terms of environmental protection.

Planning permission is still required, regardless of whether a permit or licence has been issued. Planning permission need not be granted before a permit is issued, thus decoupling the two regimes. If a permitted site is to be enlarged, then the permit can also be enlarged. Under the old system a waste management licence could not be extended, and another licence would be needed, and thus several licences could apply to one facility. Under Regulation 4 of the PPCR 2000, the regulator must determine whether the applicant is a fit and proper person to carry out a specified waste management activity. The definition of fit and proper person is given in Section 8.6.2 of this guide.

8.4. Best Available Techniques and Best Practicable Environmental Option

Conditions under the IPPC permitting regime are intended to reduce and control emissions and wastes and are based on the concept of Best Available Techniques (BAT). BAT is defined in the Pollution Prevention and Control (England and Wales) Regulations (2000) under regulation 3 as

> the most effective and advanced stage in the development of activities and their methods of operation which indicates the practical suitability of particular techniques for providing in principle the basis for emission limit values designed to prevent and, where that is not practicable, generally to reduce emissions and the impact on the environment as a whole (*sic*).

BAT involves balancing the environmental benefit with the practicability and cost to the operator.[5] BAT relies on technological solutions, environmental

---

[5] The term 'Best Available Techniques Not Entailing Excessive Cost' (BATNEEC) is no longer used, because the issue of excessive cost is now included in the term 'available' in BAT.

management techniques and staff training. The risk associated with a particular activity can change over time as new technology is developed. Just think back to what was not known in the 1900s, and where industry would be now if today's plans were based on what was known then.

Schedule 2 of the PPCR 2000 lists the considerations for BAT. These include the use of low-waste technology and the production of less hazardous substances, increased recovery and recycling, process comparison, the use of methods which have been previously tried with success on an industrial scale, technological advances and scientific developments, the effects and volume of the emissions, the length of time needed to introduce the BAT, raw material use (including water) and energy efficiency, the minimisation of wastes, emissions and environmental risk. The likely costs and benefits of measures and the precautionary principle must also be considered. The EA is proposing to publish BAT guidance in the summer of 2004, covering 10 key BAT areas:

- the waste hierarchy (please see Chapter 1)
- characterisation, sampling and checking
- selection of treatment technologies
- liquid waste immobilisation processes
- intractable waste
- accumulations of waste
- accident risk
- emissions to sewer
- odour associated with fugitive emissions
- site restoration.

The inclusion of the waste hierarchy means that to fulfil BAT a disposal option cannot be selected when a viable recovery alternative exists. For the latest consultation details visit www.environment-agency.gov.uk/yourenv/consultations.

Best Practicable Environmental Option (BPEO) is the option that provides the best benefit or least damage to the environment as a whole at acceptable cost, in the long term as well as the short term. BPEO was first developed as a concept in the 12th Report of the Royal Commission on Environmental Pollution, published in 1988. Section 7 of the Environmental Protection Act 1990 requires that BPEO be used for minimising pollution as a whole in respect of substances released in a process subject to IPC[6] (now IPPC).

---

[6] Further reading: Tromans S. R. and Hawkins R. G. P. (1987), *Best Practicable Environmental Option – A New Jerusalem?*, UKELA, London; Royal Commission on Environmental Pollution (1988), 12th Report, Stationery Office, London.

8.5. Particular types of permits and licences

8.5.1. Landfill permits

The Landfill Regulations 2002 SI 1559 make provisions for the issue of landfill permits in accordance with the Pollution Prevention and Control (England and Wales) Regulations 2000 SI 1973 (PPCR 2000). The IPPC regime stipulates that:

- there can be no unacceptable discharges to groundwater, regardless of how long ago the wastes were disposed of
- if no hydrological separation exists between existing and future waste deposits, then the permit will be declined.

These requirements are difficult to meet in the case of newly engineered landfilled cells overlying old deposits.

Under the Landfill Regulations 2002, operators of all existing landfill sites were required to submit a Conditioning Plan by 16 July 2002. The EA used the Conditioning Plans to assess whether the landfill sites could continue operating under the new regime. An IPPC permit application based on the Conditioning Plan was then subsequently prepared and submitted to the EA.

Schedule 4 of the PPCR 2000 sets out a specific permit application procedure for landfill sites. In summary, the application must contain:

- the waste description
- the site capacity
- the site description (including hydrology and geology)
- operating, monitoring and control details
- post-closure care procedures
- financial provisions for the above.

For further details, consult the DEFRA website and Landfill Regulatory Guidance Note 6, *Interpretation of the Engineering Requirements of Annex 1 of the 99/31 Landfill Directive*. Draft EA guidance has recently been published on the surrender of landfill permits or licences and requirements for completion. The consultation documents are available from the EA website.

8.5.2. End of life vehicles permits

The End of Life Vehicles Regulations 2003 SI 2635 (ELVR 2003) provide an example of the level of detail required to obtain a licence for a waste recovery activity. The ELVR 2003 currently make provisions for permits to be issued under the waste management licensing system. This will shortly be updated and brought into line with the new permitting regime.

Under Part VII, Regulation 45 of the ELVR 2003 all sites treating (scrapping) ELVs must obtain a waste management licence under the WMLR

161

1994.[7] The licence is issued by the EA on the condition that the site conforms to specified technical requirements (summarised in Table 8.3) and the general requirements laid down in Article 4 of the 75/442 Waste Framework Directive (please see Chapter 1). A waste management licence is not needed for the recovery of depolluted vehicles. A vehicle is depolluted when all of the operations specified in Schedule 5, Part 2 of the ELVR 2003 are complete.

8.5.3. Waste electrical and electronic equipment permits

The hope must be that the implementation deadline of August 2004 will be met to restore confidence, not only in local authorities but also in the EC. It may well be that a more cautious approach is being taken to the issuing of WEEE permits, but those involved in this recycling task should have regard to the consultation papers setting out the details and the timetable.

8.5.4. Hazardous waste permits

The EA has produced draft guidance on the recovery and disposal of Hazardous and non-Hazardous waste under the IPPC permitting regime. Hazardous waste is defined in the 91/689 Hazardous Waste Directive. The EA guidance aims to minimise the amount of operator and regulator work required, and improving IPPC permitting application consistency by providing:

- an operator's framework and methodology for addressing the relevant PPCR 2000 aspects
- indicative standards for BAT
- a structure for operator responses to issues arising during the application process—this will make any departures from the standards easily recognisable and comparable between applications.

The EA publication *Guidance for the Recovery and Disposal of Hazardous and Non Hazardous Waste: Integrated Pollution Prevention and Control (IPPC)* is available at www.environment-agency.gov.uk/commondata/105385/waste_bat_guidance_582354.pdf.

8.6. The waste management licensing system

The waste management licensing regime is regulated under ss.35–44 of the Environmental Protection Act 1990 (EPA 1990) and the WMLR 1994,[8] as amended by the Waste Management Licensing (Amendment) Regulations 1995

---

[7] The ELVR 2003 amended the Waste Management Licensing Regulations 1994 to include the licensing of sites for the treatment of ELVs. This will shortly be changed to the new permitting system.

Table 8.3: Summary of requirements under Schedule 5, Part 2 of the ELVR 2003

Site requirements for keeping ELVs	Site requirements for treating ELVs	Treatment operations for the depollution of ELVs
(a) Impermeable surfaces, spillage collection facilities, decanters, and cleanser–degreasers	(a) All requirements listed under the keeping of ELVs	(a) The removal of the battery or batteries
(b) Equipment for the treatment of water (including rainwater) in compliance with all applicable legislation concerning health and environmental matters	(b) Storage facilities appropriate for dismantled spare parts, including impermeable storage facilities for spare parts that are contaminated with oil	(b) The removal of the liquefied gas tank
	(c) Containers appropriate for the storage of batteries (whether electrolyte neutralisation is carried out on-site or elsewhere), filters, and condensers containing any PCB or PCT or both	(c) The removal or neutralisation of all potentially explosive components (e.g. air bags)
	(d) Storage tanks that are appropriate for the separate segregated storage of any fluid from a waste motor vehicle	(d) The removal and separate collection and storage of all fluids contained in the vehicle, but excluding any fluid which is necessarily retained for the reuse of the part concerned
	(e) Storage for used tyres without excessive stockpiling, and minimising any risk of fire	(e) The removal, so far as is feasible, of all components identified as containing mercury

[8] Northern Ireland's waste management licensing regime was brought fully into line with the UK in November 2003 under the Landfill Regulations (Northern Ireland) 2003. *De jure*, if not, *de facto*.

SI 288, 1996 SI 1279 and 2003 SI 595. A waste management licence is needed for the treatment, keeping or disposal of Controlled waste.

A licence is not needed if the activity is:

- listed as exempt under schedule 3 of the WMLR 1994, or
- already covered by the Integrated Pollution Prevention and Control (IPPC) permitting regime (some of the key waste management activities subject to the IPPC regime are listed in Table 8.2).

IPPC permitting is progressively replacing waste management licensing, but is not yet fully implemented. IPPC already applies to landfill sites and incineration, and some limited recovery operations. However, for the present the WMLR 1994 still apply to the waste management activities not yet subject to IPPC. (For the latest position on the transfer from waste management licensing to the IPPC permitting regime visit the EA and DEFRA websites.)

There are two types of waste management licence:

- a site licence for the treatment, storage, recovery or disposal of Controlled waste in or on land
- a mobile plant licence for the treatment, recovery or disposal of Controlled waste using mobile plant.

Waste management licensing can be complex, and is site-specific. For further details it is recommended that the local EA office should be contacted on 08459 333 111.

8.6.1. Exemptions from licences

Schedule 3 of the WMLR 1994 provides a list of activities exempt from licensing. The Waste Management Licensing (Amendment) Regulations 1995 SI 288 also provide for specific licensing exemptions. Exemptions tend to include:

- specified recovery activities
- waste placed in a receptacle awaiting contracted collection
- storage of construction and demolition waste to be used on site.

A useful summary of Schedule 3 exemptions is given in the EA online document *Exemptions from Needing a Waste Management Licence* (www.environment-agency.gov.uk/commondata/105385/ld3_exemptions_ta_ 627862ble) (this table is not relevant in Scotland, further details for which can be obtained from SEPA, www.sepa.org.uk).

All exempt activities must still be carried out without:

- endangering human health or harming the environment
- unacceptable risk to water, air, soil plants or animals
- causing a nuisance, e.g. through noise or odours
- adversely affecting the countryside or places of special interest.

The WMLR 1994 exemptions can still be subject to conditions, and waste not specifically named in the list will not be exempt. The exemptions stipulate the waste types, quantity limits, time limits for storage, methods of recovery and pollution control measures. Usually thresholds are specified for the amount of a given material that can be processed under the exemptions; for large quantities of material a licence will be needed. Often several exemptions may be required for different activities affecting one material, for example one for the storage of glass cullet prior to manufacture, and a second for its sorting, crushing and washing. Exemptions do not apply if the activity involves Special/Hazardous waste, unless specifically stated in Schedule 3.

Exempt activities need to be registered with the regulatory body, which must be provided with:

- information on the activity
- details of who is carrying out the activity
- the site address.

The regulatory body responsible for granting the authorisations are specified in Schedule 3, and is usually either the EA or the local authority.

The reuse of construction and demolition rubble on site is listed in the Schedule 3 exemptions; however, a PPC permit will be needed for certain activities such as concrete crushing.[9] Storage is allowed of up to 20,000 tonnes of waste concrete awaiting the permitted crushing activity at any time. In practice, contractors involved in demolition projects subject to tight programmes are dissuaded from crushing and reusing concrete because markets for the crushed material may be unpredictable, and storage requirements unknown in advance. PPC permits for processing or permission to store material may be needed at short notice. Contractors have found that the system can be subject to unpredictable delays and inconsistency, or involve costly conditions, which can be difficult to incorporate into a construction programme.

8.6.2. Who can hold a waste management licence?
Under s.74 EPA 1990 a person must be deemed to be 'fit and proper' to hold a waste management licence:

- the applicant must not hold a criminal record
- the activities must be managed by a technically competent person
- adequate financial provision must be made to discharge any duties or obligation arising from the licence.

---

[9] Concrete crushing must be authorised by the local authority as a Part B activity under the IPPC permitting regime.

The licence holder will be responsible for the obligations of the licence. Under regulation 4 of the WMLR 1994 the manager of a waste treatment, storage or disposal facility must hold an approved qualification to demonstrate technical competence. This can be obtained by undertaking a Certificate of Technical Competence (COTC) issued by the Waste Management Industry Training and Advisory Board (WAMITAB). The April 2003 revised standards have an emphasis on the safety and maintenance of plant located at the waste facility.

A person over the age of 55 having more than 5 years' experience as the manager of a facility could in the past be issued with a Certificate of Qualifying Experience (CQE), which entitled the holder to a 10-year transitional exemption from the need to hold a COTC. However, as of 10 August 2004 this exemption, known colloquially as grandfather rights, will no longer apply. People previously covered by the CQE will need to obtain a COTC by 10 August 2004 to continue in a waste facility management role. For further details visit www.wamitab.org.uk.

Any broker who arranges for the treatment, recovery or disposal of the waste on behalf of another person must be a registered broker of Controlled waste with the EA.

8.6.3. Application for a waste management licence

A waste management licence is issued by the EA under the EPA 1990. In 2002–2003, 7000 waste sites and activities were subject to EA licences. Planning permission must be obtained before a licence can be issued. Before granting or refusing a licence, the EA must consult the local planning authority to check that the planning permission is in place (under the IPPC permitting regime, one does not have to be obtained before the other) and notify the Health and Safety Executive of the planned activities. A licence will be refused if the EA believes that the activities will pollute the environment, harm human health, or seriously damage local amenities, or it will impose the necessary conditions to prevent pollution.

The information required for a licence application is listed in Schedule 1 of the WMLR 1994, which includes:

- contact and company details
- a detailed site plan
- a description of the activities involving the treatment, keeping or disposal of Controlled waste
- an indication of the quantity of waste to be handled on site
- the nature of the waste (a report is needed giving the results of sample analyses)
- details of likely contaminants.

Box 8.2: Blighted by flies

Licensing conditions can cover all manner of operational details. In a recent example, the EA criticised the management of a tip (*sic*) after residents complained of consecutive summers blighted by plagues of flies.

Source: *Halesowen News and Country Express*, 16 October 2003.

No doubt the flies were very real, but residents will anticipate them from a tip or a dump, less from a licensed engineering landfill site if it is well supervised with good internal disciplines and quality control.

The EA has standard licence application procedures, and the same form is used for new licences, transfers, modifications and surrenders. The form can be downloaded from the EA website (www.environment-agency.gov.uk/netregs). However, before applying, the local EA office should be contacted on 08459 333111. Guidance is also available from the DEFRA publication *Applying for a Waste Management Licence* (www.defra.gov.uk/environment/ waste/management/licence/index.htm).

8.6.4. Licence terms and conditions

Section 35 of the EPA 1990 states that the regulatory authority will issue the waste management licence on given terms and subject to specified conditions. The conditions specify any precautions that must be taken to prevent harm to human health, the environment or local amenities, and may require the holder to carry out works required before the licence can be granted. Requirements can be imposed before the activities can begin. They can also be imposed before an activity can be certified to have ceased.

Waste management licence terminology is different to that used in the terms recited in contracts. In Box 11.1 the continuing saga of 'Able UK unable' is briefly recited. At first, in September 2003, the EA mistakenly thought it had the power to grant Able UK Ltd a modification to its site licence to recycle US navy ships at Hartlepool. The modification in the licence increased the handling allowance from 24,500 tonnes per year to up to 200,000 tonnes per year. Unfortunately, this constituted an alteration to the site licence terms, and not just to the site licence conditions. Waste management licence terms, which are fundamental, cannot be lawfully altered. Licence conditions can be altered under s.37(1) EPA 1990. Therefore, a whole new site licence had to be sought for the increased tonnage.

8.6.5. Revocation and suspension of licences

Under s.38 EPA 1990 the EA can revoke a waste management site licence where:

- the holder, broker or contractor has ceased to be a fit and proper person, or
- activities would cause pollution or harm unable to be prevented by imposing more licence conditions.

Further details are given in the Environmental Licences (Suspension and Revocation) Regulations 1996 SI 508. According to the 2004 ENDS Report (347), one licence was revoked in the years 1996–2000, but since then 37 licences at 34 sites have been revoked: 13 for failing to comply with licence conditions, 10 because the licence holder died or the company was dissolved, and six where the licence fees were unpaid. Surprisingly, the first ever revocation for not being a fit and proper person came in November 2003, when a Merseyside transfer station operator was convicted of a string of waste-burning offences, and given a 3-year conditional discharge with costs of £30,000.

8.6.6. Modification, transfer, appeals and surrender of a licence

Under s.37 EPA 1990 conditions of an existing licence may be modified.[10] An application may be made by the licence holder, or the EA may impose a modification on an existing waste management licence. New conditions will usually be imposed under a modification. The case of Able UK Ltd, who applied to modify their site licence to treat waste ships at their Hartlepool recycling site, is summarised in Box 11.1. A copy of the EA original notice of modification for Able UK Ltd can be viewed at www.environment-agency.gov.uk/commondata/ 103599/able_notice_of_mod_594869.doc. It was later ruled that the changes requested could not be made under a modification, and instead a whole new licence had to be sought.

If an applicant or licence holder wishes to appeal against a rejection or modification, an appeal can be made under s.43 EPA 1990 to the DEFRA Secretary of State through notice in writing. Information must be provided on the grounds for appeal, along with other relevant information such as the consents, planning permissions, and a certificate of lawful use of the development, along with a copy of the application (if rejected) or the existing licence (if suspended or revoked). Usually appeals will be determined by an inspector appointed by the Planning Inspectorate, but the DEFRA Secretary of State may intervene in high-profile cases. Details are provided in Regulation 7 of the WMLR 1994. Notice of appeal forms can be obtained from the Planning Inspectorate, and guidance on the appeals process is available from the Planning Inspectorate website (www.planning-inspectorate.gov.uk/pins/appeals/environmental_appeals/ waste_man_licences_appeal_procedure_01.htm).

---

[10] The term 'conditions' in the context of waste management licensing has a different meaning to when it is used in the context of contractual arrangements. For further information please see Section 10.4.1 of this guide.

The Waste Management Licences (Consultation and Compensation) Regulations 1999 SI 481 amended the EPA 1990 (adding s.35A). Section 35A of the EPA 1990 applies in cases where a licence holder needs the consent of another person to carry out works in order to comply with requirements imposed by the licence. Anyone who grants rights to a licence holder to enable the holder to comply with his licence conditions is entitled to claim compensation from the licence holder. For example, conditions may be imposed on a landfill site[11] to carry out monitoring of groundwater within a 3-mile radius of the site, and access may be required from local landowners in order to comply.

Under s.40 EPA 1990 a licence can be transferred to another person (the transferee). The transferee must fulfil the requirements to hold a licence (please see Section 8.6.2 above). The transfer can be made regardless of whether it is partly revoked or suspended. Under s.39 EPA 1990 a licence may be surrendered and a certificate of completion issued by the EA. The EA has to approve the surrender of a site licence, because there have been many instances of long-term environmental impacts arising from historical landfills many of which were *ab initio* old-fashioned tips and dumps. The impact of a legitimately closed landfill site can be long-term and far-reaching, and at the beginning of the closure probably impossible accurately to estimate within 20–30 years. The biodegradation rate will be uncertain and can extend over generations. In addition, those sites that were tips or dumps may contain chemical wastes deposited before the Deposit of Poisonous Waste Act 1972 in containers which will not naturally stand the test of time. The potential pollution that could be caused by subsurface seepage is unpredictable. The EA may well determine certain measures which the site licence holder must undertake, and only time will tell whether those measures will prevent pollution for the next 50 years and longer. The licence surrender can only occur when the licence holder has demonstrated that the condition of the site is such that no pollution or harm to human health or amenity can be expected from it. Section 39 of the EPA 1990 states the procedures for considering an application to surrender a site licence and the issuing of certificates of completion.

8.6.7. Financial provision and insolvency of licence holder

Recent court decisions have determined that a waste management licence is 'onerous property', and thus can be disclaimed by the liquidator. Hence, creditors, and not the EA, will have the first claim on the waste management licence financial provisions, often held in a ring-fenced bank account (escrow). A High Court ruling, subject to an appeal, was made in November 2003 in favour of a

---

[11] Landfill sites have recently been subject to the new PPC permitting regime, but were previously covered by waste management licensing.

company's creditors, leaving the EA not entitled to the £375,000 provision for a West Yorkshire site abandoned in 2001.

The EA believes that whilst a waste management licence is in force, costs for any EA emergency work should be recovered from the licence holder, rather than the financial provisions. In future, a closed-purpose trust will take the place of an escrow account, and the trust will be for the operator to use for remediation subject to the EA controls.

After the introduction of the Landfill Regulations 2002 SI 1559, landfill sites now come under the new IPPC permitting regime (see above). As a result of the change in the regulations (often more expensive to comply with) many landfill sites previously covered by the waste management licensing system had to be abandoned, and a fund supported by landfill tax revenue has been required to manage some of these sites. Since existing sites will have to be upgraded under the PPC permitting regime there will be a higher risk of insolvency.

The EA also believes that because the 99/31 Landfill Directive is more explicit than the EPA 1990, it will no longer be possible for liquidators to disclaim a permit as opposed to a licence as onerous property. It has requested DEFRA to provide greater clarity so as to remove the risk that funding from the operator's financial provision will not continue to be available at abandoned sites.

It may well be that DEFRA will have to set up a body to manage abandoned sites, since such a role assigned to the EA would more than stretch the EA's resources, and it would not be compatible with the role of the EA as regulator.

8.7. Monitoring of facilities subject to a licence or a permit

The 75/442 Waste Framework Directive (as amended by the 91/156 Waste Directive) requires regulators to undertake appropriate periodic inspections of

Box 8.3: Rise in local air pollution control inspectors

All 388 local authorities responded to a DEFRA survey on local authority inspection rates on complementing Local Air Pollution Control (LAPC). Local authorities should inspect most sites twice a year. Earlier, DEFRA had named and shamed 31 poorly performing councils.

It is now offering a carrot-and-stick policy. Six awards will be given for Best Practice in pollution control, e.g. management planning, innovative approaches achieving compliance. The average number of inspectors for processes other than petrol stations and small old waste burners rose from 1.5% in 2000–2001 to 1.9% in 2002–2003.

Source: DEFRA LAPC Statistical Survey 2002–2003.

authorised facilities. The Environment Agency uses the Operator Pollution Risk Appraisal (OPRA) procedure to assess the risk a waste management facility poses to the environment. It also determines the necessary management systems to control the risks. The regulation and monitoring of sites is prioritised by comparing OPRA outputs. It also affects fees and charges for licences or permits. OPRA has recently been renamed Environmental Protection OPRA, or (EP) OPRA. For further information see the 2004 EA guidance documents *Waste Management Licensing: Risk Assessment Inspection Frequencies* and *Licensed Waste Management Facility: Site Inspection Methodology*, available from the EA website (www.environment-agency.gov.uk).

Chapter 9

Environmental criminal and civil law simplified and the control of fly-tipping

A crime is an offence against the state in contravention of the current criminal law and, if a conviction results either in the magistrates' court or before a judge and jury in a Crown Court or other criminal court, can involve a fine, custodial sentence or community service. The object of a criminal charge is to punish the offender, not to compensate the victim, although compensation orders under the Powers of Criminal Courts (Sentencing Act) 2000 may be made. The offence could be relatively trivial, e.g. driving just over the tolerated speed limit, or serious, such as causing death through dangerous driving. Magistrates' courts in England and Wales hear and decide, with the help of their clerks, the least serious of offences, and have limited sentencing powers. Crown Courts under the Courts Act 1971 sit with a judge and jury and hear the more serious (indictable) offences.

Under civil law a party that has been wronged can sue for a suitable remedy, such as financial compensation for damages or an injunction. Civil law includes the law of tort (the French for 'you are wrong' is '*vous avez tort*'). Under the law of tort an individual can protect their private interests, e.g. through an action based on negligence (see below) or libel. Civil law includes contract and commercial law, family law, e.g. divorce and adoption, and the law of property.

Public law is concerned with the functions of governmental organisations, including the regions and local authorities. Public law is sometimes called constitutional or administrative law.

The sources of law which provide a structure for the criminal, civil and public law are:

- Statute law, which is Acts passed by both Houses of Parliament. This is new legislation (e.g. the Water Act 2003), and is able to supersede the provisions of earlier Acts or hitherto established case law. An example is the tax payer who has, perfectly and properly, construed the meaning of a section in a Finance Act to his personal or his company's financial advantage, but the Chancellor's Treasury drafters in the next Finance Act have then introduced a fresh section to close the previously unforeseen loophole. Some EU law is directly enforceable in the UK through the European Communities Act 1972 (please see Chapter 1).

- Common law, which comprises rules arising from previous cases, customs and common practice.

9.1. The criminal law

When reviewing the often esoteric judgements in high-profile cases such as Mayer Parry and Palin Granit (please see Chapter 2), it is easy to forget that these are essentially cases subject to the criminal law. The companies were prosecuted for contravening the environmental and regulatory regimes of their particular country, and that country's criminal court referred the case for a legal analysis to the European Court of Justice (ECJ), but not for a possible conviction, since that is not within the ECJ's remit. At the ECJ there is no requirement for professional law practice experience to qualify for selection, and the court consists of academic lawyers, professional parties and public servants, mostly, naturally, coming from very different legal systems to that of the UK.

Strict liability under criminal law occurs where there is no requirement in the particular Act that the prosecution should prove that the accused intended or could have foreseen that his acts might have resulted in the commission of an offence. There has been a trend towards imposing strict liability in relation to environmental offences, so as to place a serious duty on those who have responsibility for potentially polluting activities. An example is the principal offence relating to the pollution of Controlled waters under s.85 of the Water Resources Act 1991, which imposes liability on any person who causes or knowingly permits the entry of any poisonous, noxious or polluting matter to Controlled waters (please see Chapter 12).

For a possible environmental offence the general remedy is either a criminal prosecution under a specific Act, e.g. a breach of the Water Resources Act 1991 by a farmer allowing nitrates to pollute a river, or a waste manager contravening a condition of a recycling facility waste management licence, resulting in a breach of the Environmental Protection Act 1990 (EPA 1990).

Penalties for environmental offences in the last decade imposed by magistrates' courts and the Crown Court have generally thought to be too light to deter. The pendulum may be beginning to swing the other way. There is now a perceptible trend for directors and senior management to appear in the dock personally charged for their responsibility in corporate mismanagement. Regulation 17 of the Landfill Regulations 2002 SI 1559 states that where an offence committed by a body corporate is 'proved to have been committed with the

Box 9.1: Naming and shaming damages business

In a recent Environment Agency (EA) conference, United Utilities was named as the one of the worst environmental offenders. The company received 10% of the £3 million fines issued in 2003. The Chief Executive Officer of United Utilities stated that 'I have no doubt in my mind that bad environmental performance damages your bottom line'. He added that 'The national media had a field day'. The company has since invested in environmental measures to improve its environmental performance.

Source: *Environment Business News Briefing*, 7 November 2003.

The proof will be in the pudding.

consent or connivance of, or to have been attributable to any neglect on the part of, any director, manager, secretary or other similar officer of the body corporate, he as well as the body corporate shall be guilty of that offence and shall be liable to be proceeded against and punished accordingly.'

There can be appreciable social disgrace reflected among peer groups in being fairly charged with an environmental offence even if the Magistrates' Bench or Crown Court jury are not finally persuaded to convict. Potential social disgrace can be an effective deterrence, although certainly not amongst the hardened criminal fraternity — who are not absent, alas, from the UK environmental scene.

9.1.1. Fly-tipping

One of the more common waste mismanagement criminal offences is fly-tipping, which is the illegal deposit or disposal of waste in an unauthorised manner and location. It pollutes public spaces in both urban and rural areas, is a health risk, especially to children, and can cause significant environmental damage. Its clean-up poses a heavy financial burden on local authorities and affected land owners. Under s.33(1) EPA 1990 a person shall not:

- deposit controlled waste, or
- knowingly (see below) cause, or
- knowingly permit controlled waste to be deposited
  - in or on any land or
  - by means of any mobile plant

except in accordance with an appropriate waste management licence or permit, nor treat keep of dispose of waste in a manner likely to

- cause pollution of the environment or
- harm to human health.

Box 9.2: Dumping costs property developer £25,500

A Wiltshire Company and one of its directors were fined £7500 in November 2003 after the EA received a public complaint about a 2 m high pile of old beds, plastic pipes and broken furniture. The property developer and farmer who owned the site was fined £2500 for depositing waste at an unlicensed site. Both were ordered to pay costs of £9000.

Source: The ENDS Report 347.

Perhaps cheap at the price? Somebody must have known what was going on.

These offences do not apply to a householder's waste on their own premises.[1]

Allowances are made for waste placed in a receptacle awaiting scheduled collection, such as the office litter bin or a transfer station. It is important to distinguish between a statutory rule to include materials as waste under the licensing or permitting system and, what can be confusing, the approximately 45 statutory exemptions from the waste management site licensing rules, as explained in Chapter 8. Under regulation 3 of the Landfill Regulations 2002 SI 1559 any site which is used for the temporary storage of waste intended for disposal for more than 1 year is classified as a landfill, and thus requires a landfill permit under the Landfill Regulations 2002. As a general rule, waste intended for recovery or treatment can be stored for up to 3 years without a permit.

Some activities, such as storing crushed concrete awaiting reuse on a construction site, are listed as exempt from licensing under Schedule 3 of the Waste Management Licensing Regulations 1994 (subject to specified conditions). A list of exemptions is available from the EA website (www.environment-agency.gov.uk/commondata/105385/ld3_exemptions_ta_627862ble).

There is a difference between knowingly causing and knowingly permitting, in that the operator of a water reclamation plant will be treated as causing the discharge of polluting substances from its works, even though the offending substances were discharged upstream and then into the sewage system without the operator's knowledge or consent, e.g. see the *National Rivers Authority* v. *The Yorkshire Water Services Ltd* 1993.[2]

There are many discussions in law journals on the meaning of the terms 'knowingly', 'cause' and 'permit'.[3] In summary, the key differences are:

---

[1] For the full text of the EPA 1990 visit www.hmso.gov.uk.

[2] House of Lords Judgement, Session 1997–1998, 5 February 1998 (www.parliament.the-stationery-office.co.uk).

[3] In the context of waste on land, and the wording of s.33 EPA 1990 there is a practical discussion in *Garner's Environmental Law*, Binder 1, Division II/117A, issue 74.

Box 9.3: Firm fined for pollution caused by thieves

A generator was stolen from an unsecured construction site, resulting in a spillage of diesel into a ditch 10 m from a drinking-water aqueduct. Ashtead Plant Hire, who were the luckless victims of the theft, were fined £5000 for the incident for which they were only indirectly, but ultimately, responsible.

Source: *Environment Business News Briefing*, 18 December 2003.

- 'Cause' involves a positive act (but not necessarily criminal intent), e.g. instructing a member of staff to deposit some Controlled waste within the factory curtilage. Causing pollution is a strict liability offence.
- 'Permitting'[4] does not require a positive act, but it does require an awareness or turning a blind eye on the part of the defendant before he can be said to permit something.
- 'Knowingly' means that the company has a knowledge of the breach and is aware of the deposit, and a knowledge that it is not in accordance with the terms of the licence.

The following penalties apply for fly-tipping:

- £20,000 or 6 months in prison from a magistrates' court
- an unlimited fine and 2 years imprisonment from a Crown Court
- up to 5 years imprisonment (or either of the above) if the offence involves Special/Hazardous waste.

The s.33(7) EPA 1990 defence of acting under instruction from an employer may in the future be abolished (and it should be), although other defences that:

- all reasonable precautions were taken
- it was an emergency action to avoid real public danger

will remain. Special measures to counter fly-tipping were taken in the Control of Pollution (Amendment) Act 1989 (see Chapter 11), under which all owners of vehicles transporting Controlled waste in the course of a business or for profit must be registered with the EA.

In 2002, the Department for Environment, Food and Rural Affairs (DEFRA) issued a consultation on fly-tipping, which included the concepts of:

- a waste duty of care for householders
- new powers to allow local authorities to investigate fly-tipping cases, and to

---

[4] Note that 'permitting', of course, is also the term applied to the licensing of waste management facilities under the new Integrated Pollution Prevention Control regime (please see Chapter 8).

- require occupiers to remove tipped waste from the land on which it had been tipped.

Developers planning large-scale demolition and/or construction projects would have to produce site waste management plans for the local authority to ensure that legal disposal routes for site waste were in place before work was carried out. An excellent idea, not before its time. Construction, demolition and excavation activities account for the greatest proportion of fly-tipped waste in urban areas, and is one of the main fly-tipping growth areas, accounting for a quarter of annual incidents.

All waste collection authorities must develop a strategic approach to dealing with fly-tipping, including joint working between councils and other bodies such as the police. The Scottish Fly-tipping Forum, for example, brings together regulators, land owners and waste firms. It is hoped that the forum will produce the expected results, and not become a lethargic talking shop which steadily declines in its efficacy, as many in the UK have previously done.

Forceful new measures are needed, with accurate and truthful reporting of their efficacy, since there are approximately 50,000 reported fly-tipping incidents per year in England and Wales costing £150 million per year.[5] It is also noteworthy that:

- prior to 2002 fly-tipping was not distinguishable from other waste offences on the EA database
- in 2002 the EA prosecuted 252 offences with £228,620 in fines
- in 2003 (to October) 210 offences were prosecuted, with £225,702 in fines.

Those local authorities, particularly in urban areas, who have been struggling against the real villains will have been cautiously encouraged by the Anti-Social Behaviour Act 2003, whereby waste collection authorities are empowered to stop, search and seize vehicles suspected of unlawful deposit of waste. The Act requires the EA and local authorities to provide DEFRA with summary data on the fly-tipping incidents, in order to target resources more effectively. DEFRA has funded the EA development of a fly-tipping database, which was launched in April 2004, and there are proposals for a national fly-tipping abatement force.[6]

---

[5] *Fly-tipping Strategy and Consultation on Statutory Direction for the Environment Agency and Waste Collection Authorities on the Unlawful Disposal of Waste*, February 2004 (www.defra.gov.uk/corporate/consult/antisocial-flytipping/index.htm).
[6] After the decline of the power of the Drugs Tsar, perhaps the Fly-tipping Tsar will have greater success.

Box 9.4: Guy Fawkes cover-up leads to fines

In November 2002 a demolition firm invited local residents to participate in bonfire night celebrations around a large bonfire: according to reports it burned for 4 days, and consisted of three lorry loads of demolition waste, containing timber, cables and old carpet. Local residents reported the smoke and smell to the EA, who investigated and successfully prosecuted the Bournemouth-based company responsible for the fire. Trojan Developments was fined £5000 for burning the Controlled waste, and the individual who lit the fire was ordered to pay a total of £1072.

Source: *Resource Management and Recovery*, 23 January 2004.

9.1.2. Smoke, burning and bonfires

One of the direct or indirect consequences of fly-tipping can be the burning of such materials, thus forming both informal and formal bonfires, e.g. for 5 November celebrations. Here the Clean Air Act 1993 is relevant. The Office of the Deputy Prime Minister (ODPM) has warned that bonfires may add to background air pollution levels, and that putting waste on bonfires could be illegal. Waste site management licence holders may jeopardise their site licence if caught burning waste on bonfires. The Clean Air Act 1993 specifically restricts the emission of dark smoke from any chimney and the emission of dark smoke (darker than shade 2 on the Ringelmannn Chart) from any industrial or trade premises, whether or not from a chimney. According to s.79(7) EPA 1990, smoke includes soot, ash and gritty particles.

There are quite complex exemption rules for burning waste without a waste management licence. Under Schedule 3 of the Waste Management Licensing 1994 SI 1056 there are storage limits for waste without a licence prior to burning.[7] Wood bark or other plant matter (but not including treated wood) can be burnt in the open where it was produced on railway or drainage or EA land, or on other land as a result of demolition work. The persons burning must be burning their own waste and burning less than 10 tonnes every 24 hours. This is a complex and detailed area of waste management law, so advice before beginning any burning operation at all, after scrutinising any relevant licences or permits, should be sought from the local EA office.

The burning of waste in landfills has always been a recurrent problem, not least because historically in the lawless days before the Deposit of Poisonous Waste Act 1972 it was a practical way to retain tipping void space. The fires

---

[7] A summary of all waste management licence exemptions is given on the EA website, and is currently available at www.environment-agency.gov.uk/commondata/105385/ld3_exemptions_ta_627862ble.

179

became more frequent after the 1972 Act, and often included the site hut since the fire coincidentally could destroy any consignment documentation or, more likely, conceal the absence of any, if the statutory authorities, more often than not in those days the National Rivers Authority, were having a drive to enforce the notification provisions of the Deposit of Poisonous Waste Act 1972.

A more straightforward cause of site fires was the controlled burning of cable covering in order to recycle the inner copper wiring. Today, even recently well-engineered landfill sites can suffer from subsurface spontaneous combustion, as biodegradation can cause significant temperature rises, and oxygen is drawn in through the permeable waste. Such fires can be notoriously difficult to approach in order to control and manage, and the EA should be notified and the written and signed-off emergency procedures followed, immediately combustion is noticed.

9.2. The civil law

Under civil law, a person or company that has been wronged can sue another person for compensation for loss or damage. The use of the civil law in the environmental context is principally in the areas of nuisance and negligence, where the evidence between the claiming plaintiff and the defendant will be assessed by a judge, not with a jury. The burden of proof is different in that the plaintiff must in general terms prove his case on the balance of probabilities, as opposed to the prosecution's duty in criminal cases to satisfy the jury beyond all reasonable doubt.[8]

There can also be liability even if a defendant in a civil action had taken all reasonable care to prevent damage occurring. This is sometimes called no fault liability or strict liability (please see the example in Chapter 12). Proponents of the imposition of strict liability maintain that it can provide an incentive for businesses to take enhanced precautions to prevent damage from occurring. The 1866 case of *Rylands* v. *Fletcher* has important implications for contemporary environmental liability. It established that a person has strict liability for any damage caused for anything brought onto his land which is likely to cause damage if it escapes, irrespective of fault if the damage was foreseeable. Foreseeability of the damage actually caused is a prerequisite of liability, normally for nuisance and negligence, but also for cases falling under the *Rylands* v. *Fletcher* rule, a rule whose strictness in varying physical circumstances and social climates has changed through the years, thus demonstrating

---

[8] In criminal law, guilt must be proved beyond all reasonable doubt. However, the Government is currently considering moves to allow proof on the balance of probabilities to apply to terrorist suspects currently held without trial under the Terrorism Act 2000. The debate continues.

the flexibility of English case law. Others in the EU with different systems of law would aver that the law should be more certain.

9.3. Nuisance

An interference with someone's use or enjoyment of their land, or the amenities of their locality or community, can amount to nuisance. The law recognises three types of nuisance:

- private nuisance at common law
- public nuisance at common law
- statutory nuisance under the EPA 1990.

9.3.1. Private nuisance at common law

Private nuisance is an unlawful interference with a person's use or enjoyment of land or some right over it, or in connection with it (e.g. through the generation of noise, odour, vibration or dust). It is concerned with infringement of private property rights, and this tends to limit its applicability as a means of redress for environmental harm. To succeed in private nuisance, a plaintiff must have an interest in the land affected by the nuisance.

Cambridge Water (Box 9.5), as it is informally known, was a case involving solvents leaking from a leather factory which polluted a groundwater aquifer.

Box 9.5: Liability for damage to a neighbour: an important case

In 1994, the Cambridge Water Company (CWC) brought a civil action in private nuisance against Eastern Counties Leather plc (ECL), the operator of a leather tannery, to recover £1 million it had incurred in providing an alternative water supply when its existing supply failed to meet the quality standard set by the 80/778 Drinking Water Directive.

The claim failed because ECL did not know, and could not reasonably have foreseen in 1976 that the migration of the chemical through the cracked concrete tannery floor would have caused the pollution of groundwater and the damage suffered by CWC many years later. Similar damage is, however, in 2004 much more likely to be held to be reasonably foreseeable. But even if the claim for compensation had succeeded, ECL would only have had to pay CWC's cost of commissioning a new water abstraction point, and not for the clean-up of the groundwater. The environmental damage itself would not have had to be remediated.

Source: House of Lords 1994 Judgement in *Cambridge Water Company* v. *Eastern Counties Leather plc* (1994) 1 ALL ER 531. (For those interested in how the law works in practice and how the environment is managed, this is an easy and most interesting case to read. It is available from several online sources, e.g. www.swarb.co.uk/c/hl/1993camb-east.html.)

The House of Lords held that the distinct principles earlier cited in the well-known Victorian case of *Rylands* v. *Fletcher* should still be applicable, but only when the particular pollution pathway was not foreseeable. However, the existence of the factory was deemed to be a non-natural use of the land. It is possible, therefore, that a landfill or an incinerator is also a non-natural use of land to which civil liability without fault might be applicable.

Ten years later, in *Transco* v. *Stockport Metropolitan Borough Council (MBC)* 2003, the House of Lords was invited to review the applicability of the *Rylands* v. *Fletcher* strict liability rule, but declined to do so. Hence this part of the civil environmental law of liability is still uncertain. In the Transco case water was supplied through a large pipe to a block of flats belonging to Stockport MBC. The water had been leaking for some time and had damaged a Transco gas pipeline some distance away. No negligence was alleged by Transco against Stockport MBC, and since this was a one-off event, it did not fall within the normal principles of nuisance law, which requires some element of continuous interference. So, was Stockport MBC strictly liable? The House of Lords decided that it was not, and that the existence of the large pipe was necessary to carry out its statutory duty to supply water to its rate payers, and so would not be a non-natural use of the land.

9.3.2. Public nuisance

A public nuisance at common law is both a tort and a crime. It has been defined as a nuisance which materially affects the reasonable comfort and convenience of life of a particular class of people, e.g. a row of houses. Unlike private nuisance, a proprietary interest in land is not required, but a plaintiff will have to show that he has suffered substantial direct damage over and above that suffered by the relevant group of people as a whole.

Under the common law of public nuisance, waste accumulation (usually refuse or putrescibles[9]), the deposit of waste on land resulting in odours, dust or other interference to a neighbour, or the escape of waste resulting in the pollution of neighbouring land, can all result in an action in tort.

9.3.3. Statutory nuisance

The law of statutory nuisance has no place under civil law, but it is included here to contrast with private and public nuisance, summarised above. The offence of statutory nuisance was first introduced in the Public Health Act 1936, under which local authorities could bring a prosecution against a party allowing an offensive smell to annoy neighbours, or allowing his property to get into such disorder that rats and other vermin cause damage to his neighbour's health and

---

[9] This does not include piles of inert material.

property. Local authorities from 1939 to 1945 were, however, preoccupied with more pressing matters (please see Chapter 1). Hence the Regulations were slow to be enforced, and there was little case law, so the offence remained undeveloped until the 1950s.

Statutory nuisance continues now as a criminal offence under Part III s.79 EPA 1990. Failing local authority action, an individual may apply to the magistrates' court. Public nuisance is a common law criminal offence, but can also be a tort, and under the Local Government Act 1972, local authorities have the power to prosecute under public nuisance. The Attorney General may also prosecute, and an individual can, with the consent of the Attorney General, apply to take out an injunction. All statutory nuisances must have an element that is prejudicial to health (s.79(1) EPA 1990), although actual prejudice to health is not necessary, since just a material interference with personal comfort can be held to be prejudicial to health. A part of a successful prosecution is that the damage caused by the nuisance is shown to have been reasonably foreseeable. Putrefying rubbish (not inert) which has accumulated on land may amount to a statutory nuisance under s.55 of the Town and Country Planning Act 1990.

9.4. Negligence

The tort of negligence occurs when:

- one party owes a duty to another
- there is a breach of that duty and, as a result,
- damage occurs which could reasonably have been foreseeable.

For example, the owners of a composting plant have a duty to monitor and record the results in liaison with the local environmental health and EA officers for any aerial pollution that might cause harm to the health of the neighbours and their children. If illness occurs, liability can result, but only if there has been found to have been a breach of the duty of care[10] by the managers and owners of that composting plant and that the cause of the foreseeable illness was shown on the balance of probabilities to have been the composting plant. No easy task, because, for example, contributory negligence could be alleged against a neighbouring water treatment plant. Likewise, if a consulting engineer who designs or supervises the construction or installation of a landfill site gas control system without proper professional care and an explosion results in which neighbours

---

[10] The duty of care in negligence preceded, by some 400 years, the statutory phrase Duty of Care under s.34 (see Chapter 10) of the EPA 1990. The EPA 1990 phrase was borrowed from the historical law by the Royal Commission on Environmental Pollution in 1985.

are injured, then that landfill engineer could well be liable for the ensuing personal injuries and physical damage.

Liability, generally, is not strict or absolute, but is based on the concept of reasonable care and skill. A local authority may be liable in negligence if it unreasonably fails to remove rubbish from land of which it is the occupier, when that land adjoins the highway, where foreseeable injury results. For example, a boy was injured by an exploding aerosol can in detritus left as the result of a dustman's strike (see *Woolfall* v. *Knowsley Borough Council* 1992, Garner's Environmental Law, Division 0, p. 0/5). In general, no compensation can be recovered for purely economic loss.

9.5. Environmental liability

Most extant environmental law is based on the principle of prevention, traditionally through the licensing and permitting regimes. Regulatory bodies do have the power to seek the remediation of environmental damage under some existing UK legislation. There is strict liability under the:

- Pollution Prevention and Control Regulations 2000 SI 1973. If pollution occurs as a breach of permit conditions, the regulator can stipulate steps for that pollution to be remedied. The regulator can also take emergency action to prevent imminent pollution and reclaim the costs from the operator.
- Part II of the EPA 1990 (as amended by the Waste Management Licensing Regulations 1994 SI 1056). Landfill operators must avert or remedy environmental damage for licensed activities.
- Contaminated land section set out in Part IIA of the EPA 1990. Anybody who causes or knowingly permits activities to result in contaminated land has strict liability for environmental harm or water pollution. Local authorities have the power to remediate and reclaim the costs, or serve a remediation notice.

Liability for environmental damage may however be wider in the years to come. In January 2002 the European Commission adopted a proposal for a Directive on Environmental Liability with regard to the Prevention and Restoration of Environmental Damage (Cod 020017). A framework political agreement was reached in June 2003, and a common position agreed in September 2003.[11] The Directive may be adopted in 2004, with an implementation deadline in 2007. This Directive concerns the broader public interest in protecting the

---

[11] See Macrory R. and Woods M. (2003), *Modernising Environmental Justice — Regulation and the Role of an Environmental Tribunal*, DEFRA, London.

quality of life of the environment itself. It is based on the polluter pays principle (please see Chapter 1), making companies and relevant individuals liable for damage caused to the environment itself (e.g. deterioration of a water body, damage to land or reduced biodiversity), affecting facilities such as:

- reclamation and recycling plant sites
- landfill sites
- incineration plants
- installations producing dangerous chemicals or releasing heavy metals into water or the air.

The proposed Directive recognises that the environment is unable to assert and enforce any rights of its own to be protected, or to be remediated when it is damaged. It provides a framework for the public authorities to do this on behalf of the environment and its citizens.

Offenders found to be acting contrary to the Directive's Articles could be ordered to pay for:

- remediation of the damaged environment directly
- measures to prevent imminent damage
- reimbursement of the competent authorities who, in default, remediate the damage or take action to prevent damage.

The regime would be enforced by competent authorities (please see Chapter 4) in the public interest. This would include:

- stipulating remediation standards
- taking remedial action
- recovering the costs from the offender.

Defences might include:

- compliance with permitting conditions
- authorised emissions that were not considered to be harmful at the time of permitting, and where the best available scientific and technical knowledge were applied
- natural phenomena
- damage resulting from armed conflict.

Each Member State of the EU would have a subsidiary responsibility for remediation. The public and non-governmental organisations (NGOs) directly affected by actual or potential damage may request action or a judicial review of the competent authority's actions.

But every new law has a cost as well as an anticipated benefit. The Union of Industrial and Employers' Confederations of Europe is concerned that the new Directive would result in undefined and unquantifiable liability claims for environmental damage, which could result in bankruptcy and insurance problems for companies of all sizes. It was recently reported that professional indemnity insurance for environmental consultants, particularly those working in waste management, has increased in some cases by six times from 2003 to 2004.

For the latest Government position visit www.defra.gov.uk/environment/ liability.

9.6. An environmental court

There has also been a continual movement over the last 2 years, controversial in some quarters, towards a specialist environmental court to hear all civil environmental cases, and backed by changes to court rules to relieve the financial burden on applicants bringing public interest cases. This follows on from several recent special studies which have seemingly supported the reform of the legal system, especially the creation of an environmental tribunal and the use of civil fines for environmental offences. The UK Government originally promised to ratify the pan-European Aarhaus Convention in 2001, but has so far failed to do so. This convention would enable members of the public with a sufficient interest, to question the substantive and procedural legality of environmental permitting decisions as well as acts or omissions by private or public bodies in breach of environmental law.

The principal difficulty is that the Government is reluctant to ratify the Aarhaus Convention, because this would mean significant reforms of its judicial review system. Another historical stumbling block is the application of the current rules on costs whereby the losing side in a civil case pays the winner's costs. In late 2003 Able UK (please see Box 11.1) informed Friends of the Earth that its legal fees for a 1-day judicial review hearing in the US Navy ship decommissioning case would amount to £100,000. In the event, Able UK lost that round of the litigation, although other rounds are expected to follow in 2004–2005.

Box 9.6: A special environmental court?

> The Macrory Report published by University College, London, funded by DEFRA, recommended an environmental tribunal, following the 1989 Carnwarth Report on the planning relationship with environmental enforcement. Certain environmental cases are believed by some to be too technically complex for the Magistrates' and sometimes the High Courts. New proposals are being discussed for an appeals body, and eventually an environmental court with perhaps an increased workload for environmental lawyers.

The NGOs' hope is that the courts themselves should have the power to waive the loser pays all principle when the subject matter of the case is decided by the judge to be in the public interest. Of course, the sequential difficulty might be that the side which did not find favour with the first judge would appeal that judge's decision, and then go to the Court of Appeal, perhaps the House of Lords, to determine whether the case was in the public interest or not. What is that sound, please? Could it be lawyers smiling?

Chapter 10

Health and safety, the Duty of Care Regulations and basic contractual considerations

It is important to be aware of the complementary nature of health and safety at work legislation with environmental legislation, particularly the Environmental Protection Act 1990 (EPA 1990). Section 34 of the EPA 1990 Duty of Care as explained in Section 10.3 below could well have been a Health and Safety at Work Regulation, in that clearly the containment and integrity and clear documentation of all waste loads could be considered a typical health and safety matter. A fundamental understanding of and close attention to contemporary health and safety at work practices is essential, the ethos of which was so well and simply expressed in the Robens Report.[1]

This chapter also covers the bare bones of waste management contracting. The contract serves, *inter alia*, as a discharge of a health and safety at work obligation between the waste producer and the waste contractor (the transporter and/or disposer). It provides not only a record of the waste description but also sets out how it is to be handled, transported and treated and when the ownership of the waste material is passed on.

10.1. The relationship between the Health and Safety Executive and waste management

10.1.1. Health and safety at work

The Health and Safety at Work etc. Act 1974 (HASAWA 1974) provides for the health, safety and welfare of all persons at work, and for protecting others against risks to health and safety in connection with the activities of persons at work. All employers have a duty to:

---

[1] Committee for Health and Safety at Work (1972), *Report 1970–1972* (Chairman Lord Robens), The Stationery Office (Cmnd 5034), London.

- Write and update a health and safety policy and bring it to the attention of all employees. Even more important, an active and respected health and safety manual will contain continually updated standard operating procedures for every aspect of the organisation's work, however small. Fires prey on the SMEs, if only because there will be no 24-hour safety patrol.
- Provide and maintain safe plant and work systems.
- Ensure the safe use, handling, storage and transport of articles and substances.
- Provide information, instruction, training and supervision.
- Provide a safe working environment.
- Ensure that the public are not exposed to unacceptable risk as a result of the employer's activities (there is no such concept as zero risk, in the same way that there is no concept of zero waste; please see Chapter 5).
- Not charge for anything provided for the employee's personal safety which is required by a specific law.
- Consult safety representatives.
- Provide welfare facilities

HASAWA 1974 likewise places duties on employees to:

- take reasonable care for themselves and others
- cooperate with the employer in the execution of the employer's health and safety duties
- not interfere with or misuse anything provided for health and safety benefit.

HASAWA 1974 is criminal law and imposes duties not just on employers and employees, but on:

Box 10.1: £200,000 fine for employee's death during plant overhaul

In 2001 a fitter at a scrap metal processing plant was struck on the head by a two-chain sling, lifting a large steel plate. Mayer Parry Recycling Ltd was prosecuted by the Health and Safety Executive (HSE) under s.2(1) HASAWA 1974, requiring employers to take all reasonable care for the health and safety of their workforce. The HSE Principal Inspector said: 'This fine properly reflects the seriousness of the offence and hopefully will send a strong message to the industry to tighten up health and safety management, particularly when considering lifting operations, which can have such a devastating affect when they go wrong.'

Source: Health and Safety Executive Press Release (www.hse.gov.uk).

Box 10.2: Criminal prosecution for perimeter fence inadequately maintained

> In 2001 children broke through a landfill perimeter fence. A boy fell 18 m to his death. A coroner recorded an accidental death verdict. At the inquest it was clear that people could access the site through a part of the fence.
>
> HSE prosecuted because the company had failed to operate the site in order to ensure that, so far as is reasonably practicable, even trespassing children were not exposed to risks. The Environment Agency (EA), just 3 days before, had noted that the perimeter fence was adequate to prevent people from entering the site but had not inspected the particular section of fence near where the accident had happened.
>
> This tragic example demonstrates the complementary role of the EA and HSE. BIFFA's health and safety support manager said: 'This is a timely reminder to check all perimeter fences, barriers and warning signs.' And so it was.
>
> Source: *Resource Management and Recovery*, 13 June 2003.

- the self-employed
- designers
- manufacturers
- importers
- materials' suppliers
- people in control of premises
- members of the public.

In 1993 six health and safety at work Regulations were introduced under the HASAWA 1974. The six pack, as the Regulations are known, was introduced to implement EU Health and Safety Directives, which standardised requirements across the EU in order to promote fair competition between Member States. The Regulations cover:

- management of health and safety at work
- manual handling operations
- display screen equipment
- workplace (health, safety and welfare)
- provision and use of work equipment
- personal protective equipment.

Waste management facilities are subject to regular inspections by the HSE inspectors, who are answerable to the Health and Safety Commission. All of the activities associated with these operations require a risk assessment under the Management of Health and Safety at Work Regulations 1999 SI 3242.

For further information on the health and safety at work Regulations visit www.hse.gov.uk or consult your local HSE office (08701 545500).

10.1.2. The Construction (Design and Management) Regulations

The Construction (Design and Management) Regulations (CDM) 1994 SI 3140 were introduced to improve safety management in construction industry projects. They set out responsibilities for health and safety aspects of design and construction projects. For further information read the HSE Information Sheet *Construction (Design and Management) Regulations 1994: The Role of the Planning Supervisor* (www.hse.gov.uk/pubns/cis40.pdf).

10.1.3. Technical competence for the management of facilities

Under s.74 EPA 1990, waste facilities must be managed by a fit and proper person as defined by requirements set out by the Secretary of State. This requirement was defined in the Waste Management Licensing Regulations 1994 SI 1056 as 'technical competence'. A waste facility manager must obtain a Certificate of Technical Competence, which is issued by the Waste Management Industry Training and Advisory Board. The standards have an emphasis on the safety and maintenance of plant located at the waste facility. (Please see also Section 8.6.2.)

10.1.4. Other Regulations relating to health and safety

When an application for a waste management licence for the treatment, recovery, storage or disposal under the Waste Management Licensing Regulations 1994 is made, the EA will notify HSE of the proposed activity. For further information on licensing, please see Chapter 8.

Under the Reporting of Injuries, Diseases and Dangerous Occurrences Regulations 1995 SI 3163 (RIDDOR), injuries, diseases and dangerous occurrences must be reported to HSE. This provides the local HSE office with details of occurrences which it might not have come across otherwise, but could indicate a less than satisfactory corporate health and safety management system. For further information visit www.riddor.gov.uk.

The Control of Major Accident Hazards Regulations 1999 SI 743 (COMAH) apply principally to the chemical industry, some storage activities, explosives and nuclear sites. COMAH aims to reduce the risk and mitigate the effects of major accidents involving hazardous substances. These Regulations are enforced by the EA and HSE.

The Notification of Installations Handling Hazardous Substance Regulations 1982 SI 1357 (NIHHS) are also relevant, and the notification of installations handling Hazardous substances must be made to the local HSE office.

The Control of Substances Hazardous to Health Regulations 2002 SI 2677 (COSHH) apply to potentially harmful substances. Under COSHH:

Box 10.3: Appropriate fines

Firth Vickers Centrispinning Ltd, a foundry operator with 300 employees, was fined £100,000 and £6600 costs when molten metal escaped from a spinning machine and seriously burned three employees. Similar incidents had occurred previously, but without serious injury. The company was convicted under s.2 HASAWA 1974, which requires employers to ensure the safety of their employees. An appeal was dismissed, and the Court of Appeal concluded that:

- the company was complacent since it had foreknowledge of the potential dangers and had received complaints
- the history of inaction regarding previous incidents was relevant
- the sentence fairly reflected the criminality of the company.

Source: *R* v. *Firth Vickers Centrispinning Ltd* (1988), *Croner Health and Safety Briefing*, Issue 270, 10 December 2003.

- an assessment or risk must be carried out by a competent person if workers are to be exposed to substances hazardous to health, then
- the employer must prevent or control the risk by product substitution, ventilation, improved work methods, etc.
- if those do not work, then personal protective equipment (PPE) may be used as a last resort. PPE must never be thought of as a prophylactic to replace an integrated safe system of work based on risk assessment procedures
- proper control measures must be employed, and records of all examinations, tests and repairs kept for at least 5 years.

Likewise, monitoring for employee exposure and records, and health surveillance, and, of course, information, instruction and training, are necessary. Under the Management of Health and Safety at Work Regulations 1999 SI 3242 employers must make a suitable and sufficient assessment of the risks to the health and safety of their employees and anyone affected by their work activities. Arrangements must be made for health surveillance and procedures for imminent danger.[2]

---

[2] Under the Management of Health and Safety at Work Regulations 1999 SI 3242 a risk assessment must be carried out for new and expectant mothers, including women of child-bearing age. The assessment must have regard to the working conditions and agents specified in Annexes I and II of the 92/85 Directive on the introduction of measures to encourage improvements in the safety and health at work of pregnant workers and workers who have recently given birth or are breast-feeding. Typical risks include load handling, noise and vibration, and chemical and biological agents, many of which are prevalent in waste management activities.

Other regulations to be aware of are the:

- Control of Lead at Work Regulations 2002 SI 2676, which applies to all work activities, including waste, containing a significant lead proportion
- Fire Precautions Act 1971 and the Fire Certificates (Special Premises) Regulations 1976, which are self-explanatory
- Dangerous Substances (Notification and Marking of Sites) Regulations 1989 SI 304, which apply to sites holding a total of over 25 tonnes of dangerous substances, when notification must be given to the local HSE office
- Health and Safety (Safety Signs and Signals) Regulations 1996 SI 341.

10.2. Documentation for the transportation of waste

Chapter 11 explains the law concerning the transport of Controlled and Hazardous waste, e.g. the Carriage of Dangerous Goods by Road and Rail Regulations. This chapter is more concerned with the day-to-day municipal, commercial and industrial Controlled wastes. A false distinction is sometimes drawn between dry waste and liquid waste, which, alas, flies in the face of the rainy realities of British weather, which at times is subject to global cooling[3] and warming (please see Chapters 1 and 4).

There are several documents which, according to the nature of the substance of the load, have to be carried for load identification, not only at the customer's check-in and check-out gates but also for the ever more frequent stop and spot checks by statutory authorities on the highway similar to the weighing of vehicle loads. Documents may be statutory forms provided by the competent authority, or internal company operations control documents, which demonstrate compliance with health and safety, Duty of Care and other legal requirements. The waste management statutory documents are the:

- Duty of Care Waste Transfer Note (WTN) (required for all Controlled waste transfers under s.34 EPA 1990)
- Special Waste Consignment Note (required under the Special Waste Regulations 1996) and soon to be subject to the 91/689 Hazardous Waste Directive.

---

[3] In 1968–1972 there was an acceptance in some scientific circles that the world should expect global cooling and a consistent decline in the world's temperatures for at least the next 50 years. This concept returned in 2004 some 30 years later with the prognosis that global warming will melt the Greenland and other ice sheets, thus diluting and altering the warming efficacy of the Gulf Stream.

10.2.1. Special (Hazardous) waste

The documentation and procedures for the consignment of Special (Hazardous) waste are detailed in Chapter 11. Please note that the consignment note has five copies: the top copy must be received by the EA 3 days in advance, and the bottom four copies must be retained with the waste. A Special Waste Consignment Note is shown in Appendix C. Look out for any amendments under the forthcoming Hazardous Waste Regulations, anticipated to come into force in 2005.

10.2.2. Company operations control documents

A company may produce internal operations control documents, which are developed and revised over the years to incorporate the provisions of the Duty of Care, Carriage of Dangerous Goods documentary requirements and the Health and Safety at Work etc. Act. Other companies may have different documents to cover these aspects. A clear and precise example of an operations control document is reproduced in Appendix D.

The purpose of the operations control document is to enable the company to act in accord with health and safety regulation, and show that it is taking reasonable care of its employees and any third parties (e.g. cyclists). The documentation can be used in emergencies to tell the emergency services what to do, e.g. if the tanker is lying in a ditch, perhaps to warn fishermen downstream to stop fishing. There are other health and safety documents such as the TREMCARD and HAZCHEM warning signs, outlined in Chapter 11, which link waste management and health and safety.

The TREMCARD (Transport Emergency Card TEC) is kept in the driver's cab. Any other documents, e.g. those describing the next load that the vehicle will be carrying later that day, must be safely locked away inside or outside of the cab. Emergency services arriving in a hurry at an accident scene must not be misinformed unwitting as to the nature of the load or the reason for the driver or operator's breathing difficulty.

10.3. The Duty of Care Regulations

The Duty of Care Regulations could well have been drafted as regulations under the Health and Saftety at Work Act etc. 1974 (HASAWA 1974). However, since they were derived from the Royal Commission on Environmental Pollution 11th Report in 1985 (well worth reading, 10 years on) they were implemented under environmental law. The Environmental Protection Act 1990

---

[4] See *Croner's Waste Management*, January 2004. This loose-leaf encyclopaedia is well worth a place in one's library, always providing a topical account of many environmental laws including the Duty of Care. Tel. 0208 547 3333.

(EPA 1990) set out the statutory requirements for the s.34 Duty of Care,[4] which applies to Controlled waste (please see the definition of Controlled waste in Chapter 3). The Duty of Care,[5] for the present, does not apply to agricultural, mines and quarries, explosives and radioactive waste (please see Chapter 3). As explained in Chapter 9 the phrase 'duty of care' is an integral part of the tort of negligence,[6] which has a different meaning to the s.34 EPA 1990 Duty of Care, and can be confusing for the layperson.

The s.34 EPA 1990 Duty of Care applies to anyone who imports, produces, carries, keeps, treats,[7] disposes of or is a broker of Controlled waste. All these groups have a duty to take all reasonable and applicable measures to:

- prevent anybody else whom they may or may not know from illegally depositing, keeping, treating or otherwise disposing of the waste
- prevent the escape of waste
- ensure that waste transfer occurs only to an authorised person or for authorised transportation purposes
- enable others, by a written waste description, amounting to a simple contract and transport terms, to avoid contravention of s.33 EPA 1990 (please see Chapter 9) and thus comply with the Duty of Care.

It is the consignor's duty to check with the EA or SEPA that the carrier is registered[8] or exempt from registration. Exempt carriers are:

- charities and voluntary organisations
- waste collection authorities
- ship operators
- householders
- persons authorised to hold or deal with animal by-products.

Under the Duty of Care Regulations 1991 all Controlled waste movements must be accompanied by a Duty of Care Waste Transfer Note (WTN) (please see Chapter 11 for further details). Appendix D provides an example of a company-specific operations control document, which satisfies the requirements of the Duty of Care 1991 WTN requirements. The WTN must provide sufficient information to allow the waste to be:

---

[5] In Chapter 9 it was explained that the duty of care owed under the tort of negligence is a wholly different concept from the S.34 EPA 1990 statutory Duty of Care. With careful choice of words this confusion could have been avoided.

[6] One of three inherent parts of proving negligence is that there has to be a duty of care owed by one party to another and a breach of that duty.

[7] Simplified requirements have been introduced for scrap metal recyclers.

[8] Registered waste carriers under s.2 of the Control of Pollution (Amendment) Act 1989 (please see Chapter 11).

- handled safely
- disposed of or recovered within the law.

Regulation 19 of the Landfill Regulations 2002 SI 1559 amends the Environmental Protection (Duty of Care) Regulations 1991 so that waste must be identified on the WTN by reference to the appropriate six-digit codes in the European Waste Catalogue.

The WTN should contain the following information:

- quantity of waste
- six-digit European Waste Catalogue codes for the wastes
- type of container
- time and place of transfer
- name and address of the transferor or transferee
- whether the transferor is the producer or importer of the waste
- which authorised transport purpose applies
- categories into which the transferor or transferee falls (e.g. waste producer or registered carrier)
- licence number and name of the licensing authority for a waste management licence holder
- registration certificate for a registered carrier with unique reference numbers.

Clients may sometimes request that the Standard Industrial Classification (SIC) code is also provided, which identifies the business sector from which the waste is generated. SIC codes are given in the *Indexes to the United Kingdom Standard Industrial Classification of Economic Activities 1992*, published by the Office for National Statistics in 1997.

The EA may prosecute for insufficient information on the WTN. The written description of the waste and copies of the WTN must be kept by both parties for 2 years. A single WTN is allowed to cover multiple consignment transfers within a 1-year period, provided that the description and all other details are the same for all consignments.

The forthcoming Hazardous Waste Regulations (anticipated to come into force in 2005) will give the EA power to issue fixed-penalty notices for failure to have a Special waste consignment note (please see Chapter 11). Likewise, £300 fixed-penalty notices can be issued for failure to produce:

- valid WTNs
- written descriptions of waste as required by the Duty of Care Regulations (as amended), or
- waste carrier registration details.

It is possible that in the future carriers' windscreen tax discs will be overstamped with waste registration details. This will certainly help waste producers, particularly small businesses, in checking that contractors are registered carriers, since many say they are, though some are not.

An essential part of the Duty of Care Regulations is that the waste must not be allowed to escape through insecure un-netted containers, accidental spillages, vandalisation, or loose waste blowing out of skips. Containers must be in good condition, secure and accurately labelled. There are two vital elements of the Duty of Care:

- the security of the waste
- a correct contractual description.

Further details are set out in the Environmental Protection (Duty of Care) Regulations 1991 SI 2839. Guidance is provided in *Approved Code of Practice (ACOP) Waste Management: The Duty of Care—A Code of Practice*, available from The Stationery Office or www.defra.gov.uk/environment/waste/management/doc/pdf/waste_man_duty_code.pdf. Have it on your desk when the Inspector comes to call, and make certain it is genuinely well thumbed

Box 10.4: Living a lie in a builder's skip

95% of all builders' skips that are said to contain inert waste have a false description. They can contain the remains of builders' sandwiches, mortar clinging to demolished bricks, rotten wood from attics, as well as paint residues from decorators' cans.[9] This is a far more important point than most directors realise, since a novice manager to the industry will see on his very first day a criminal offence misdescription not only tolerated but encouraged. Perhaps skips containing inert waste should be labelled on two sides 'This skip contains 95% inert waste and is subject to turn-out and scrutiny at the recycling yard or landfill site.'

But unfortunately builders' skips often get transported with one inside the other, and the labels or signs can be easily erased. It is only when public and private industry realises that a regular form of random test checking of, say, one in 25 builder's skips arriving at a site being exposed to video cameras on a hard standing to the side of the entrance gate, that there will be real integrity *ab initio* in waste management. Inconceivable, you aloofly think? Well then go to Lima or Santiago airport Customs and Immigration where a button must be pressed, which lights up red or green at random. If a red light is shown, out come the contents of your suitcase. Lights don't take bribes.

---

[9] The Customs and Excise officers responsible for landfill taxation now recognise this, and a reasonable amount of active waste contamination is acceptable for the purpose of landfill tax payment on inert consignments, which are subject to the lower rate of tax (please see Chapter 5). Let us hope that the absorption by The Treasury of Customs and Excise will not dull the cutting-edge and percipience of most Customs and Excise officers.

Table 10.1: An indication of the decision process to be undertaken by the waste producer and contractor

Waste producer	Waste contractor
(1) Can the material be minimised or eliminated at the production source or before?	(1) What is the true nature of the material, and what is the quantity (am I being told the truth?)
(2) Why is it waste? Can I properly avoid it being classified as waste?	(2) If I accept to contract the management and engineering of this material, can it be sent to regional markets for reuse, recovery or recycling?
(3) Is there a local or regional market for the materials to be reused, recovered, or economically[a] recycled?	(3) If not, will it need specialist handling, treatment or disposal? For example, Hazardous waste such as asbestos
(4) Do we need to engage a contractor for specialist services and incur additional fees and service charges?	(4) What will be the economics and the statutory duties for the acceptance and transport of the material? Who should be notified? What is my Standard Operating Procedure for it?

[a] However, in Scotland at the Glasgow SEPA Conference in March 2004, the Chairman in his address and visual aids stated that 'ReMaDe has clearly established that producing recyclate comes before market creation'. Where then is it to be stored prior to sale?

through and coffee stained. The adoption of the six-digit European Waste Catalogue classification[10] is not yet shown in the statutory code of practice, although this is to be amended shortly to include the recent developments. For further information read the Landfill Directive Regulatory Guidance Note 14, *The Duty of Care and the European Waste Catalogue*, available from www.environment-agency.gov.uk.

10.4. The bare bones of waste management contracting

10.4.1. Some basic principles for waste contractors and producers
The proper management of materials, seemingly of no further use, requires the simple approach to some decision processes indicated in Table 10.1.

No matter how well designed the recycling plant, excellently engineered the incinerator or robust the landfill site, everything (criminal and civil law) depends

[10] Note that Code 99 for waste 'not otherwise specified' is not allowed by the EA.

upon whether those waste materials have been correctly identified and agreed, since they are subject to the s.34 EPA 1990 Duty of Care, well before leaving the waste producer's premises. So there must be a clear and mutually under-stood and respected contract. Often the contract begins on a verbal basis, but with the statutory documentation these days, it will end in a written signed contract.

But, alas, the reality is that waste producers often take the cheapest route, even in 2004. Do not forget that, despite the historically inherited ill-discipline amongst some SME waste contractors, if waste producers had taken the trouble to describe their waste, selected and contracted with efficient contractors and disposers, and monitored the results, then s.34 EPA 1990 Duty of Care would not have been necessary.[11]

But what should be in that simple written contract, often seemingly printed in the same colour ink as the paper on the back of the consignment note in the hope that it won't be read? The terms of service reflect the details of the contract, which may have been initially agreed on the telephone, and provide that neces-sary written formality which can both apportion civil liability if anything goes wrong, and criminal liability if one party has unfortunately been sailing on the margin. Simple waste management contracts should typically include the terms of service shown in Box 10.5, which necessarily have had to be summarised as briefly as possible. They will have to be tailored and supplemented for each particular circumstance.

The terms in Box 10.5 are indicative, but only indicative, of the general content of a waste management contract. Operational contractual terms should be taken very seriously indeed. They can often prevent accidents and amputa-tions by defining performance liabilities well in advance. Do not forget to bring the terms to the attention of the customer before the price is agreed or the contract completed.[12] Contract terms cannot retrospectively be included after a contractual agreement has been reached, unless both parties agree to renegotiate and make a new contract. Also, if there is an unfortunate accident, the fact that such simple and transparent contractual terms have been drawn up will hold both parties initially in good stead with the HSE inspector, because at least a sensible attempt has been made to define mutual responsibilities.

Terms of a contract can legally be classified as conditions or warranties. Breach of conditions can result in the contract being rescinded, i.e. dissolved by the courts, whereas a breach of a warranty can generally only give rise to a claim for damages. Unfortunately, the language of waste management licensing does not follow these clear distinctions. Note the differences summarised in Section 8.6.4.

---

[11] The Royal Commission on Environmental Pollution (1985), 11th Report, *Managing Waste: The Duty of Care*, The Stationery Office, London.

[12] The customer is sometimes called the 'profferee', because he is being proffered or offered the terms of a contract, including the price, which he can accept or refuse, or suggest a counter-offer.

Box 10.5: A brief summary of some indicative terms in a servicing contract between a waste manager and a waste producer

(a) Duties of the waste management contractor

The waste management contractor undertakes to:

- service according to the specification provided by the waste producer
- provide the necessary equipment and plant and the site disciplines as nominated in the contract
- act in accord with all up-to-date regulations and statutory codes of practice.

(b) Duties of the waste producer

The waste producer undertakes to:

- provide an accurate description of the waste
- ensure that the constituents are compatible within the waste (i.e. to avoid chemical reactions between the contents)
- not to cause damage to the equipment, plant or vehicles
- provide safe access for the contractor at all reasonable times.

(c) Changes in the specification

In the event of a change to the producer's waste description there must be:

- an immediate notification to the contractor's managers and driver/ operators with suspension of the contract
- full and adequate notice given in advance if the change is known
- a new negotiated contract with revised description and agreed charges
- a possible interim payment.

(d) Statutory notices

The service of statutory notices will be the responsibility of the waste producer.

(e) Safety discipline

The waste producer will provide:

- safe access for the contractor's vehicle(s) and adequate supervision of the driver/operator
- notice of special site conditions and site emergency procedures
- responsibility for the conduct of his personnel.

(f) Title to the waste

The time and place where title to the waste materials passes from the producer to the contractor must be defined, for example at the entrance of the waste producer's site.

(g) Insurance cover

Considerable care must be taken by both parties that their individual insurance cover is applicable to all operational eventualities.

(*Box 10.5 continued overleaf*)

201

Box 10.5: Contd

(h) Delays and operational changes

The servicing of waste materials must provide for:

- the occurrence of delays of either party beyond their reasonable control
- a defined contingency plan if the servicing site has to be changed
- procedures for unexpected operational changes.

(i) Apportioning responsibility

The contract will define who has responsibility, *inter alia*, for:

- containers being stolen, accidentally lost or damaged
- loss or damage to the equipment, plant or vehicles
- obtaining the relevant highway permits if a container is deposited on the highway, including the proper continuous illumination throughout lighting-up times if necessary[a]
- the suitability of containers including warning and waste description signs.

(j) Payment

Payment terms may, for example, be:

- 30 days, no deferment of actual payment for a counter claim, plus 2% from invoice date
- there can be no waiver of payment or any term unless in writing, signed by an authorised manager clearly responsible for the contract.

(k) Remedy for a contractual breach

Provision should be made in the contract for the remedies for any breach of contract. In the event of bankruptcy, receivership or administration the contract should define the consequences in simple terms.

(l) Possible subcontracting

The terms of a possible or otherwise assignment of the contract work or sub-contracting should be agreed if considered reasonable.

[a] For example, flashing warning lights may be needed. Depositing any form of waste container on a highway or road without adequate continuous illumination during the hours of darkness or daylight fog is the equivalent of digging a hole in a road which is unlit. The consequences for even the most prudent of motorists can be tragic.

10.4.2. Public sector contracts

The roles and responsibilities of local authorities are outlined in Chapter 4. Under s.51 EPA 1990 waste disposal authorities can make arrangements for contractors to dispose of waste collected by the waste collection authorities. Rules for waste disposal companies are set out in Part II of Schedule 2, 'Waste Disposal Authorities and Companies', of the EPA 1990, which specifies the terms of waste disposal contracts and procedures for putting waste disposal contracts out to tender. The terms must be designed to minimise environmental pollution or harm to human health and maximise recycling.

Public sector tender requirements have been amended by the EU public procurement rules. Public procurement is the contracting of works, supplies and services by central, regional and local government and other public agencies or bodies such as the fire or police service, the NHS, universities, and joint public–private utilities. The EU Procurement Directives were developed to promote fair and transparent competitive tendering, untainted by prior corruption allegations, for public sector projects throughout Europe and associated countries in Scandinavia, Eastern Europe and North Africa. The total value of public sector projects in the EU is about £500 billion per year, or 12% of the EU GDP.[13] These are often large projects, such as a materials recovery facility for a local authority or an incinerator for a hospital. A summary of the EU Procurement Directives and the corresponding UK Regulations is shown in Table 10.2.

The public procurement regulations apply when a project exceeds financial thresholds specified by the Directives. The threshold depends on the type of company contracting the work. A full list of EU public procurement thresholds and exemptions is available at www.publictender.co.uk/eu-thresholds.html.

Under European law all applicable public procurement contracts must be advertised throughout Europe. There are three main tendering procedures, the:

- open procedure, where the contract requirement is advertised, and all applicants may tender
- restricted procedure in which the contract requirement is advertised, but only a select number of applicants (between five and 20) are invited to tender
- negotiated procedure, which is used only in exceptional circumstances.

Contracts are advertised in the *Official Journal of the European Communities* (OJEC) (www.ojec.com). Detailed Directive procedures do not need to be followed for contracts falling below the specified financial threshold, although the process must still be fair and transparent.

For further information on public procurement visit www.publictender.co.uk/eu-procurement.html.

10.4.3. Civil engineering contracts

The legal framework for civil engineering project management procedures is set out in the New Engineering Contract (NEC), which was developed during the 1990s by the Institution of Civil Engineers. The NEC is made up of a series

---

[13] Source: www.publictender.co.uk/eu-procurement.html.

Table 10.2: Summary of European Procurement Directives and some relevant corresponding UK Regulations

EU Procurement Directive	UK Regulations
93/97 Works Directive as amended by the 97/52 Directive	Public Works Contracts Regulations 1991 SI 2680 as amended
93/36 Supplies Directive as amended by the 97/52 Directive	Public Supply Contracts Regulations 1995 SI 201 as amended
92/50 Services Directive as amended by the 97/52 Directive	Public Services Contracts Regulations 1993 SI 3228
	Public Supply Contracts Regulations 1995 SI 201
	Utilities Contracts Regulations 1996 SI 2911
93/38 Utilities Directive as amended by the 98/4 Directive	Utilities Contracts Regulations SI 1996 2911 as amended
89/665 Public Sector Remedies Directive as amended by the 97/52 Directive	Public Works Contracts Regulations 1991 SI 2680
	Public Supply Contracts Regulations 1995 SI 201
	Public Services Contracts Regulations 1993 SI 3228 as amended
92/13 Utilities Remedies Directive	Utilities Contracts Regulations 1996 SI 2911

Box 10.6: Waste contract deemed illegal by the European Court of Justice (ECJ)

The European Commission recently took infringement proceedings against six Member States who were in breach of EU procurement law. For example, in April 2003 the ECJ ruled that the award of a waste disposal contract by a German local authority was in breach of the 92/50 Services Procurement Directive. The authority had conducted negotiations with a contractor before having advertised the contract. The contract was deemed to have been awarded illegally, and that breach would continue throughout the period of contract, which thus had to be terminated. Germany was given the option to meet the request or face a daily fine for continued infringement.

Source: ECJ cases C-20/01 and C-28/01.

of standard contract documents, support services and software. For further information visit www.newengineeringcontract.co.uk.

The design of waste management facilities has until recently been carried out according to the relevant British Standards (BS). However, these are currently being replaced by the Eurocodes, and the BS will be withdrawn between 2008 and 2010. The Eurocodes are a set of 10 harmonised documents, which are being prepared by the Comité Européan de Normalisation (CEN) from 2002 to 2005 to help Member States meet the requirements of the 89/106 Construction Products Directive, the 92/50 Services Directive, and the 93/37 Works Directive. They also aim to improve competitiveness and health and safety in the construction industry. Once implemented the Eurocodes will be mandatory for all public sector projects. For further information visit www.eurocodes.co.uk.

Chapter 11

The consignment and movement of waste

11.1. The transportation of Controlled waste within the UK

The purpose of the Control of Pollution (Amendment) Act 1989 (COP(A)A 1989) and Controlled Waste (Registration of Carriers and Seizure of Vehicles) Regulations 1989 is to make fly-tipping more difficult and traceable through a compulsory registration scheme for waste carriers, which is closely allied to and forms the first step in the implementation of s.34 of the Environmental Protection Act 1990 (EPA 1990) Duty of Care Regulations.[1] Under COP(A)A 1989 all vehicles must be registered if they carry waste for profit, save for the exemptions listed below.[2] The COP(A)A 1989 applies to road, rail, air, sea, or inland waterway transport, but not to the moving of waste by pipelines, or direct transport into or out of the UK (the later being covered by other Regulations). The Environment Agency (EA) or the Scottish Environment Protection Agency (SEPA) manage registration and fee applications, normally valid for 3 years; all partners must register.

11.1.1. Registration of waste carriers

Section 1 of COP(A)A 1989 creates the offence of carrying Controlled waste for profit by anyone that is not a registered carrier to or from any place in Great

---

[1] The carrier registration scheme is implemented by the Controlled Waste (Registration of Carriers and Seizure of Vehicles) Regulations 1991 SI 1624, as amended by the Waste Management Licensing Regulations 1994 SI 1056, and the Controlled Waste (Registration of Carriers and Seizure of Vehicles) (Amendment) Regulations 1998 SI 605.

[2] The National Assembly of Wales (Transfer of Functions) Order 1999 SI 672 gives power to the National Assembly of Wales to administer this Act.

[3] The Act does not apply in Northern Ireland.

Britain.[3] Registered carriers of Controlled waste under s.2 COP(A)A 1989 are one of the five groups who are authorised to receive a transfer of waste under the s.34 EPA 1990 Duty of Care Regulations. The registration is that of the carrier (the company or individual who is the registered owner of the vehicle) and not of the vehicle itself. So the correct question to ask is 'in whose name and under whose control has the carriage being undertaken?' Thus, a person who transported Controlled waste for a registered carrier under a hire contract is not guilty of a section 1 offence.

A breach of COP(A)A 1989 can result in the loss of registration and the seizure of vehicles. It is a defence to prove that:

- waste was carried in an emergency, notified at the time to the EA
- the carrier was acting under employer instructions.

Carriers of Controlled waste have to be very responsible, because if they have been convicted under the COP(A)A 1989 there may be a refusal of an application for a licence in the future. They must show clear evidence in revised management systems to ensure that there should be no repetition of the offences for which they have been convicted.

Any individual or company wishing to transport or broker the transport of Controlled waste by

- road
- rail
- air
- sea
- inland waterways

must register with the EA.[4] The carriage of the producer's own waste does not tend to require registration unless it is construction and demolition waste. Other exemptions are vehicle ferry operators, who are exempt in respect of waste carried in the cargo of vehicles on the ferry, and Government departments and councils.

Under Schedule 4 of the Waste Management Licensing Regulations 1994 SI 1056 there is a simplified scheme of registration for:

- waste collection authorities, waste disposal authorities and the EA
- charities and voluntary organisations
- British Railways Board wholly owned subsidiaries.

---

[4] A single registration based on the main place of business will cover transportation throughout the UK. For Northern Ireland registration is with the Environment and Heritage Service, and for Scotland SEPA.

The EA can refuse or revoke registration only if:

- the carrier has been convicted of certain offences, with a wide environmental scope listed in Schedule 1 of the Regulations
- the EA considers it undesirable that the carrier should continue to transport controlled waste. The carrier can appeal to the Secretary of State. The Secretary of State generally decides in the carrier's favour the first time around—nobody likes to take a rice bowl away.

Under the Duty of Care Regulations 1991 the following must be completed every time waste is transported:

- a Waste Transfer Note for Controlled waste (copies must be retained for 2 years)
- a consignment note for Special (Hazardous) waste.

The general rules for transporting Controlled waste are to ensure that:

- the waste is contained and to prevent its escape (it is advisable not to rely on the packaging of the previous holder of the waste—repack waste and relabel if necessary)
- a visual inspection is made when the waste is accepted in order to check the accuracy of the waste description on the Waste Transfer Note (please see Appendix D)
- waste must be taken to a site possessing the correct permit or licence or exemption, which should be checked with the site manager in advance
- offences must be reported to the EA, before they come to the EA's notice.

11.1.2. Operator licences (O-licences)

In order to begin a waste transportation business, renewable operator licences (O-licences) must be obtained for operating vehicles. Applications must be made to the Vehicle Operator Services Agency (VOSA). VOSA was formed in April 2003 to improve road safety and the environment and enforce compliance with commercial operator licensing requirements. It is the merger of the Vehicle Inspectorate and the Traffic Area Network divisions of the Department for Transport. The application must be carefully prepared, preferably with the help of independent transport administrators. For further information and application forms visit www.vosa.gov.uk or telephone 0870 6060440.

11.1.3. The Duty of Care and the necessity for documentation

Everybody every minute of their lives owes a duty of care (see negligence, Chapter 9) towards a third party, as when driving, sleeping (i.e. owning a reasonable alarm system) or even playing games determined by fair tackles. An operations control document (OCD) (please see Appendix D) is a unique company document that has been developed over many years to incorporate the provisions of the Duty of Care, Carriage of Dangerous Goods documentary requirements and the Health and Safety at Work etc. Act 1974. Waste management companies devise their own different documents to cover these aspects. It provides a description of the waste, and is linked with the finance side and checking, gatekeepers' reference, etc. Waste producers should ask to see OCDs as part of their s.34 EPA 1990 Duty of Care. If a waste contractor does not have an OCD system, think again.

The OCD information will contain, *inter alia* the:

- waste producer's name and address
- general description of the waste and principal components
- quantity and frequency, e.g. 20 tonnes weekly
- physical form, e.g. brown liquid
- maximum temperature and density, e.g. ambient and 1.45 g/cc
- collection point and method of site storage
- licensed treatment recycling or landfill site destination
- handling and safety notes and safe working procedures
- method of loading and class of personal protective equipment (PPE).

The essentials of PPE are:

- overalls
- a safety helmet
- gloves
- goggles or visor
- ear defenders
- a high-visibility coat
- safety boots.

Further details on the Duty of Care are given in the Duty of Care Regulations 1991 and *Waste Management: The Duty of Care. A Code of Practice*, available from The Stationery Office or www.defra.gov.uk/environment/waste/management/doc/pdf/waste_man_duty_code.pdf.

Manual handling

Everyone has a different capability for lifting, pushing or pulling loads depending on their age, gender, physical condition or medical history, so no specific weight limits can be set. Incorrect posture and excessive repetition of movement can be important factors, and the general essentials are to:

- plan the task
- prepare, e.g. the object is securely closed or the load divided into manageable packages

- assess, e.g. floors are not slippery or wet
- apply good lifting and handling techniques, e.g. kinetic lifting.

11.2. The consignment of Hazardous waste

The transport of dangerous goods across Europe has had to comply with international Regulations (known as the ADR Regulations) for some time, and there are no exceptions for waste. In 2004, potentially in the early summer, there is to be a changeover to using ADR for UK domestic journeys. These will be implemented through a new Carriage of Dangerous Goods Statutory Instrument, which will also simplify the existing regulatory framework.

The up-to-date historical framework has been included here to give an outline of current practice in the UK. There is also the usual uncertainty as to when exactly Regulations will be implemented and the old Regulations phased out. The reader should stay informed of the latest legal developments, and it is recommended that the relevant websites at the end of this section are explored. If still in doubt contact HSE's InfoLine on 08701 545500, or write to HSE Information Services, Caerphilly Business Park, Caerphilly CF83 3GG.

The current, although shortly to be replaced, Regulations for the transportation of dangerous goods are principally the:

- Carriage of Dangerous Goods by Rail Regulations 1996 SI 2089 (CDG-Rail Regulations)
- Carriage of Dangerous Goods (Classification, Packaging and Labelling) and Use of Transportable Pressure Receptacles Regulations 1996 SI 2092
- Carriage of Explosives by Road Regulations 1996 SI 2093
- Carriage of Dangerous Goods by Road (Driver Training) Regulations 1996 SI 2094
- Carriage of Dangerous Goods by Road Regulations 1996 SI 2095 (CDG-Road Regulations)
- Carriage of Dangerous Goods (Amendment) Regulations 1999 SI 303
- The Transport of Dangerous Goods (Safety Advisors) Regulations 1999 SI 257.

The CDG-Road Regulations are a comprehensive set of instruments covering road movements of all dangerous substances (except explosives and radioactive substances). The similar CDG-Rail Regulations cover rail transport.

A useful good practice guidance on the carriage of dangerous goods is the HSE publication *Are you Involved in the Carriage of Dangerous Goods by Road or Rail?*, available at www.hse.gov.uk/pubns/indg234.pdf or from HSE Books, PO Box 1999, Sudbury CO10 6FS, or email public.enquiries@hse.gov.uk.

11.2.1. How do I determine whether my wastes are dangerous?

Most goods are not considered sufficiently dangerous to need special precautions during transport. However, some wastes have properties which mean they could present a danger while being carried, such as being:

- explosive
- toxic
- corrosive
- flammable.

In order to classify the wastes as dangerous it is necessary to identify the hazards first. Some common dangerous goods include wastes that have already been classified, but many have not. For example, radioactive waste materials are administered under the Radioactive Material (Road Transport) Regulations 2002 (RAMRoad or RAMRail), and the Classification and Labelling of Explosives Regulations 1983 (CLER 1983) are self-explanatory.

All other dangerous wastes must be assigned an appropriate entry in the July 1999 Approved Carriage List (ACL). The Health and Safety Executive (HSE) Approved Carriage List Pack is a comprehensive guide which includes a hard copy of the ACL (L90) and the Approved Requirements and Test Methods for the Classification and Packaging of Dangerous Goods for Carriage. These provide information on:

- classification
- packaging
- labelling.

The CDG-Road Regulations 1996 (as amended) cover:

- the inspection of vehicles containing dangerous substances carried by road
- documentation
- the roles and responsibilities of the driver
- the operator and consignors
- safety equipment necessary for loading, packing and transporting dangerous substances.

Some, but not all, dangerous goods or wastes are listed by name in the ACL. If the goods are not listed, then the dangerous properties will need to be established, in particular the most dangerous ones, before the appropriate entry can be identified. Once the ACL entry has been identified, it is possible to find the information to comply with other requirements such as the need to package and label the goods properly. This information includes:

- the proper shipping name or designation of the wastes
- the corresponding UN number

- the packing group
- appropriate danger signs
- any subsidiary hazard signs required.

The CDG Road and Rail Regulations do not apply in certain circumstances, for example:

- the goods/wastes are not used at work
- the goods/wastes are not carried by road or rail
- the goods/wastes are being moved between adjacent premises
- only very small quantities by road are being carried.

All Special wastes are dangerous goods (e.g. oily wastes and bonded asbestos), however Article 5(1) of the 91/689 Hazardous Waste Directive states that all Hazardous wastes should be packaged and labelled in accordance with international and community standards. This ought to be interpreted only if they fulfil the dangerous goods criteria specified in the ADR Regulations. Eventually the term Special will be replaced by the term Hazardous, to come in line with the 91/689 Directive, and new Hazardous Waste Regulations are anticipated to come into force in 2005 (please see Chapter 3).

11.2.2. The packaging of dangerous goods for transport

Dangerous wastes should be packaged so that they do not escape during handling and carriage. This is a basic requirement of the Duty of Care as well as the Carriage of Dangerous Goods Regulations. Packages must be able to withstand normal transport conditions, e.g. vibration, humidity, pressure or heavy braking and the normal stresses of loading and unloading, so that the risk of leakage is minimised. In all but a few cases all containers must be of a type approved by the UK competent authority—these are known as UN-approved packages/receptacles.

11.2.3. The Transport of Dangerous Goods (Safety Advisors) Regulations 1999

Directive 96/35, on the appointment and vocational qualification of safety advisors for the transport of dangerous goods by road, rail and inland waterway, and Directive 2000/18, on the minimum examination requirements for safety advisors for the transport of dangerous goods by road, rail or inland waterway, require the EU Member States to implement legislation to ensure that undertakings which transport dangerous goods by road, rail or inland waterways, including loading and unloading, to appoint Dangerous Goods Safety Advisors (DGSAs). DGSAs must obtain a vocational training certificate (VTC) after a written examination approved by the competent authority. VTCs are EU mutually recognised; DGSAs had to be appointed by the 1 January 2000. These

Regulations were made after extensive consultation by HSE and the Department for Transport (DfT),[5] signed by a Transport Minister.[6]

For further information visit www.dft.gov.uk.

11.2.4. The Carriage of Dangerous Goods by Road Regulations 1996

The CDG-Road Regulations indicate specific duties for drivers of vehicles carrying dangerous substances to:

- know the applicable regulations
- be provided with written information on their load
- lock away all other information
- understand the main hazards of the load being carried
- know the precautions during loading and unloading
- take all precautions necessary to avoid fire or explosion
- not to overfill the tank or overload the vehicle
- ensure all valves, tank openings, etc., are closed before starting a journey
- ensure that hazard warning panels and compartment labels (see below) reflect the correct load information, and are removed when the load has been unloaded, and the tank has been cleaned and purged
- see that hazard warning panels are kept clean and free from obstruction
- understand what action to take in an emergency
- park always in a safe place away from the general public
- supervise generally the vehicle carrying dangerous goods.

11.2.5. The Special Waste Regulations 1996 in the context of transport

Special waste is defined in Chapter 3. It has essentially the same properties which qualify a chemical as dangerous under the Chemical (Hazard Information and Packaging for Supply) Regulations (CHIP) 1994 SI 3247. The waste producer must notify the EA three working days before Special waste can be collected through the consignment note. An example of a Special waste consignment note is shown in Appendix C. The consignment note is uniquely numbered, has five sections and five copies. The five sections are:

- Part A—the consignment details
- Part B—the description of the waste
- Part C—the carrier's collection certificate

---

[5] The DfT (Dangerous Goods Board) appointed the Scottish Qualification Authority to perform the duties of training, examination and certification as agent to the competent authority.
[6] A similar leg was introduced into Northern Ireland (NI SI 2000 119 and 171).

- Part D—the consignor's certificate
- Part E—the consignee's certificate.

The five copies are

- 1st (white)—the pre-notification copy (to be received by the EA three working days in advance)
- 2nd (green)—the consignor's copy (contractor's copy)
- 3rd (orange)—the carrier's copy (completed by the carrier driver in the cab)
- 4th (pink)—the consignee's copy (the landfill, incineration, etc., site to which the waste is taken)
- 5th (yellow)—the consignee's EA office copy (sent to the local EA office).

All except the white pre-notification copy must travel with the waste. All copies are distributed from the bottom up, except the top pre-notification copy. The logic here is that the EA gets the two best copies. The documents are retained on a register for 3 years. The pink consignee's copy must be kept for the site lifetime.

There is a simplified procedure, called a 'season ticket', where several identical consignments of waste are sent from the same waste producer to the same disposal site or recycling facility over a period of a year. There is no need to send a pre-notification copy of the consignment note to the EA, so only four copies are required for each waste consignment. Care must be taken that this concession is not inadvertently abused, and liaison with the EA is advised.

11.2.6. The Carriage of Dangerous Goods by Road (Driver Training) Regulations 1996

The CDG-Road Regulations apply to drivers carrying dangerous goods on a vehicle with a permissible maximum weight exceeding 3.5 tonnes. Employers must ensure that their drivers have been trained and hold a Valid Training Certificate (VTC) issued by the Driver and Vehicle Licensing Agency (DVLA) when the driver has passed the examinations for the relevant vehicle type and the classes of dangerous goods.

Drivers' duties are to:

- carry the VTC at all times and have it available throughout the whole of the carriage
- produce the VTC to a policeman or goods vehicle examiner on request.

The certificate is valid for 5 years. In the fourth year the driver must be retrained and pass fresh examinations.

215

11.2.7. The CDG-Road Regulations in operation

The CDG-Road Regulations comprehensively cover road movements of all dangerous substances except explosives and radioactive substances. In summary, and only in summary, the rules require the operator to have knowledge of:

- the substances being carried
- the possible hazards
- what to do in an emergency
- how to load and unload the particular substance
- how to ensure that the tank is not overfilled
- the rules about hazard warning panels
- precautions necessary to prevent fire and explosion
- supervising and parking rules
- how to use safety equipment
- where to keep written information in the cab on the substance being carried
- where to place information relating to other substances in a secure container, so with a vehicle in a ditch and the driver unconscious the emergency services will not be confused as to the load and can select with confidence their own rescue and containment procedures.

11.2.8. The ADR Regulations

Two international agreements exist to govern the transport of dangerous goods by rail and road, known as RID (Règlements Internationale Relatif au Transport des Marchandises Dangereuses par Chemin de Fer) and ADR (Accord Européen Relatif au Transport International des Marchandises Dangereuses par Route), and these are updated every 2 years. RID and ADR are reflected in two recent EU Framework Directives:

- the 2003/28 ADR Framework Directive, adapting for the fourth time to technical progress Council Directive 94/55 of 21 November 1994 on the approximation of the laws of the Member States with regard to the transport of dangerous goods by road (excluding parts relating to the carriage of radioactive material by road)
- the 2003/29 RID Framework Directive, adapting for the fourth time to technical progress Directive 96/49 of 23 July 1996 on the approximation of the laws of the Member States with regard to the transport of dangerous goods by rail.

The ADR Regulations have for some time applied to the transportation of dangerous goods, including wastes, by road in Europe and Scandinavia. These are now being brought in to control domestic movements of waste. The new Regulations will:

- simplify the regulatory framework through a single set of regulations replacing 14 separate pieces of legislation
- implement the 2003/28 ADR and 2003/29 RID Framework Directives and also complete the implementation of the 1996/36 Transportable Pressure Equipment Directive.

The Carriage of Dangerous Goods and Use of Transportable Pressure Equipment Regulations 2004 SI 568 will merge all the requirements for the carriage of dangerous goods by road and rail, and replace or partly replace the following 14 existing UK Regulations:

- Gas Cylinders (Pattern Approval) Regulations 1987 SI 116
- Pressure Vessels (Verification) Regulations 1988 SI 896
- Packaging of Explosives for Carriage Regulations 1991 SI 2097
- Carriage of Dangerous Goods by Rail Regulations 1996 SI 2089 (some minor parts will remain)
- Carriage of Dangerous Goods (Classification, Packaging and Labelling) and Use of Transportable Pressure Receptacles Regulations 1996 SI 2092
- Carriage of Explosives by Road Regulations 1996 SI 2093
- Carriage of Dangerous Goods by Road (Driver Training) Regulations 1996 SI 2094
- Carriage of Dangerous Goods by Road Regulations 1996 SI 2095 (some minor parts will remain)
- Carriage of Dangerous Goods (Amendment) Regulations 1998 SI 2885
- Carriage of Dangerous Goods (Amendment) Regulations 1999 SI 303
- Transport of Dangerous Goods (Safety Advisors) Regulations 1999 SI 257
- Transport Pressure Vessels Regulations 2001 SI 1426
- Packaging, Labelling and Carriage of Radioactive Material by Rail Regulations 2002 SI 2099
- Carriage of Dangerous Goods and Transportable Pressure Vessels (Amendment) Regulations 2003.

And will also replace or partly replace the following approved documents:

- the Approved Carriage List
- the Approved Requirements and Test Methods for Classification and Labelling of Dangerous Goods for Carriage
- the Approved Vehicle Requirements
- the Approved Tank Requirements
- the Approved Explosives Vehicles Requirements
- the Approved Requirements for the Packaging, Labelling and Carriage of Radioactive Material by Rail.

The Carriage of Dangerous Goods and Use of Transportable Pressure Equipment Regulations 2004 SI 568 are available online at www.hmso.gov.uk/si/si2004/2004568.htm. The new Regulations directly cross-reference the 2003/28 ADR Directive and the 2003 version of ADR/RID, the main features of which are set out in Table 11.1.

Classification of dangerous goods

Dangerous goods/waste may not be carried by road until:

- they have been classified according to the requirements set out in ADR 2.1
- they have been assigned a UN number, proper shipping name, description, subsidiary risk and packing group (Dangerous Goods List, see below)
- specified requirements on the Dangerous Goods List have been met
- they have complied with any relevant test methods set out in ADR 2.2 and 2.3.

The main UN classes are shown in Table 11.2.

The Dangerous Goods List

The Dangerous Goods List is given in ADR Table A, Chapter 3.2. It contains a list of dangerous goods in UN class order, and provides the relevant information on the:

- UN number
- proper shipping name and description
- class

Table 11.1: Contents of the 2003/28 ADR Directive 2003

Annex A	
1	General provisions
2	Classification
3	Dangerous Goods List special provisions and exemptions to dangerous goods packed in limited quantities
4	Packaging and tank provisions
5	Consignment procedures
6	Construction and testing of packages, intermediate bulk containers and large packages and tanks
7	Conditions of carriage, loading, unloading and handling
Annex B	
8	Vehicle crews, equipment, operation and documentation
9	Construction and approval of vehicles

Table 11.2: UN classes of dangerous substances

Class	Summary
1	Explosive substances and articles
2	Gases
3	Flammable liquids
4.1	Flammable solids, self-reactive substances and solid desensitised explosives
4.2	Substances liable to spontaneous combustion
4.3	Substances which on contact with water emit flammable gases
5.1	Oxidising substances
5.2	Organic peroxides
6.1	Toxic substances
6.2	Infectious substances
7	Radioactive material
8	Corrosive substances
9	Miscellaneous dangerous substances and articles

- classification code
- packing group
- labels
- special provisions
- the specification for a limited quantity (see exemptions below)
- type of tank approved for transport.

Exemptions

Under ADR there are exemptions, partial exemptions and relaxations, all of which are subject to some conditions and qualifications. Typical exemptions include:

- the carriage of dangerous goods/wastes for private individuals where the goods have been packaged for retail sale, and are to be used for domestic, personal or leisure use
- the carriage of machinery or equipment not specifically listed in the Dangerous Goods List
- carriage undertaken by or under the supervision of the emergency services, e.g. breakdown vehicles towing vehicles carrying dangerous goods
- emergency transport to save human life or protect the environment
- when limited quantities of dangerous goods are being carried (packaging and marking requirements must be met) (specified quantities are given in the Dangerous Goods List – Table A)

219

- the carriage of gases and liquids used as fuel in the tanks of road-going vehicles (or trains)
- carriage other than by road.

Further information on ADR

Groups likely to be affected by the new Regulations are mainly those who:

- classify dangerous goods
- consign dangerous goods for carriage
- package and label dangerous goods
- will be affected by the new provisions for the first time (e.g. those transporting fuel oil)
- Dangerous Goods Safety Advisors.

Further information on the new developments is available from:

- HSE (www.hse.gov.uk, InfoLine 08701 545500, or write to HSE Information Services, Caerphilly Business Park, Caerphilly CF83 3GG).
- The consultation document *Proposals for the Carriage of Dangerous Goods and Use of Transportable Pressure Equipment Regulations* (available at www.hse.gov.uk/consult/live.htm or from HSE Books on 01787 881165).
- The HSE publication *Are You Involved in the Carriage of Dangerous Goods by Road or Rail?* (www.hse.gov.uk/pubns/indg234.pdf), Feb. 1999.
- The Carriage of Dangerous Goods and Use of Transportable Pressure Equipment Regulations 2004 SI 568.
- The international agreements on ADR and RID (available from www.unece.org/trans/danger/publi/adr/adr2003/ContentsE.html and www.hse.gov.uk, respectively). A CD-ROM for ADR can be ordered from www.unece.org/trans/danger/publi/order.htm.
- The 2003/28 Directive adapting for the fourth time to technical progress the 94/55 Directive on EU laws for the transport of dangerous goods by road is available from www.unece.org/trans/danger/publi/adr/adr2003/ContentsE.html. Amendments to ADR have not been included in the text.
- The 2003/29 Directive adapting for the fourth time to technical progress on EU Laws for the transport of dangerous goods by rail is also available from www.http://europa.eu.int/eur-lex/pri/en/oj/dat/2003/1_090/_09020030408en00470047.pdf.
- The 99/364 Directive on transportable pressure equipment (Schedule 13 of the Carriage of Dangerous Goods and the Use of Transportable Pressure Equipment Regulations 2004 SI 568).
- The Reporting of Injuries, Diseases and Dangerous Occurrences Regulations 1995 SI 3163.
- The Multilateral Agreement M90 (www.unece.org/trans/danger/multi/agree.wpf/m0090_e.htm).

- The National Chemical Emergency Centre (F6 Culham, Abingdon, Oxfordshire OX14 3ED, Tel. 0870 190 6621, Fax. 0870 190 6614, email ncec@aeat.co.uk, or visit the website at www.the-ncec.com).

11.3. Emergency response and labelling of dangerous waste

11.3.1. Domestic journeys

Dangerous wastes in packages need to be labelled according to their classification, with the labels clearly visible so that everyone involved is aware of the potential hazards. It is particularly important that the emergency services attending an incident can see that dangerous wastes are present, and what dangers to health, safety and environment the wastes present. Labelling requirements for dangerous wastes for domestic transport, other than for explosives and radioactive material, are contained in regulation 8 of the Carriage of Dangerous Goods (Classification, Packaging and Labelling) and Use of Transportable Pressure Receptacles Regulations 1996 SI 2092, as amended by the Carriage of Dangerous Goods (Amendment) regulations 1999 SI 303.

Drivers of tankers must display on the tank itself various pieces of information on panels for use in an emergency, and to ensure with certainty that the panels are:

- attached immediately prior to loading
- kept in place, clean and free from obstruction
- removed only when the tank has been cleaned and/or purged.

Emergency Action Codes (EACs), also known as Hazchem codes, give details of:

- the fire extinguishing media
- the level of PPE
- whether the spillage should be contained or may be diluted
- whether there is a possibility of violent reaction
- whether the substance poses a public safety hazard.

EACs assist the emergency services at the scene of accidents involving substances in bulk. If an EAC is not available, it should not be assumed that the hazard is low. For a clear explanation of the signs, symbols, codes and keys used visit www.the-ncec.com/hazchem/index.html. The new Carriage of Dangerous Goods Regulations will contain a derogation, which will enable the continued use of the UK's EAC and Hazchem system, for domestic journeys only.

The number and position of the panels depend on the type of tank. Road tankers and tank trailers require three Hazchem panels, one at the rear, one on each side as close as possible to the front of the tank, plus a plain orange board on the front of the vehicle. Tank containers require four Hazchem panels, one each side and one on each end of the tank container.

The transport emergency card, or TREMCARD as it is often called, contains information vital to the safe treatment of people exposed to the dangerous goods in question, and more specific information about how to deal with spillages and fires. TREMCARDs are most important when dealing with incidents involving dangerous goods in drums/packages, because the external vehicle placarding will provide no useful information to the emergency services.

There are many other sensible precautions to be taken depending on the particular circumstances, but the above descriptions indicate how wide the duties of careful, reasonable anticipation and supervision are for employers and employees.

The National Chemical Emergency Centre operates a national 24-hour response centre, and is supported by the Department for Environment, Food and Rural Affairs (DEFRA). For further information visit www.the-ncec.com/emergency/index.html.

11.3.2. Trans-European journeys

The transportation of dangerous goods by road through Europe must comply with the ADR Regulations. The driver must be provided with instructions in writing in the languages of the driver and those of the countries visited. The ADR Hazard Identification Number (HIN) or Kemler code should be used on vehicles carrying dangerous goods in bulk or tankers travelling across Europe.

In summary, for:

- journeys within the UK—use Emergency Action Codes (EACs) or Hazchem codes (actions to be taken when dealing with the hazards)
- journeys across Europe—use the Hazard Identification Number (HIN) or Kemler code (advice on the nature of the hazard).

The international HIN is different from the national EAC, since it gives the danger presented by the goods as opposed to the action required to mitigate the consequences of an accident. For an excellent explanation of the signs and symbols used in the ADR visit www.the-ncec.com/hazchem/index.html.

Software is available to help comply with the ADR information requirements by generating TREMCARDS which contain the necessary information—this is available from www.tremcards.com/index.html.

11.4. Transfrontier shipment of waste

11.4.1. International law for the transfrontier shipment of waste

EC Regulation 259/93 on the supervision and control of shipments of waste within, into and out of the European Community, amended by Regulation 257/2001, controls international waste movements. This Regulation has direct effect in the UK, and applies to all waste, whether Hazardous or not. Its aims are to:

- prevent Hazardous waste export to non-OEDC (Organisation for Economic Cooperation and Development) countries
- ensure all shipments between OECD countries are properly monitored and are acceptable to the national regulatory authorities.

Waste shipments are divided into:

- waste final disposal
- shipments for recovery.

The disposal[7] of waste requires a notification to the:

- exporting countries
- importing countries
- transit countries.

Only when the three consents have been obtained can the shipment progress. When disposal has finished, the national authorities must again be informed. Authorities can refuse imports of waste for disposal on the grounds of:

- conflict with national waste strategies
- the EC proximity principle.

Since January 1998, under the Basel Convention, on which EC regulation is based, all Hazardous waste shipments to developing countries are banned by Regulation 120/97. For further information on the Basel Convention visit www.basel.int.

11.4.2. The international classification system for the shipment of waste for recovery

Wastes for recovery are divided according to the OECD classification system:

- red list wastes are the most hazardous, and are subject to the full notification procedure, namely the prior written consent of the authorities is required for each shipment
- amber list wastes are subject to a more streamlined procedure, where the consent of the competent authorities is assumed, provided no objections are made
- green list wastes (shipped for recovery) are not normally subject to the 259/93 Regulation.

---

[7] Note that under UK law the export of waste for disposal is banned, except under very special circumstances. Approach the EA on enquiry with all relevant documents filed and well presented.

For further information visit www.europa.eu.int/comm/trade/miti/envir/
waste.htm?lang=_e.

11.4.3. The Waste Transfrontier Shipment Regulations

The Waste Transfrontier Shipment Regulations 1994 SI 1137 (TFSR 1994) are
administered by the EA as the competent authority for the import and export of
waste, although the Secretary of State for the Environment is the competent
authority to whom UK transfers of waste must be notified. See regulation 3 in
the TFSR 1994.

A shipper of waste into or out of the UK must apply to the EA for a certificate that a financial guarantee or equivalent in insurance will cover the shipment cost (regulation 7 of the TFSR 1994). If the waste consignment cannot be
delivered to its destination, the EA can ensure the return of the exported waste
to the UK, and the repatriation of waste if wrongly imported (regulation 8 of
the TFSR 1994). The EA can also ensure the environmentally sound disposal
or recovery of waste illegally imported into the UK. Offences under the EC
Regulation, punishable with an unlimited fine or 2 years in prison, are relevant
offences under the Waste Management Licensing Regulations 1994,[8] Control
of Pollution (Amendment) Act 1989 (COP(A)A 1989) and the Integrated
Pollution Prevention and Control permitting regime, and can result in disquali-
fication from any waste management activity (regulation 12 of the TFSR
1994).

These Regulations are set against the background of the 1996 Department of
the Environment (now DEFRA) UK Government policy on international waste
shipments, UK Management Plan for Exports and Imports of Waste which
states that:

- exports of waste for disposal are banned
- waste may be exported for recovery to OECD countries, and under
  limited circumstances to non-OECD countries
- waste may only be imported for disposal if it cannot be environmentally
  soundly managed either in or nearer to its country of origin, or
- if waste can be imported for high-temperature incineration from certain
  EU Member States, where such facilities would be uneconomic, e.g.
  Ireland. In an emergency, waste can be imported from any country for
  incineration.

The TFS Regulations 1994 are available online at www.legislation.
hmso.gov.uk/si/si1994/Uksi_19941137_en_1.htm. See also the EA publication

---

[8] If convicted of a criminal offence, a person no longer qualifies as a 'fit and proper person', and
is therefore not entitled to hold a waste management licence (please see Section 8.6).

Box 11.1: Able UK unable

In September 2003 Able UK was granted a waste management licence modification by the EA to recycle 13 ex-US navy ships in a contract worth £10 million. The EA judged the company 'to have the capacity to carry out the work while fulfilling all of our requirements to protect the environment'.

In December 2003 a High Court Judge ruled for Friends of the Earth that the licence modification was not valid. A week later, local residents won a case which made the original planning application also not valid. Meanwhile, the Secretary of State for the Environment, who had originally allowed the passage of the ships, deemed that it was totally illegal for the ships to dock at Hartlepool, but then reverted to her original decision 3 days later. Meanwhile, Hartlepool Council decided that it was unhappy about the ships being scrapped in the borough, and the EA, which originally approved the recycling of the 13 ships, also performed a U-turn, deciding that its original advice to Able UK was contrary to good law. Instead of a licence modification, the changes actually necessitated a complete new licence application for consideration.

Able UK's managing director stated that 'We now find ourselves having to examine how we should proceed, recruitment of local people to work on the vessels is on hold, and yet our company has the experience, the track record and the facilities to carry out the recycling of these and other vessels in the best possible environmentally friendly and safe conditions.'

Meanwhile, Able UK must renegotiate all the legal proceedings, giving Hamburg and Rotterdam plenty of time to prepare their bids and take the work to the Continent, to the detriment of Teeside emplyment and the honing of future skills. Watch this space.

Sources: *The Evening Standard*, 12 November 2003; *The Times*, 13 November 2003; *The Times*, 9 December 2003; and *The Guardian*, 16 December 2003.

The Transfrontier Shipment of Waste—How to Complete a Notification and Movement Tracking Form (www.environment-agency.gov.uk/commondata/105385/transfrontier_ship_waste.pdf).

Practical illustrations in the difficulties of restraining transfrontier movements of waste materials, whether liquid or dry, generally are drawn from transfrontier movements within the Low Countries, France and Germany, where transfrontier movements by road and rail should obviously be more difficult to inspect than those entering England via the Channel Tunnel or possibly through our harbours.

A practical illustration of the difficulties of restraining certain transfrontier movements is the Northern Ireland Environment and Heritage Service (EHS) transfrontier control. The EHS deploys its transfrontier control system against a background that imports of waste into the UK for disposal are illegal under the

Box 11.2: Illegal shipment caught by vigilant officials

A ship containing 24 tonnes of waste cabling, for which the operators had been contracted to recover from the North Sea bed, was stopped by Dutch trading officials, and its contents intercepted as suspicious cargo. The illegal export was not accompanied by documentation, and the company was not a registered waste broker. The ship was sent back to Portland in Dorset, and the company later fined.

Source: *Environment Business News Briefing*, 12 February 2004.

1996 management plan for exports and imports of waste. However, the powers transferring responsibility for regulating transfrontier waste shipments from Northern Ireland's 26 local authorities to the EHS have yet to be implemented. It is as well for the UK to remember that when it sometimes criticises certain EU countries, its own Northern Ireland 26 local authorities do not all have full-time waste regulation officers. Responsibility for waste site licensing was finally transferred from those 26 councils to the EHS some 10 years after those in Britain were transferred to the EA.

There have been improvements in the Republic of Ireland's waste management systems since their Waste Management Act 1996 established a new national regulatory system. The number of landfills operating fell from 95 to 33 between 1995 and 2003, and it is not surprising, therefore, that it is estimated that there could be a 1 million tonne shortfall in capacity in 2004. Therefore, the Republic's landfill fees have tripled in the past 4 years, sometimes in the range of £100–135 per tonne, encouraging the waste from Dublin and its surrounding catchment area to travel north of the border. Increasingly sophisticated illegal networks are using forged papers and number plates to deliver considerable amounts of the Republic's waste to the Northern Ireland landfills. Not a happy scene.

Northern Ireland is not the only target of this illegal trading. Dutch authorities have recently returned 51 containers incorrectly classified as green list segregated waste suitable for recycling to the Republic; there is an appreciable return trade also awaiting reshipment from Antwerp back to the Republic.

The Merchant Shipping (Dangerous Goods and Marine Pollutants) Regulations 1997 SI 2367 require compliance with the International Maritime Dangerous Goods Code, which relates to the classification packaging, labelling, transport unit loading and placarding.

11.4.4. Import and export of radioactive waste

The European Council Regulation 1493/93 and the Transfrontier Shipment of Radioactive Waste Regulations 1993 SI 3031 apply to the import and export of radioactive waste. For further information on radiocative waste visit www.environment-agency.gov.uk/netregs/ or www.europa.eu.int/comm/ energy/nuclear/radioprotection/doc/legislation/931493_en.pdf?lang=_e.

Chapter 12

Waste mismanagement and water quality

Waste mismanagement can have the most deleterious effect on surface, ground and estuarine water quality, and there is some overlap between the waste and water regulatory regimes. The regulatory framework for water has recently undergone significant reform under the 2000/60 Water Framework Directive, which has been described by the Department for Environment, Food and Rural Affairs (DEFRA) as the most substantial piece of EU legislation to date.[1] The 2000/60 Directive has been implemented under the Water Act 2003, which may well have a restraining influence on waste management practices over the next decade, particularly in areas such as landfill engineering. Waste defined under the 75/442 Waste Framework Directive (as amended) does not include waste water, such as trade effluents.

12.1. Emergent control of surface water and groundwater

After the Second World War the level of water pollution in the UK's rivers was looked on as a necessary function of the war effort and the postwar export drive to right the country's serious balance of payments problems. There was a consequential low level of expectation, particularly in the light of the considerable capital expenditure involved in attaining even a low level of the alleviation of existing pollution. The UK approach to the control of water pollution has been to make discharges into Controlled waters a criminal offence in the absence of a legal defence, which is likely now, after recent case law, only to be that the discharge was authorised by a consent from a regulatory body. This is because with the increased emphasis on environmental standards, the criminal offence

---

[1] See www.defra.gov.uk/environment/water/wfd/.

has now become a strict criminal offence[2] (please see Chapter 9) in that neither criminal intent nor negligence are relevant. For example, a waste tanker tyre blow-out is no defence, but a lightening strike might possibly be. The first question by the visiting Environment Agency (EA) or Health and Safety Executive (HSE) inspector would be to ask for the risk assessment and then the whereabouts of the lightening conductor.

The Rivers (Prevention of Pollution) Act 1951 and the 1961 Act for Scotland stated in s.2(1)(a) that 'a person commits an offence ... if he causes or knowingly permits to enter a stream any poisonous, noxious or polluting matter'. This section was enforced with limited resources by the National Rivers Authorities (NRA) under the Water Resources Act 1963. The NRA's constant vigilance in many parts of England and Wales led to the Deposit of Poisonous Waste Act 1972 (please see Chapter 1), and for that they should always be remembered. That was the first Act to be enforced in any country in the world with such a deposit to be illegal and punishable with possible stiff penalties if a mitigation after conviction was unsatisfactory.

There has been legislation to control industrial effluent discharges to sewers, among them the Public Health Act 1936, then the Public Health (Drainage of Trade Premises) Act 1937, and finally the Water Act 1989. All the effluent control provisions have been amended, and are now in the Water Industry Act 1991. It is important briefly to recall the history of surface and groundwater control (as has been more fully recited in Chapter 1) because the historical dumping and tipping practices have left a legacy in contaminated land and polluted groundwater. It is easy to be wise after the event, and frown on all such practices, but they are partly understandable against a background of indiscriminate wartime bombing and then the V1s and V2s, and, almost as indiscriminate, armoured live ammunition manoeuvres carried on for well over 2 years before D-Day over considerable areas of UK pristine farm land and forest. Likewise, similar practices in and around naval dockyards and to some extent airfields, followed over recent years by the closing down of much of the UK steel and other metal-working industries, have left a difficult legacy of brownfield land, sometimes grossly polluted.

In 1996 the NRA, which had controlled water pollution since 1989 was transferred to the EA under s.2 of the Environment Act 1995. The Water Industry Act 1991 controls the 10 water companies under the Director General of water services known as OFWAT.

---

[2] *R* v. *Dovermoss Ltd*, Court of Appeal 1995. Rivers streams and ditches do not cease to be watercourses simply because they are dry. If polluting matter is put into a dry watercourse, then an offence is committed. So just a risk of water pollution can mean guilt. A tough regime of which too few in England and Wales are aware — they should be.

12.2. The Water Resources Act 1991, section 85

Section 85 of the Water Resources Act 1991 provides for five interrelated criminal offences of polluting Controlled waters. The most important (s.85(1)) is the offence to 'cause or knowingly permit any poisonous, noxious or polluting matter or any solid waste matter to enter any controlled waters.' On summary conviction the penalty can be up to 3 months imprisonment or £20,000, and on indictment 2 years and an unlimited fine. In fact, civil liability for clean-up costs and damages incurred following water pollution incidents may be as effective as criminal liability, although without the social opprobrium or the inability to qualify as a fit and proper person.[3]

Controlled waters are defined under s.104 of the Water Resources Act 1991 as:

- relevant territorial waters (waters which extend 3 miles seaward)
- coastal waters (up to high tide)
- any enclosed dock which adjoins coastal waters
- inland freshwaters, including rivers, canals and lakes
- groundwater, which is any waters contained in underground strata.

12.3. Groundwater

The Groundwater Regulations 1998 SI 2746 partially implement the 80/68 Groundwater Directive and apply to all of Great Britain. The 80/68 Directive is also implemented under the Waste Management Licensing Regulations 1994 SI 1056 and in particular regulation 15, and the Water Resources Act 1991 Part III. The Groundwater Regulations 1998 SI 2746 apply to waste disposal arising from agricultural and industrial activities that are described within the 80/68 Directive. The Regulations give powers to the EA, the Scottish Environment Protection Agency (SEPA) and DEFRA to control direct or indirect discharge of substances set out in Lists 1 and 2 of Schedule I. At present, List 1 and 2 substances cannot be discharged unless a discharge consent is obtained under Part III of the Water Resources Act 1991 or an Integrated Pollution Control authorisation under Part I of the Environmental Protection Act (EPA 1990) (as amended by the new Integrated Pollution Prevention and Control regime, please see Chapter 8). The 80/68 Directive is to be replaced by a new Groundwater Directive, and will be repealed in 2013. The new Directive will apply to all polluting substances, not just those limited to Lists 1 and 2. Any present problems can be complex. Please seek the very best advice.

---

[3] A waste management licence can only be held by a fit and proper person (please see Chapter 8).

12.4. The Water Framework Directive

The 2000/60 Water Framework Directive serves a similar role to the 75/442 Waste Framework Directive. It sets out fundamental aims and key principles which pull together all aspects of water regulation, and provides a framework for national legislation and possible future Daughter Directives. The 2000/60 Water Framework Directive aims to coordinate emissions limit values with the Integrated Pollution Prevention and Control regime. 2004 is the first year of the DEFRA 11-year Water Framework Directive implementation timetable, the cost of which was originally estimated (in 1999) to be between £1.9 and £9.0 billion.

The main aims of the 2000/60 Directive are to:

- prevent the deterioration of aquatic ecosystems
- enhance the status of aquatic ecosystems
- reduce pollution, particularly from certain priority substances
- protect groundwater and reduce groundwater pollution
- reduce the effects of floods and droughts.

A key feature is the need to 'enhance the status' of aquatic ecosystems. Most environmental legislation aims to protect or prevent, and it is unusual for a law to require actual improvement of the environment. The 2000/60 Directive aims to improve water management by integrating strategies on a large supra-catchment scale,[4] and it adopts a hazard–risk approach. An ambitious programme, subject to proof.

Table 12.1 summarises some of the key deadlines in the DEFRA 2000/60 Water Framework Directive implementation programme. The programme will include consultations, reviews and reporting, and the plans will be updated in 2015. The competent authority for the Directive in England and Wales is the EA, and in Scotland SEPA.

12.5. Water quality under the Water Framework Directive

Under the 2000/60 Water Framework Directive water quality is evaluated differently depending on whether it is surface or groundwater:

- surface water quality is termed ecological status, and is based on physical ecological effects, which are the outcome of pollution
- groundwater quality is quantified by measuring the actual amount of pollutants present, i.e. chemical levels, and is termed chemical status.

---

[4] In the UK the large catchment areas are known as river basin districts.

232

Table 12.1: Some key 2000/60 Water Framework Directive deadlines

Date	Deadline
December 2004	Analysis of surface and groundwater characteristics, review of human environmental impact and economic analysis to be completed
December 2005	Criteria for identifying trends in groundwater pollution to be established
December 2006	Monitoring programmes to be operational Environmental quality standards for surface water affected by discharges to be established
December 2007	75/440 Surface Water Directive to be repealed
2010	Water pricing policies to be in place
December 2013	The following Directives will be repealed: • 76/464 Discharge of Dangerous Substances Directive • 79/928 Shellfish Waters Directive • 78/659 Freshwater Fish Directive • 80/68 Groundwater Directive The 2000/60 Water Framework Directive is to be supplemented by a new Groundwater Directive
2015	Good ecological or chemical status to be achieved for all inland and coastal waters

The scores for ecological or chemical status are bad, poor, moderate, good and high. 'High' relates to pre-industrialised quality. The 2000/60 Water Framework Directive requires EU Member States to achieve good ecological or chemical status in all inland and coastal waters by 2015. Most difficult to attain.

Ecological status can be subject to many influencing factors, such as an unexpectedly warm summer or other natural phenomena resulting in fish kill or thriving populations. Chemical status is based on the direct measurement of chemicals and their levels. Although these can also be affected by a range of natural factors (e.g. salinity influenced by highest astronomical tides or a storm surge), the chemical levels are measured directly and are therefore more traceable or attributable to a source or cause than the ecological indicators.

The term heavily modified water bodies (HMWBs) was introduced in the 2000/60 Directive, and refers to water bodies that have been subject to engineering (e.g. for navigation, storage or drainage). The Directive recognises that restoration to good ecological status might not be achievable in the long term without preventing the continuation of that use, or detriment to social and

233

Box 12.1: Good ecological status undefined

The 2000/60 Water Framework Directive consists of 20 pages setting out radical new requirements for water quality, presently unfathomable. High ecological status refers to a pristine aquatic system. So good ecological status (GES) is defined as a deviation or distortion from this pristine status. There are no truly pristine habitats in the UK—achieving UK GES by 2015 would need 50% of the country to revert to semi-natural vegetation, somewhat akin to set-aside land. GES is to be defined by ecology, not by oxygen levels, pH, nutrients or salinity.

The UK EA is collaborating with other EU regulators on the EU Common Implementation Strategy (CIS), which comprises 10 working groups. The timetable for achieving GES has been estimated to be 11 years, but consideration should be given to:

- the technical feasibility
- whether the expense is proportionate.

economic benefits. Instead, HMWBs must achieve good ecological potential instead of good ecological status.

12.6. The Water Act 2003

The extensive existing UK water regulatory regime is not sufficient to implement the 2000/60 Directive. The Water Act 2003 is therefore implementing the 2000/60 Water Framework Directive, and aims to:

- reform the water industry's regulatory arrangements
- reform the abstraction licensing system
- open up competition in water supplies to major customers
- review pollution from abandoned coal mines and contaminated land
- consider the structure of discharge consents.

The Water Act 2003 amends key areas of three environmental Acts:

- Section 78A of the EPA 1990 on contaminated land. The word 'significant' has been added; for example: the contamination must cause 'significant pollution' of Controlled waters.
- Water Resources Act 1991. The Act amends the Water Resources Act 1991, which relates primarily to a reform of the abstraction licensing system. Changes include the creation of two new types of abstraction licence, transfer and temporary licences, with exemptions for abstractions of less than $20\,m^3$ per day.
- Water Industry Act 1991. The amendments to the Water Industry Act 1991 relate to the duties of water companies, who must now prepare and

Table 12.2: Some key legislation relating to water and waste management

New Water Directives	Directives to be repealed under the 2000/60 Directive	Relevant Directives that still apply	Relevant UK law in force
2000/60 Water Framework Directive	76/464 Discharge of Dangerous Substances Directive	96/61 Integrated Pollution Prevention and Control Directive	Water Act 2003 (implements the 2000/60 Directive)
New Groundwater Directive	75/440 Surface Water Directive	99/31 Landfill Directive	Pollution Prevention and Control Act 1999
	78/659 Freshwater Fish Directive	86/278 Sewage Sludge Directive	Water Resources Act 1991 (as amended by the Water Act 2003)
	79/928 Shellfish Waters Directive	92/43 Habitats Directive	Water Industry Act 1991 (as amended by the Water Act 2003)
	80/68 Groundwater Directive	79/409 Birds Directive	EPA 1990 (as amended by the Water Act 2003)
		91/676 Nitrate Directive	Landfill Regulations 2002 SI 1559 Water Environment (Water Framework Directive) Regulations 2003 SI 3242 Groundwater Regulations 1998 SI 2746 Regulation 15 of the Waste Management Licensing Regulations 1994 SI 1056

publicise drought plans and water resource management plans, improve water conservation, increase competition in the supply of water services and arrange with the strategic health authorities for the fluoridation of water supplies.

The EU Common Implementation Strategy (CIS) aims to coordinate a common approach to implementing the 2000/60 Directive between Member States. The CIS guidance is not legally binding, and was developed with input from the EA and SEPA. Through the CIS, Member States are currently undertaking pilot testing on selected river basins, which in the UK is the River Ribble in the North-West region. The project aims to determine how the Directive will be implemented in the UK, and to provide a prototype individual river basin management plan. The catchment in this case covers 820 square miles. For further information visit www.environment-agency.gov.uk/ribblewfd.

The Water Resources Act 1991, Water Industry Act 1991 and the EPA 1990 sections that have not been amended still apply, in addition to a number of other Acts and secondary legislation which may affect waste management practice in relation to water. The Water Act 2003 is being implemented with new secondary legislation (e.g. the Water Environment (Water Framework Directive) Regulations 2003 SI 3242, the Water Environment (Water Framework Directive) (Northumbria River Basin District) Regulations 2003 SI 3245 and the Water Environment (Water Framework Directive) (Solway Tweed River Basin District) Regulations 2004).

Some of the key changes under the 2000/60 Directive and other relevant existing legislation are summarised in Table 12.2.

Table 12.2 is not comprehensive, and therefore regard should be had to updates available from the DEFRA and EA websites. A full text of the 2000/60 Water Framework Directive is available at europa.eu.int/eurlex/pri/en/oj/dat/2000/l_327/l_32720001222en00010072.pdf.

An overview of the Water Act 2003 is set out in the explanatory notes to the Act, which are available at www.legislation.hmso.gov.uk/acts/en2003/2003en37.htm. For further information visit www.defra.gov.uk/environment/water/wfd/.

Chapter 13

The end of the beginning

The benefits of even-handed enforcement of a sensible, well-thought-through and coherent environmental regulatory regime certainly cannot be underestimated, and can be far more rewarding than those who view the law simply as a tool of enforcement could ever envisage. Not only can such a regime protect the environment and benefit human health but it can increase efficiency, reduce production costs and recognisably control risks. Any such improvement can be reflected in local authority or corporate morale, thus indirectly raising the quality and calibre of prospective new recruits.

In the Preface to this practical guide some of the tsunami of approaching UK and EU future legislation was listed. It is as well to remind UK political parties across the spectrum that we have acquired the habit of legislating too easily, both in the EU and the UK. It helps nobody; in fact it is harmful to pile law upon law without regard to the cumulative effect of measures which, and this must be emphasised, individually may be laudable. There are many laws which have been introduced because a previous law on a similar subject has only been partially implemented.[1] There are limits to what legislation can achieve; every new legislation involves detriment as well as benefit.

---

[1] For example, the statutory nuisance provisions under the Public Health Act 1936 were not effectively enforced, as explained in Chapter 1. These were later replaced with some change in the detail by Part III, s.79 of the Environmental Protection Act 1990. Likewise, the 90/313 Directive on freedom of access to environmental information, implemented through the Freedom of Access to Environmental Information Regulations 1992 SI 3240, was not uniformly administered and applied to achieve its stated purpose. The Royal Commission on Environmental Protection 10th Report 1984 stated that there was a presumption in favour of unrestricted access for the public to information, which the pollution control authorities obtain by virtue of their statutory powers. The European Convention on Access to Information, Public Participation in Decision Making and Access to Justice in Environmental Matters (the Aarhaus Convention) was the next legislation to be passed and then implemented in the UK by the Freedom of Information Act 2000. The 90/313 Directive was replaced in January 2003 by the 2003/4 (*sic*) Public Access to Environmental Information Directive. Yet many people complain that environmental information is no more accessible by the UK public than it was 10 years ago.

Box 13.1: Do not say that you were not warned ...

> European law is like an incoming tide.
> It flows into the estuaries.
> And up the rivers.
> It cannot be denied.
>
> Lord Denning, 1972
>
> Source: Hawkins R. G. P., NAWDC (now ESA) Lectures 1972–1993

This general acceptance that all new environmental laws will be even-handedly enforced, and thus improve the environment, is necessarily encouraged by environmental consultants and lawyers who, recognising the business opportunities, wish to explain to their clients the effect of the incoming laws on their present or future business. Some are perhaps less enthusiastic than others to comment on whether the directives and UK laws are operable and their efficacy quantifiable. It has not proved possible, for example, to persuade many institutes, institutions and associations, who perhaps in all honesty should know better, to scrutinise as a matter of course whether proposed directives are really necessary in their context before their EU adoption.

Again in the Preface to this book the House of Commons February 2004 All Party Select Committee on the End of Life Vehicles and Waste Electrical and Electronic Equipment Directives concluded that the Department for Environment, Food and Rural Affairs (DEFRA) management had been characterised by a lack of guidance and clarity. They also questioned whether DEFRA possessed adequate specialist skills, particularly in terms of legal capacity. Two years previously, the House of Common Environment Food and Rural Affairs Committee in their report on hazardous waste, published on 26 July 2002, proposed in the last sentence of their summary: 'We recommend that the Government instigates a thorough review of the process by which environmental legislation is arrived at in the European Commission.'

How the UK and EU future environmental and planning laws will be implemented and consistently enforced and monitored and, most important of all, be respected by those whom they affect cannot be within the ambit of this practical guide. But it is as well to recall that hope pays no dues to reason. European environmental control has often been the subject of a Commissioner's wishful thinking, nourished by intravenous optimism, yet out of touch with field operational enforcement reality. For example, there has been no calculation of recycling rates by reference to useable outputs from recyclable materials.

So, it is hoped that the next edition of this practical guide will be the same size, or even contain fewer pages, but we are not all that sanguine. Are you? In any event, please let us know those matters which you think should not have been included in this guide, and those which you consider to have been omitted, and any comments, adverse or otherwise.

Appendix A

Some relevant legislation and international conventions

The field of waste management covers a broad range of disciplines, including biochemistry, chemical engineering, civil engineering, emissions control, financial analysis, geotechnical engineering, hydrogeology, transportation economics and noise abatement. There is a thin line dividing these subjects from intrinsic waste management law, and certain topics that are related to waste management are subjects in their own right. For example, employment law and contract management are covered by appropriate specialist texts.

The following pages summarise much of the principal law that influences public and private sector waste management industry decisions. The schedules are as complete as is reasonably possible, but are by no means final. The reader should not take the tables as complete and up to date, but check with his or her professional sources or library and the relevant websites (Appendix E lists some useful websites). The Directives and UK Acts are in chronological order, but because an inquiring reader will probably know the subject matter for which he or she is searching, the secondary legislation has been listed in alphabetical order, which hopefully will be of some help for quick referral.

Some EU Directives

(In chronological order.)

75/442	Waste Framework Directive (as amended)
75/439	Waste Oil Directive
76/403	Disposal of PCBs and PCTs
76/464	Discharge of Dangerous Substances Directive
78/659	Freshwater Fish Directive
79/409	Birds Directive
79/928	Shellfish Waters Directive
80/68	Groundwater Directive
80/778	Drinking Water Directive

85/337	Environment Impact Assessment Directive
86/278	Sewage Sludge
87/217	Prevention and Reduction of Environmental Pollution by Asbestos
87/101	Disposal of Waste Oils
89/106	Construction Products Directive
89/369	Prevention of Air Pollution from Waste Incinerators
89/429	Prevention of Air Pollution from Waste Incinerators
89/665	Public Sector Remedies Directive
90/313	Freedom of Access to Information on the Environment
90/425	Animal Waste
90/667	Animal Waste
91/157	Batteries and Accumulators
91/156	Waste Directive (amending the 75/442 Waste Framework Directive)
91/676	Nitrate Directive
91/689	Hazardous Waste
91/692	Standardising and Rationalising Reports on the Implementation of Certain Environmental Directives
92/43	Habitats
92/50	Services Procurement
92/85	Introduction of Measures to Encourage Improvements in the Safety and Health at Work of Pregnant Workers and Workers who have Recently Given Birth or are Breastfeeding
93/36	Supplies Procurement
93/38	Utilities Procurement
93/97	Works Procurement
93/86	Batteries and Accumulators
94/31	Hazardous Waste
94/62	Packaging and Packaging Waste
96/35	Appointment and Vocational Qualification of Safety Advisers for the Transport of Dangerous Goods by Road, Rail and Inland Waterway
96/59	Disposal of PCBs and PCTs
96/61	Integrated Pollution Prevention and Control
97/11	Environmental Impact Assessment
98/8	Risk Assessment
99/31	Landfill Directive
99/364	Transportable Pressure Equipment
2000/18	Minimum Examination Requirements for Safety Advisers for the Transport of Dangerous Goods by Road, Rail or Inland Waterway
2000/59	Implementation of the Strategy for Port Reception Facilities for Ship-generated Wastes and Associated Issues
2000/76	Waste Incineration Directive
2000/53	End of Life Vehicle Directive

2000/60 Water Framework Directive
2001/42 Strategic Environmental Assessment
2001/77 Electricity from Renewable Sources
2002/49 The Assessment and Management of Environmental Noise
2002/95 Restrictions of Hazardous Substances
2002/96 Waste Electrical and Electronic Equipment
2003/28 ADR and 2003/29 RID Framework Directives for the Carriage of Dangerous Goods
2003/30 Biofuels
2003/87 Emissions Trading

Some EU Regulations and decisions

880/92   Ecolabelling
259/93   Supervision and Control of Shipments of Waste Within, Into and Out of the European Community, amended by Regulation 257/2001
93/98   Control of Transboundary Movements of Hazardous Waste and their Disposal (Basle Convention)
94/3   European Waste Catalogue
94/575   Supervision and Control of Shipments of Waste
94/774   Supervision and Control of Shipments of Waste
94/904   Hazardous Waste List
96/660   Supervision and Control of Shipments of Waste
97/138   Packaging and Packaging Waste
2037/2000   Ozone Depleting Substances
2076/2002   Withdrawal of Products Containing Certain Substances
1600/2002   6th Community Environmental Action Programme
2150/2002   Waste Statistics
2099/2002   Establishing a Committee on Safe Seas and Pollution Prevention from Ships
2003/33   Waste Acceptance Criteria

European agreements

2003 European Agreement concerning the International Carriage of Dangerous Goods by Road
2003 European Agreement concerning the International Carriage of Dangerous Goods by Rail

Some EU Directives in the pipeline

Biowaste
Environmental Liability
Groundwater

Household Hazardous Waste
Management of Waste from the Extractive Industries
Registration, Evaluation and Authorisation of Chemicals (REACH)
Waste Oils

Some principal Acts

(In chronological order.)

Explosives Act 1875
Health and Safety at Work etc. Act 1974
Control of Pollution Act 1974
Refuse Disposal (Amenity) Act 1978
Local Government (Scotland) Act 1982
Local Government Act 1985
Income and Corporation Taxes Act 1988
Environmental Protection Act 1990
Town and Country Planning Act 1990
Planning (Hazardous Substances) Act 1990
Planning (Listed Buildings and Conservation Areas) Act 1990
Planning and Compensation Act 1991
Water Resources Act 1991
Water Industry Act 1991
The Radioactive Substances Act 1993
Environment Act 1995
Dogs Fouling of Land Act 1996
Finance Act 1996
Merchant Shipping and Maritime Security Act 1997
Government of Wales Act 1998
Scotland Act 1998
Waste Minimisation Act 1998
Local Government Act 1999
Pollution Prevention and Control Act 1999
The Employment Act 2002
Anti-Social Behaviour Act 2003
Household Waste and Recycling Act 2003
Regional Assemblies (Preparations) Act 2003
Finance Act 2003
Waste Emissions Trading Act 2003
Water Act 2003
Planning and Compulsory Purchase Act 2004

Some important secondary legislation

(In alphabetical order by subject matter where possible.)

Animal By-Products Regulations 2003 SI 1482

Asbestos (Licensing) (Amendment) Regulations 1998 SI 3233

Control of Asbestos at Work Regulations 2002 SI 2675

Control of Asbestos in Air Regulations 1990 SI 556

Batteries and Accumulators (Containing Dangerous Substances) Regulations 1994 SI 232

Batteries and Accumulators (Containing Dangerous Substances) (Amendment) Regulations 2001 SI 2551

Building Regulations 1991 SI 2768

Carriage of Dangerous Goods and Use of Transportable Pressure Equipment Regulations 2004 SI 568

Chemicals (Hazard Information and Packaging for Supply) Regulations 1996

Classification and Labelling of Explosives Regulations 1983 SI 1140

Coal Mines (Respirable Dust) Regulations 1975 SI 2001

Construction (Design and Management) Regulations 1994 SI 3140

Contaminated Land (England) Regulations 2000 SI 227

Controlled Waste Regulations 1992 SI 588

Controlled Waste (Amendment) Regulations 1993 SI 566

Controlled Waste (Registration of Carriers and Seizure of Vehicles) Regulations 1991 SI 1624

Controlled Waste (Registration of Carriers and Seizure of Vehicles) (Amendment) Regulations 1998 SI 605

Control of Major Accident Hazards Regulations 1999 SI 743

Control of Pollution (Amendment) Act 1989 SI 1618

Control of Pollution (Licensing of Waste Disposal) (Scotland) Regulations 1977 2006

Control of Substances Hazardous to Health Regulations 2002 SI 2677

Crop Residues (Burning) Regulations 1993 SI 1366

End of Life Vehicles Regulations 2003 SI 2635

Energy from Waste Plants (Rateable Values) (England) Order 2000 SI 952

Environmental Information Regulations 1992 SI 3240

Environmental Licences (Suspension and Revocation) Regulations 1996 SI 508

Environmental Protection (Disposal of Polychlorinated Biphenyls and other Dangerous Substances) (England and Wales) Regulations 2000 SI 1043

Environmental Protection Disposal of Polychlorinated Biphenyls and other Dangerous Substances (England and Wales) (Amendment) Regulations 2000 SI 3359

Environmental Protection (Duty of Care) Regulations 1991 SI 2839

Environmental Protection (Waste Recycling Payments) (England) Regulations 2004 SI 639

Farm Waste Grant (Nitrate Vulnerable Zones) (England) Scheme 2003 SI 562

Greenhouse Gas Emissions Trading Scheme Regulations 2003 SI 3311

Landfill (England and Wales) Regulations 2002 SI 1559

Landfill Tax (Contaminated Land) Order 1996 SI 1529

Landfill Tax Regulations 1996 SI 1527

Local Government (Best Value) Performance Indicators Order 2000 SI 896

Management of Health and Safety at Work Regulations 1999 SI 3242

Merchant Shipping (Dangerous Goods and Marine Pollutants) Regulations 1997 SI 2367

Merchant Shipping and Fishing Vessels (Port Waste Reception Facilities) Regulations 2003 SI 1809

Merchant Shipping (Prevention of Pollution by Garbage) Regulations 1998 SI 1377

Notification of Installations Handling Hazardous Substance Regulations 1982 SI 1357

Oil Storage Pollution Control Regulations 2001 SI 2954

Packaging (Essential Requirements) Regulations 2003 SI 1941

Packaging of Explosives for Carriage Regulations 1991 SI 2097

Pollution Prevention and Control (England and Wales) Regulations 2000 SI 1973

Pollution Prevention and Control (Scotland) Regulations 2000 SI 323

Pollution Prevention and Control (Designation of Council Directives on Large Combustion Plants, Incineration of Waste and National Emission Ceilings) Order 2002 SI 2528

Producer Responsibility Obligations (Packaging Waste) Regulations 1997 SI 648

Producer Responsibility Obligations (Packaging Waste) (Amendment) Regulations 1999 SI 1361

Producer Responsibility Obligations (Packaging Waste) (Amendment) England and Wales 2000 SI 3375

Producer Responsibility (Packaging Waste) Amendment (Scotland) Regulations 2002 SSI 147

Removal and Disposal of Vehicles Regulations 1986 SI 183

Removal of Refuse Regulations 1967 SI 1240

Removal, Storage and Disposal of Vehicles Regulation 1989 SI 336

Reporting of Injuries, Diseases and Dangerous Occurrences Regulations 1995 SI 3163

Sludge (Use in Agriculture) Regulations 1989 SI 1263

Special Waste Amendment (Scotland) Regulations 2004 SI 112

Special Waste Regulations 1996 SI 972

Special Waste (Amendment) Regulations 1996 SI 2019

Special Waste (Amendment) Regulations 1997 SI 251

Town and Country Planning (Applications) Regulations 1988 SI 1812

Town and Country Planning (Environmental Impact Assessment) Regulations 1999 SI 293

Town and Country Planning (Environmental Impact Assessment) (Amendment) Regulations 2000 SI 2867

Town and Country Planning General Development Order 1988 SI 1813

Town and Country Planning (General Permitted Development) Order 1995, SI 418

Town and Country Planning (Use Classes) Order 1987 SI 764

Transfrontier Shipment of Radioactive Waste Regulations 1993 SI 3031

Transfrontier Shipment of Waste Regulations 1994 SI 1137

United Kingdom Ecolabelling Board (Abolition) Regulations 1999 SI 931

Waste and Contaminated Land (Northern Ireland) Order 1997 SI 2778

Waste Electrical and Electronic Equipment Regulations 2004

Waste (Foot-and-Mouth disease) (England) Regulations 2001 SI 1478

Waste (Foot-and-Mouth disease) (England) (Amendment) Regulations 2001 SI 3189

Waste Incineration (England and Wales) Regulations 2002 SI 2980

Waste Management Licences (Consultation and Compensation) Regulations 1999 SI 481

Waste Management Licensing Regulations 1994 SI 1056

Waste Management Licensing (Amendment) Regulations 1995 SI 288

Waste Management Licensing (Amendment) Regulations 1996 SI 1279

Waste Management Licensing (Amendment) Regulations 2003 SI 595

Waste Regulation and Disposal (Authorities) Order 1985 SI 1884

Some relevant international conventions

London Convention 1972 (formerly the London Dumping Convention, amended 1996), a global convention controlling the dumping of wastes at sea under licence

Marpol Convention 1973 on the prevention of pollution from ships (modified by the Protocol of 1978)

Montreal Protocol 1987 on substances that deplete the ozone layer

Basel Convention 1989 on transboundary movements of hazardous waste

Aarhus Convention 1998 on participation in decision making and access to justice in environmental matters

Appendix B

Some relevant House of Commons and House of Lords Parliamentary Select Committee reports 2001–2002 to 2003–2004

Committee	Report title	Session	Date	Reference	Website
Environmental Audit Committee	*Environmental Crime*	2002–2003	12.12.03	New inquiry	www.parliament.uk/ parliamentary_committees/ environmental_audit_committee/ eac_12_12_03.cfm
	4th Special Report: *Waste— An Audit: Government Response to the Committee's Fifth Report of Session 2002–03*	2002–2003	20.10.03	HC 1081	www.parliament.the-stationery-office.co.uk/pa/cm200203/cmselect/ cmenvaud/1081/108102.htm
	5th Report: *Waste—An Audit*	2002–2003	23.4.03	HC 99-I	www.parliament.the-stationery-office.co.uk/pa/cm200203/cmselect/ cmenvaud/99/9902.htm
Environment, Food and Rural Affairs	4th Report: *End of Life Vehicles and Waste Electrical and Electronic Equipment (WEEE) Directives*	2003–2004	11.2.04	HC 103	www.parliament.the-stationery-office.co.uk/ pa/cm200304/ cmselect/cmenvfru/103/103.pdf
	Agriculture and EU Enlargement	2002–2003	–	New inquiry	www.parliament.uk/ parliamentary_committees/ parliamentary_committees26.cfm
	17th Report: *Biofuels*	2002–2003	6.11.03	HC 929-I	www.publications.parliament.uk/pa/ cm200203/cmselect/cmenvfru/929/ 92902.htm
	9th Special Report: *The Future of Waste Management: Government Reply to the Committee's Report*	2002–2003	16.9.03	HC 1084	www.publications.parliament.uk/pa/ cm200203/cmselect/cmenvfru/1084/ 108402.htm

Report	Session	Date	HC No.	URL
6th Special Report: *The Water Framework Directive: Government Reply*	2002–2003	10.6.03	HC 749	www.publications.parliament.uk/pa/cm200203/cmselect/cmenvfru/749/74902.htm
8th Report: *The Future of Waste Management*	2002–2003	22.5.03	HC 385-I	www.publications.parliament.uk/pa/cm200203/cmselect/cmenvfru/749/74902.htm
4th Report: *The Water Framework Directive*	2002–2003	19.3.03	HC 130-I	www.publications.parliament.uk/pa/cm200203/cmselect/cmenvfru/130/13002.htm
7th Special Report: *Radioactive Waste: The Government's Consultation Process*	2001–2002	24.10.02	HC 1221	www.publications.parliament.uk/pa/cm200102/cmselect/cmenvfru/1221/122102.htm
11th Special Report: *Hazardous Waste: Government's Reply to the Committee's Eighth Report of Session 2001–02*	2001–2002	24.10.02	HC 1225	www.publications.parliament.uk/pa/cm200102/cmselect/cmenvfru/1225/122502.htm
12th Special Report: *Disposal of Refrigerators: Government's Reply to the Committee's Fourth Report of Session 2001–02*	2001–2002	24.10.02	HC 1226	www.publications.parliament.uk/pa/cm200102/cmselect/cmenvfru/1226/122602.htm
8th Report: *Hazardous Waste*	2001–2002	26.7.02	HC 919	www.publications.parliament.uk/pa/cm200102/cmselect/cmenvfru/919/91902.htm

251

Committee	Report title	Session	Date	Reference	Website
Environment Food and Rural Affairs (contd)	4th Report: *Disposal of Refrigerators*	2001–2002	20.6.02	HC 673	www.publications.parliament.uk/pa/cm200102/cmselect/cmenvfru/673/67302.htm
	4th Special Report: *Delivering Sustainable Waste Management: Government Reply to the Report of Session 2000–01 from the Environment, Transport and Regional Affairs Committee*	2001–2002	5.3.02	HC 659	www.publications.parliament.uk/pa/cm200102/cmselect/cmenvfru/659/65902.htm
	3rd Report: *Radioactive Waste: The Government's Consultation Process*	2001–2002	13.2.02	HC 407	www.publications.parliament.uk/pa/cm200102/cmselect/cmenvfru/407/40702.htm
The National Audit Office	*Environment Agency: Protecting the Public from Waste*	2002–2003	18.12.02	HC 156	www.nao.gov.uk/publications/nao_reports/ 02–03/0203156.pdf
Joint Committee on Statutory Instruments	*5th Road Vehicles (Registration and Licensing) Regulations 2002 SI 2002/2742; Dangerous Substances and Explosive Atmospheres Regulations 2002 SI 2002/2776*			HL Paper 25 HC 96-v	www.parliament.the-stationery-office.co.uk/pa/cm200203/cmwib/wb021221/selp.htm

Source: www.parliament.uk/parliamentary_committees/parliamentary_committees26.cfm

Appendix C

Special Waste Consignment Note: example

Cleanaway Limited

Top White	Pre notification
Second Yellow	Consignee's Agency Office
Third Pink	Consignee
Fourth Orange	Carrier
Fifth Green	Consignor

A Brambles Company

Consignment Note
Special Waste Regulations 1996

WS No.
W/T No.
Consignment Note No.
No. of pre-notice
(If different)

SECTION A CONSIGNMENT DETAILS   **PLEASE TICK IF YOU ARE A TRANSFER STATION** ☐

1. The waste described below is to be removed from   2. The waste will be taken to

3. The consignment(s) will be *one single* ☐ *a succession* ☐ *carrier's round* ☐ *other* ☐
4. Expected removal date of first consignment: last consignment:
5. Name   On behalf of (company)
   Signature   Date
6. Telephone   7. The waste producer was (if different from 1.)

SECTION B DESCRIPTION OF WASTE   **NO. OF ADDITIONAL SHEETS** ☐

1. The waste is

2. Classification
3. Physical form: Liquid ☐   Powder ☐   Sludge ☐   Solid ☐   Mixed ☐
4. Colour
5. Total quantity for removal
   Container type number and size
6. The chemical/biological components and concentrations of the waste

7. The hazards are:
8. The process giving rise to waste is:

SECTION C CARRIER'S CERTIFICATE   I certify that I today collected the consignment and that the details in A1, A2 and B1 are correct. The quantity collected in the load is:
Name   On behalf of (company) (Name, address & postcode)

Signature
1. Carrier registration No.   Date   at   hrs
Issued by   2. Vehicle registration No.

SECTION D CONSIGNOR'S CERTIFICATE   I certify that the information in B and C above are correct, that the carrier is registered or exempt and was advised of the appropriate precautionary measures.
Name   On behalf of (company)

Signature   Date

SECTION E CONSIGNEE'S CERTIFICATE

1. I received this waste at the address given in A2 on   at   hrs
2. Quantity received (include units eg kgs/ltrs/tonnes etc)
3. Vehicle registration No.   4. Management operation
I certify that waste management licence/authorisation/exemption No.
authorises the management of the waste described in B at the address given in A2.
Name   On behalf of (company)

Signature   Date

Appendix D

Operations control document: example (incorporating a Waste Transfer Note)

CLEANAWAY LIMITED	Revision 6. February 2002		Form No. 2414

CLEANAWAY LIMITED Revision 6. February 2002 Form No. 2414

Quote Ref. No.

FORM F1 OPERATIONS CONTROL DOCUMENT
INCORPORATING WASTE TRANSFER NOTE

Cleanaway Waste Carrier Reg No. ESS 314026 (GB)

WS No. TEF No.

Season Period

Disposal Site Signature	Approved Date	Driver's Name	Signature	Vehicle Regn No.
Print Name				

Producer Name & Address

Customer Name & Address (if diff.) Carrier if not Cleanaway Ltd.

Contact

Contact

Tel. No.

Tel. No.

All loads of the Waste/Material for which this form has been prepared must at all times be accompanied by this form or an identical readable copy of it. The form must be taken to the receiving site and be valid in terms of date. Driver operators must read and abide by the receiving site's instructions. This document details information required under the Environmental Protection (Duty of Care) Regulations 1991 (WASTE TRANSFER NOTE), a signed copy to be retained for 2 years.

WASTE/MATERIAL
SPECIFICATION
General Description/
Container Type

Process Source

Principal Components

Permitted concentrations for

significant constituents/

chemical analysis

Quantity and Frequency

For Cleanaway Limited
Signature:

Physical Form
Max Temperature, Max Density

Collection point and
method of site storage

Print Name:
Date:

PRINCIPAL
RECEIVING SITE

DISPOSAL AREA Technical Control Signature

Earliest Permitted Date of Deposit

Handling and Safety Notes/Safe working Procedures for loading purposes only.

This document also satisfies The Carriage of Dangerous Goods by Road Regulations 1996, which requires a signed approval to meet Regulation 13(2)(b)(vi).

V	TD	UN	E.A.C.	Class	Sec. Haz	Category	Consignor's Declaration (or on their behalf)

Signature(s): Collection Date:

Print Name: Ticket

P.S.N.

Waste Management
Licence No.

24hrs Notice Required by Receiving Site	Cover on Day of Disposal	Cover immed-iately	Technical Supervison Required	Sample Required	Washout After Discharge	Waste Code	Restricted Components

Appendix E

Some relevant websites

Asbestos: www.hse.gov.uk/asbestos
The Chartered Institute of Environmental Health: www.cieh.org.uk
The Chartered Institution of Wastes Management: www.ciwm.co.uk
The Chartered Institution of Water and Environmental Management:
    www.ciwem.org.uk
Chemicals (DEFRA): www.defra.gov.uk/environment/chemicals/eufuture.htm
The Chemical Industry Association: www.cia.org.uk
The Composting Association: www.compost.org.uk
Confederation of British Industry: www.cbi.org.uk/home.html
Croner: www.croner.co.uk
Customs and Excise: www.hmce.gov.uk
Department for Environment, Food and Rural Affairs: www.defra.gov.uk
Department of the Environment in Northern Ireland: www.doeni.gov.uk
The Department for Trade and Industry: www.dti.gov.uk
The Environment Agency: www.environment-agency.gov.uk/netregs
Environmental Data Services (ENDS): www.ends.co.uk
Environmental Industries Commission (EIC): www.eic-uk.co.uk
The Environmental Services Association (ESA): www.esauk.org
Envirowise: www.envirowise.gov.uk
European Court of Justice: curia.eu.int
European Legislation: europa.eu.int/eur-lex/en/search/search_lif.html
Government Information and Services: www.ukonline.gov.uk
Government Reports: www.parliament.the-stationery-office.co.uk
The Guardian Unlimited Special Report: www.guardian.co.uk/waste/
The Health Protection Agency: www.hpa.org.uk
The Health and Safety Executive: www.hse.gov.uk
Her Majesty's Stationery Office: www.hmso.gov.uk
The Incorporated Council of Law Reporting for England & Wales:
    www.lawreports.co.uk
The Institution of Civil Engineers: www.ice.org.uk
The Health and Safety Executive: www.hse.gov.uk

Industry Council for Electronic Equipment Recycling: www.icer.org.uk
International Solid Waste Association (ISWA): www.iswa.org
Letsrecycle.com: www.letsrecycle.com/legislation/
London ReMaDe: www.capitalwastelearning.com
The National Audit Office: www.nao.gov.uk
National Chemical Emergency Centre: www.the-ncec.com/index.html
Nuclear Waste: www.dti.gov.uk/nuclearcleanup/
The Office of the Deputy Prime Minister: www.odpm.gov.uk
Review of the Development of EU Environmental Policy from 2001–2003:
    europa.eu.int/comm/environment/industry/com2003_745_en.pdf
The Scottish Environment Protection Agency: www.sepa.org.uk
Scottish Parliament: www.scottish.parliament.uk
The Times: www.timesonline.co.uk
UK Acts: www.hmso.gov.uk
UK Environment News: www.ukenvironment.com
The United Kingdom Parliament: www.parliament.uk
UK Sustainable Development Strategy: www.sustainable-develop-
    ment.gov.uk
The Telegraph Newspaper: www.telegraph.co.uk
University College Northampton: www.northampton.ac.uk
University of Leeds: www.leeds.ac.uk
University of Southampton: www.soton.ac.uk/civilenv
The Strategy Unit Report 'Waste Not Want Not':
www.number-10.gov.uk/su/waste/report/downloads/wastenot.pdf
WAMITAB (training): www.wamitab.org.uk
Waste Strategy 2000 (England and Wales): www.defra.gov.uk/environment/
    waste/strategy/
The Waste and Resources Action Programme (WRAP): www.wrap.org.uk

Some websites appropriate to Scotland and Northern Ireland

Environment and Heritage Service Northern Ireland: www.ehsni.gov.uk
The Scottish Environment Protection Agency: www.sepa.org.uk
The Scottish Executive: www.scotland.gov.uk
Scottish Parliament: www.scottish.parliament.uk

Index

Note: Figures and Tables are indicated by *italic page numbers*, Boxes by **emboldened numbers**, and footnotes by suffix 'n' (e.g. '15n8' indicates footnote 8 on page 15)